BEN JONSON

Modern Critical Views

Henry Adams
Edward Albee
A. R. Ammons
Matthew Arnold
John Ashbery
W. H. Auden
Jane Austen
James Baldwin
Charles Baudelaire
Samuel Beckett
Saul Bellow
The Bible
Elizabeth Bishop
William Blake
Jorge Luis Borges
Elizabeth Bowen
Bertolt Brecht
The Brontës
Robert Browning
Anthony Burgess
George Gordon, Lord
  Byron
Thomas Carlyle
Lewis Carroll
Willa Cather
Cervantes
Geoffrey Chaucer
Kate Chopin
Samuel Taylor Coleridge
Joseph Conrad
Contemporary Poets
Hart Crane
Stephen Crane
Dante
Charles Dickens
Emily Dickinson
John Donne & the Seven-
  teenth-Century Meta-
  physical Poets
Elizabethan Dramatists
Theodore Dreiser
John Dryden
George Eliot
T. S. Eliot
Ralph Ellison
Ralph Waldo Emerson
William Faulkner
Henry Fielding
F. Scott Fitzgerald
Gustave Flaubert
E. M. Forster
Sigmund Freud
Robert Frost

Robert Graves
Graham Greene
Thomas Hardy
Nathaniel Hawthorne
William Hazlitt
Seamus Heaney
Ernest Hemingway
Geoffrey Hill
Friedrich Hölderlin
Homer
Gerard Manley Hopkins
William Dean Howells
Zora Neale Hurston
Henry James
Samuel Johnson and
  James Boswell
Ben Jonson
James Joyce
Franz Kafka
John Keats
Rudyard Kipling
D. H. Lawrence
John Le Carré
Ursula K. Le Guin
Doris Lessing
Sinclair Lewis
Robert Lowell
Norman Mailer
Bernard Malamud
Thomas Mann
Christopher Marlowe
Carson McCullers
Herman Melville
James Merrill
Arthur Miller
John Milton
Eugenio Montale
Marianne Moore
Iris Murdoch
Vladimir Nabokov
Joyce Carol Oates
Sean O'Casey
Flannery O'Connor
Eugene O'Neill
George Orwell
Cynthia Ozick
Walter Pater
Walker Percy
Harold Pinter
Plato
Edgar Allan Poe
Poets of Sensibility & the
  Sublime

Alexander Pope
Katherine Ann Porter
Ezra Pound
Pre-Raphaelite Poets
Marcel Proust
Thomas Pynchon
Arthur Rimbaud
Theodore Roethke
Philip Roth
John Ruskin
J. D. Salinger
Gershom Scholem
William Shakespeare
  (3 vols.)
  Histories & Poems
  Comedies
  Tragedies
George Bernard Shaw
Mary Wollstonecraft
  Shelley
Percy Bysshe Shelley
Edmund Spenser
Gertrude Stein
John Steinbeck
Laurence Sterne
Wallace Stevens
Tom Stoppard
Jonathan Swift
Alfred, Lord Tennyson
William Makepeace
  Thackeray
Henry David Thoreau
Leo Tolstoi
Anthony Trollope
Mark Twain
John Updike
Gore Vidal
Virgil
Robert Penn Warren
Evelyn Waugh
Eudora Welty
Nathanael West
Edith Wharton
Walt Whitman
Oscar Wilde
Tennessee Williams
William Carlos Williams
Thomas Wolfe
Virginia Woolf
William Wordsworth
Richard Wright
William Butler Yeats

These and other titles in preparation

Modern Critical Views

BEN JONSON

Edited and with an introduction by
Harold Bloom
Sterling Professor of the Humanities
Yale University

CHELSEA HOUSE PUBLISHERS ◇ 1987
New York ◇ New Haven ◇ Philadelphia

822.3
Blo

© 1987 by Chelsea House Publishers, a division
of Chelsea House Educational Communications, Inc.,
  95 Madison Avenue, New York, NY 10016
  345 Whitney Avenue, New Haven, CT 06511
  5014 West Chester Pike, Edgemont, PA 19028

Introduction © 1987 by Harold Bloom

Library of Congress Cataloging-in-Publication Data
Ben Jonson.
  (Modern critical views)
  Bibliography: p.
  Includes index.
  1. Jonson, Ben, 1573?–1637—Criticism and
interpretation. I. Bloom, Harold. II. Series.
PR2638.B46 1987   822'.3   86–34327
ISBN 1–55546–276–6

Contents

Editor's Note

This book gathers together a representative selection of the best criticism available upon the writings of Ben Jonson. The critical essays are reprinted in the chronological order of their original publication. I am grateful to Marijke Rijsberman and Frank Menchaca for their work as researchers for this volume.

My introduction centers upon Ben Jonson's stance, neoclassical and empirical (in the mode of Sir Francis Bacon), as a literary critic. Jonas A. Barish begins the chronological sequence of criticism with his celebrated analysis of the double plot in *Volpone,* after which Edward B. Partridge centers upon the pattern of allusions in *Epicoene,* while the poet Geoffrey Hill examines the workings of dramatic verse in *Sejanus* and *Catiline.*

Stephen Orgel, studying the Jonsonian masque, finds it to be the genre where the poet was best able to synthesize "the world he wrote for and the world he created." In a reading of *The Alchemist,* William Blisset emphasizes the remarkably dispassionate, deliberately bland, conclusion of the play, which avoids the severe moral retributions that end *Volpone.*

A comprehensive overview of Jonson is provided by Thomas M. Greene, who centers Jonson's vision of the self upon the dual image of circle and center. William Kerrigan, dissenting from our modern portrait of Jonson as sane and virtuous, returns us to the reality of the poet's abiding melancholy, to the nuances of "a little winter-love in a darke corner."

Jonson's self-revisions, so characteristic of his critical stance, are traced by A. Richard Dutton in *Every Man in His Humour.* Jonathan Haynes, studying the economics of drama in *Bartholomew Fair,* and Jonathan Dollimore, examining the historical politics of *Sejanus,* complete our exegesis of Jonson's plays for the stage. Our remaining essays return us to Jonson's masques, and lead us also to Jonson's extraordinary achievement in his verse.

Joseph Loewenstein's account of allusion in *Cynthia's Revels* is followed by Stanley Fish's readerly response to the image of the self in Jonson's poems.

John Hollander, great prosodist and prosodic authority, applies his Jonson-ian insights to Jonson's mastery of craft, finding in his precursor poet his own quest for converting form into a mode of metaphor.

In this book's final essay, previously unpublished, Marijke Rijsberman brings to Jonson's masques a fine sense of ceremonial form, one which per-ceives the justice of Jonson's passionate conviction that the literary element ought to dominate the court masque.

Introduction

I

In his conversations with (or harangues at) the Spenserian poet Drummond of Hawthornden in 1619, Ben Jonson repeated a joke of Sir Francis Bacon's:

> At his hither coming, Sir Francis Bacon said to him, He loved not
> to see poesy go on other feet than poetical dactyls and spondees.

Jonson, burly Laureate, portly Master Poet, rather grandly had marched into Scotland on foot, and greatly appreciated the Baconian compliment that poesy and Ben were identical. If Bacon presumably preferred Jonson, the Ancient, over Shakespeare, the Modern, this extraordinary evaluation was as remarkably reciprocated when Jonson gave Bacon the accolade as essayist and wisdom writer over Montaigne:

> LORD BACON: One, though he be excellent and the chief, is not
> to be imitated alone; for never no imitator ever grew up to
> his author; likeness is always on this side truth. Yet there
> happened in my time one noble speaker who was full of
> gravity in his speaking; his language, where he could spare
> or pass by a jest, was nobly censorious. No man ever spake
> more neatly, more presly, more weightily, or suffered less
> emptiness, less idleness, in what he uttered. No member of
> his speech but consisted of his own graces. His hearers could
> not cough, or look aside from him, without loss. He com-
> manded where he spoke, and had his judges angry and
> pleased at his devotion. No man had their affections more
> in his power. The fear of every man that heard him was lest
> he should make an end.

1

The art of this generous overpraise is that it is an elegant, if perhaps too neat, cento of commonplaces from Seneca, common precursor of Bacon and Montaigne. Jonson would have expected us to juxtapose this passage of *Timber, or Discoveries* with another, in which Montaigne, Shakespeare of essayists, is somewhat warily deprecated:

> Such are all the essayists, even their master Montaigne. These, in all they write, confess still what books they have read last, and therein their own folly so much, that they bring it to the stake raw and undigested; not that the place did need it neither, but that they thought themselves furnished and would vent it.

That is vigorous, nasty, and about as effective against Montaigne as were Jonson's ambivalent remarks against Shakespeare. Bacon himself, Jonson's authority, more cunningly said that the word, "essay," was "late but the thing is ancient," which is shrewdly translated by Charles Whitney as: "Montaigne, the so-called first essayist, isn't as original as everyone thinks; *my* essays in fact represent the authentic continuity with a long tradition of skeptical, probing inquiry." But to take sides with Montaigne and Shakespeare against Bacon and Jonson would be easy, vulgar, and therefore disgusting. Bacon and Jonson, both too subtle and dialectical for mere paraphrase, were fighting on the side neither of Ancients or Moderns. Modernity, as we always insist upon forgetting, is an Alexandrian concept, formulated by our grand precursor, Aristarchus, in defense of the first great Modernist poet, Callimachus. Doubtless, we cannot call Sir Francis Bacon the Nietzsche of his age, but we might begin to think of Nietzsche as the Bacon shadowing the threshold of our own era. Bacon too is concerned for the use and abuse of history for life, though he means by "life" something like civil society, the state, the future prospects of a people. Nietzsche, heroic vitalist, urged us to think of the earth, hardly a Baconian injunction, though Bacon has his own version of the Nietzschean admonition: "Try to live as though it were morning." Bacon and Nietzsche share the same resolution: do not live, work, or think as though you were a latecomer.

The heirs of Spenser in the earlier seventeenth century suffered a most acute sense of imaginative belatedness, typified by the Kabbalistic Henry Reynolds at the opening of his *Mythomystes*:

> I have thought upon the times we live in, and am forced to affirm the world is decrepit, and, out of its age & doating estate, subject to all the imperfections that are inseparable from that wrack and maim of Nature.

That is to replace history by poetry, or to read history as a Spenserian romance. Aristotle had placed poetry between philosophy and history, a stationing that Sir Philip Sidney had modified, perhaps slyly, by his apothegm that poetry took place between the precept and the example, and so could fulfill moral purposes that neither philosophy nor history could hope to serve. Bacon, in contrast, judged poetry to be a mere imitation of history, made to no end except the giving of pleasure. Spenser and Bacon were antipodes of thought and feeling, and their visions of history were almost irreconcilable. Their heirs necessarily possessed almost nothing in common. Ben Jonson and his school were divided from the Spenserians by multiple considerations, reflecting cultural choices that intricately fused religion, politics, and aesthetics.

Angus Fletcher, our great contemporary Spenserian, observes that Spenser "subordinates the insights of cyclical and scientific history to the Christian revelation of a prophetic historicism," though Fletcher shrewdly adds that this kind of poetic prophecy is as Orphic as it is Christian. I would add to Fletcher that such Orphic historicism is anti-Baconian in consequences, rather than as policy. Another major contemporary Spenserian, the late and much missed Isabel G. MacCaffrey, caught the precise agon between Spenser and the involuntary latecomer Bacon, with admirable economy: "Bacon was later to disparage poets for submitting 'the shows of things to the desires of the mind', but as both Sidney and Spenser affirm, those desires themselves bear witness to the presence of a realm of being inadequately figured by the shows of things."

Bacon's polemic against the poets presumably resulted from his desperate ambition to substitute his own historicism for the Orphic prophecies of the great poets. He too was a prophet, perhaps the most optimistic of British prophets before the young John Milton, and is rightly named as a counter-apocalyptic by Achsah Guibbory: "Like many of his contemporaries, Bacon believes that he is living in the 'autumn of the world,' that the end of time is approaching. But his sense that the end is not far off leads to a vision of progress, not an obsession with decay."

Charles Whitney, seeking to define Bacon's concept of modernity, notes the revision by misquotation that Bacon carries out in his use of the prophet Jeremiah:

> Bacon's spectacular misquotation of Jeremiah in *The Advancement of Learning*'s best-known pronouncement on tradition and innovation reveals the problematic relationship of his instauration to the religious models. (The misquotation is repeated in the *De*

Dignitate et Augmentis Scientiarum and in the essay "Of Innovations"). Failure to appreciate that complex relationship (or to note the misreading) has led commentators, among them Harold Bloom and Renato Poggioli, to construe the passage either as a bellwether of Enlightenment faith in free reason (Bloom) or as a defense of traditionalism (Poggioli). In criticizing the "extreme affection" of either "Antiquity" or "Novelty" in learned men, Bacon says:

> Antiquity envieth there should be new additions, and novelty cannot be content to add but it must deface: surely the advice of the prophet is the true direction in this matter, *State super vias antiquas, et videte quaenam sit via recta et bona et ambulate in eas.* Antiquity deserveth that reverence, that men should make a stand thereupon and discover what is the best way; but when the discovery is well taken, then to make progression. And to speak truly, *Antiquitas saeculi juventus mundi.* These times are the ancient times, when the world is ancient, and not those which we account ancient *ordine retrogrado,* by a computation backward from ourselves.

Bacon's apparently moderate view of tradition and innovation here—the reversal of ancient and modern times being a sentiment found in several earlier contemporaries—reflects the generally reconciliatory attitude about the past assumed in the *Advancement.* The present is "old," clearly, because there has been cumulative development, fruitful imitation, and emulation. Even so, it has become necessary for Bacon to distort Jeremiah considerably. The Vulgate renders him thus:

> State super vias, et videte
> Et interrogate de semitis antiquis quae sit via bona,
> Et ambulate in ea,
> Et invenietis refrigirium animabus vestris

Stand in the ways, and look, and ask for the old paths, where the good way is, and walk in it, and find rest for your soul.

Whitney interprets Jeremiah as meaning that "the right way is the old way," but that is to misread the prophet more weakly than Bacon did. Bacon's: *Stand in the old ways, and see which is the straight and good path, and walk in that,* omits asking for the old paths, because Jeremiah himself appears to mean that the good way is only one of the old paths, and the prophet's crucial emphasis is: "walk in it," which is the entire burden of normative Judaism. Bacon indeed is battling against contemporary cultural undervaluation, including the Spenserians, with their study of the nostalgias, and his polemical insistence is that the ancients were the true moderns, and the moderns the true ancients, since those who arrived later knew more, and Bacon himself knew most of all.

II

The contemporary critic-scholar Thomas M. Greene, who may be our very last Renaissance Humanist, battles his own profound sense of belatedness in a splendid essay on "Ben Jonson and the Centered Self ":

> The equilibrated energy of the centered self is most amply demonstrated by Jonson's *Timber.* The stress in that work falls on the faculty of judgment, and in fact it demonstrates this faculty at work, choosing among authors and passages, discriminating conduct and style.
>
> > Opinion is a light, vain, crude, and imperfect thing, settled in the imagination, but never arriving at understanding, there to obtain the tincture of reason.
> >
> > (8:564)
>
> The passages gathered in *Timber* are exercises of the reasonable understanding. A sentence like the one quoted seems to place the imagination in an outer layer of consciousness, where the centrifugal "opinion" can momentarily alight. The understanding is further within, at the psychic center of gravity, impervious to the flights of the butterfly-caprice. All of *Timber,* whether or not "original" in the vulgar sense, seems to issue from this center of gravity.

Greene, a well-tempered Humanist, powerful and crafty, but in the last ditch, centers upon *Timber* as a gathering of "exercises of the reasonable understanding." Thirty years ago, the great Humanist William K. Wimsatt, Jr., Greene's mentor as well as mine, asserted rather more for *Timber:*

> Jonson's stout and craftsmanly common sense about imitation, shown even more convincingly in his practice than in his precepts,

may be taken as the key to a theory of poetry which stressed hard work—imitation, practice, study, art (and with these but one poor pennyworth of *ingenium*)—a theory too which stressed poems squared off by the norm of reality. This theory celebrated the mobility and power of poetry, but it included no hymn to spontaneity or to what today we think of as the creative imagination. It included no statement even remotely parallel to that of Sidney about the free range of wit within its zodiac or that of Bacon about poetry submitting the shows of reality to the desires of the mind. Some deviation or wavering from the classic norm may appear in Jonson's treatment of such a minor article as that prescribing the unity of place—and we have seen that he is guilty of defying the authority of the antique critics. But he is the first English man of letters to exhibit a nearly complete and consistent neo-classicism. His historical importance is that he throws out a vigorous announcement of the rule from which in the next generation Dryden is to be engaged in politely rationalized recessions. One basic problem which Jonson leaves us pondering (the same as that posed implicitly once before, by a strong appreciator of poetic inspiration, Longinus) might be formulated as follows: Does an aesthetic norm of objective reality entail a *genetic* theory of conscious and strenuous artistic effort? If a poet is to give us a truthful account of general human nature, does this poet have to be a learned consumer of midnight oil, a graduate in grammar, logic, and rhetoric, and in the higher liberal disciplines? Or on the other hand: Does an aesthetic norm of personal expression entail a genetic theory of untrammeled and unstudied inspiration? If a poet is to tell the truth as he himself most really and deeply experiences it, does he have to be a rebel against tradition and conventional education, a Bohemian, long-haired, and unwashed, a defiler of ancestral ashes?

On this view, Jonson is more on the side of Ancients against Moderns than his master Bacon was, and that must be right. But how could Jonson have inaugurated English neoclassicism, when he seems to have held a Stoic or cyclical theory of history? His identification with Horace, I suspect, was not truly founded upon some supposed and rather dubious parallel between Roman and English history, despite the persuasive arguments of Achsah Guibbory in *The Map of Time*. Whatever Horace's actual temperament may have been, we know that the fierce and violent Jonson, burly Ben indeed, was not exactly a natural Stoic. Can we not surmise that Jonson's preference for the Ancients was antithetical, against the grain, a correction of the most vehement sensibility ever possessed by a major English poet. History, including the events of his own time, disgusted the passionate moralist Jonson, who turned to Stoicism and the Ancients so as to withdraw from what might have provoked him to a madness of no use to literature.

There is a great passage in *Timber* in praise of Bacon, "the late Lord Saint Albans," that can serve to sum up both of these great minds on the virtues of the Ancients, and on the possibility of becoming an Ancient in your own time:

> It was well noted by the late Lord Saint Albans, that the study of words is the first distemper of learning; vain matter the second; and a third distemper is deceit, or the likeness of truth, imposture held up by credulity. All these are the cobwebs of learning, and to let them grow in us is either sluttish or foolish. Nothing is more ridiculous than to make an author a dictator, as the schools have done Aristotle. The damage is infinite knowledge receives by it; for to many things a man should owe but a temporary belief, and a suspension of his own judgment, not an absolute resignation of himself, or a perpetual captivity. Let Aristotle and others have their dues; but if we can make farther discoveries of truth and fitness than they, why are we envied? Let us beware, while we strive to add, we do not diminish or deface; we may improve, but not augment. By discrediting falsehood, truth grows in request. We must not go about, like men anguished and perplexed for vicious affectation of praise, but calmly study the separation of opinions, find the errors have intervened, awake antiquity, call former times into question; but make no parties with the present, nor follow any fierce undertakers, mingle no matter of doubtful credit with the simplicity of truth; but gently stir the mould about the root of the question, and avoid all digladiations, facility of credit, or superstitious simplicity, seek the consonancy and concatenation of truth; stoop only to point of necessity, and what leads to convenience. Then make exact animadversion where style hath degenerated, where flourished and thrived in choiceness of phrase, round and clean composition of sentence, sweet falling of the clause, varying an illustration by tropes and figures, weight of matter, worth of subject, soundness of argument, life of invention, and depth of judgment. This is

monte potiri, to get the hill; for no perfect discovery can be made upon a flat or a level.

To discover the errors that have intervened is to awaken antiquity while making no alliances with the present, yet also is to call all former times into question. Here, at least, Jonson admirably joins himself to Bacon, and prepares the way for Milton's much more drastic transumption of the tradition.

JONAS A. BARISH

The Double Plot in Volpone

For more than two centuries literary critics have been satisfied to dismiss the subplot of *Volpone* as irrelevant and discordant, because of its lack of overt connection with the main plot. Jonson's most sympathetic admirers have been unable to account for the presence of Sir Politic Would-be, Lady Would-be, and Peregrine any more satisfactorily than by styling them a "makeweight" or a kind of comic relief to offset the "sustained gloom" of the chief action. Without questioning the orthodox opinion that the links of intrigue between the two plots are frail, one may nevertheless protest against a view of drama which criticizes a play exclusively in terms of physical action. What appears peripheral on the level of intrigue may conceal other kinds of relevance. And it is on the thematic level that the presence of the Would-be's can be justified and their peculiar antics related to the major motifs of the play.

John D. Rea, in his edition of *Volpone,* seems to have been the first to notice that Sir Politic Would-be, like the characters of the main plot, has his niche in the common beast fable: he is Sir Pol, the chattering poll parrot, and his wife is a deadlier specimen of the same species. Rea's accurate insistence on the loquaciousness of the parrot, however, must be supplemented by recalling that parrots not only habitually chatter, they mimic. This banal but important little item of bird lore offers a thread whereby we may find our way through the complex thematic structure of the play. For Sir Politic

From *Modern Philology* 51, no. 1 (August 1953). © 1954 by the University of Chicago.

and Lady Would-be function to a large extent precisely as mimics. They imitate their environment, and without knowing it they travesty the actions of the main characters. In so doing, they perform the function of burlesque traditional to comic subplots in English drama, and they make possible the added density and complexity of vision to which the device of the burlesque subplot lends itself.

His effort to Italianize himself takes the form, with Sir Politic, of an obsession with plots, secrets of state, and Machiavellian intrigue. His wife, on the other hand, apes the local styles in dress and cosmetics, reads the Italian poets, and tries to rival the lascivious Venetians in their own game of seduction.

Further, and more specifically, however, Sir Politic and Lady Would-be caricature the actors of the main plot. Sir Pol figures as a comic distortion of Volpone. As his name implies, he is the would-be politician, the speculator *manqué,* the unsuccessful enterpriser. Volpone, by contrast, is the real politician, the successful enterpriser, whose every stratagem succeeds almost beyond expectation. Sir Pol, like Volpone, is infatuated with his own ingenuity, and like Volpone he nurses his get-rich-quick schemes; but none of these ever progresses beyond the talking stage. While Volpone continues to load his coffers with the treasures that pour in from his dupes, Sir Pol continues to haggle over vegetables in the market and to annotate the purchase of toothpicks.

Lady Would-be, for her part, joins the dizzy game of legacy-hunting. Her antics caricature the more sinister gestures of Corvino, Voltore, and Corbaccio. She is jealous, like Corvino, as meaninglessly and perversely erudite as Voltore, and like Corbaccio, she makes compromising proposals to Mosca which leave her at the mercy of his blackmail. But, like her husband, Lady Would-be is incapable of doing anything to the purpose, and when she plays into Mosca's hands in the fourth act, she becomes the most egregious of the dupes because she is the blindest.

We do not learn of the existence of the Would-be's until the close of the first act, and then only in a scrap of dialogue between Mosca and Volpone. Mosca's panegyric on Celia, following his sarcasms about Lady Would-be, serves to initiate a contrast which prevails throughout the play, between the households of Corvino and Sir Politic. If Corvino's besetting vice is jealousy, that of Sir Pol is uxoriousness, and the contrast enlarges itself into a difference between the brutal, obsessive passions of Italy and the milder eccentricities, the acquired follies or humors, of England. The contrast continues to unfold in the opening scene of act 2, where Sir Politic talks to his new acquaintance, Peregrine. Peregrine, it should be mentioned, probably belongs to the beast fable himself, as the pilgrim falcon. A case for this possibility would have to be based on the habits of hawks, commonly trained to hunt other birds. One then might find propriety in the fact of the falcon's hunting the parrot in the play. In Jonson's Epigram 85, the hawk is described as a bird sacred to Apollo, since it pursues the truth, strikes at ignorance, and makes the fool its quarry. All these activities are performed by Peregrine vis-à-vis Sir Politic.

In the initial scene between them, three chief ideas are developed, all of cardinal importance to the play and all interrelated. The first is the notion of monstrosity. Monstrosity has already made its spectacular appearance in the person of Androgyno and in the passage on Volpone's misbegotten offspring. We are, thereby, already familiar with the moral abnormality of Venice and its inhabitants. The present passage, with its reports of strange marvels sighted in England—a lion whelping in the Tower, a whale discovered in the Thames, porpoises above the bridge—introduces us to an order of monsters more comic than those to be met with in Venice, but to monsters nonetheless, in the proper sense of the word. Sir Pol's prodigies are distant echoes of the moral earthquake rocking Venice, a looking glass for England whereby that country is warned to heed the lesson of the Italian state lest its own follies turn to vices and destroy it.

The enactment of the interlude in the first act, by placing the soul of the fool in the body of the hermaphrodite, has already established an identification between folly and monstrosity. Appropriately enough, then, having discussed monsters, Peregrine and Sir Pol turn to speak of the death of a famous fool, thus reinforcing the link between the two ideas. Sir Pol's excessive reaction to the event prompts Peregrine to inquire maliciously into a possible parentage between the two, and his companion innocently to deny it. The joke here, that Sir Pol is kin to the dead fool through their mutual folly if not through family, merges into a larger reflection on the ubiquity of folly, picking up that suggestion by ricochet, as it were, from the interlude in act 1. When Peregrine asks, "I hope / You thought him not immortall?" (2.1.55–56), the question implies its own Jonsonian answer: Master Stone, the fool, is not immortal, but his folly lives on incarnate in hundreds of fools like Sir Politic, much as the soul of Pythagoras, in the interlude, invested the body of one fool after another for thousands of years, only to reach its final and most fitting avatar in the person of Androgyno.

The colloquy concerning the Mamuluchi introduces the third chief motif of the scene, that of mimicry. This passage, where baboons are described in various quasi-human postures, acquires added irony from the fact that it is recited by the parrot, the imitative animal par excellence, and also from the fact that the activities of the baboons, like those of Master Stone, the fool, consist chiefly of spying and intriguing and therefore differ so little from the way Sir Pol himself attempts to imitate the Italians.

The arrival of Volpone disguised as a mountebank produces the expected confrontation between the archknave and the complete gull, the latter hopelessly hypnotized by the eloquence of the former. Volpone commences by disdaining certain imputations that have been cast on him by professional rivals. By way of counterattack, he accuses them of not knowing their trade, of being mere "*ground* Ciarlitani," or spurious mountebanks. If there is any doubt about the application of the passage to Sir Politic, it is settled by that individual's cry of admiration: "Note but his bearing, and contempt of these" (2.2.58). Sir Politic thus plays charlatan to Volpone's mountebank as, within the larger frame of the play, he plays parrot to Volpone's fox. But Volpone has brought along his own misshapen child, the dwarf Nano, as an accredited imitator. Nano, who fills the role of Zan Fritada, the zany, is the domesticated mimic, the conscious mimic, as Androgyno is the conscious fool, while Sir Pol remains the unconscious mimic and the unconscious fool.

Volpone, pursuing his attack on imitators, assails them for trying to copy his elixir: "*Indeed, very many haue assay'd, like apes in imitation of that, which is really and essentially in mee, to make of this oyle*" (2.2.149–50). What is "really and essentially" in Volpone we know already to be monstrosity, so that to imitate Volpone (as Sir Politic does) is to imitate the unnatural, and therefore, in a sense, to place one's self at two removes from nature. But Volpone believes himself, not without justification, to be inimitable. The wretched practitioners who try to duplicate his ointment end in disaster. "*Poore wretches!*" he concludes, "*I rather pittie their folly, and indiscretion, than their losse of time, and money; for those may be recouered by industrie: but to bee a foole borne, is a disease incurable*" (2.2.157–59). At this moment all that would be needed to drive home the application of Volpone's *sententia* would be a pause on his part, followed by a significant look from Peregrine to Sir Pol. But the situation conceals a further irony. Volpone's aphorism applies to himself. Before long, he, the archknave, will have proved the greatest fool, and this despite the versatility which enables him to transcend for the moment his own preferences, in order to cater to the prejudices of the public. Paradoxically, in this scene, speaking out of character, Volpone utters truths which reverse the premises of his former behavior. In act 1, gold, the great goddess, served him as sovereign remedy and omnipotent healer. For the saltimbanco Scoto of Mantua, peddling his fraudulent elixir, newer and relatively truer axioms celebrate the treasure of health: "*O, health! health! the blessing of the rich! the riches of the poore!*"

(2.2.84–85). But with the application of this facile maxim, error descends again. The new truth proves to be only a distorted half-truth. In place of gold, Volpone offers only his humbug ointment as the *"most soueraigne, and approued remedie"* (2.2.103–4). The real point, and he has made it himself, escapes him: to be a fool born is a disease incurable, and it is this disease to which he himself is destined to succumb.

The *"little remembrance"* which Volpone now presents to Celia proves to be a cosmetic powder with virtues more miraculous than those of the *oglio* itself. It is the powder *"That made* VENVS *a goddesse (giuen her by* APOLLO) *that kept her perpetually yong, clear'd her wrincles, firm'd her gummes, fill'd her skin, colour'd her haire; from her, deriu'd to* HELEN, *and at the sack of* Troy *(vnfortunately) lost: till now, in this our age, it was as happily recouer'd, by a studious Antiquarie . . . who sent a moyetie of it, to the court of* France . . . *wherewith the ladies there, now, colour theire haire"* (2.2.235–43). Thus the history of the powder parallels the metempsychoses of Pythagoras. Like Pythagoras's soul, the powder began its career as a gift from Apollo, and in its transmigrations through the goddess of love, the whore of Sparta, and the court ladies of France, it serves to underline the ancient lineage of vanity as a special case of the folly rehearsed in the interlude.

Mosca's opening soliloquy in act 3 shows that this excellent counterfeiter is himself, like his master, obsessed by the notion of imitators. His contempt for ordinary parasites suggests that there is a hierarchy of counterfeits, ranging from those who are deeply and essentially false (like himself) to those who practice falsity out of mere affectation, who are, so to speak, falsely false and therefore, again, at two removes from nature. The shift of scene back to Volpone's house produces still another variation on the theme of mimicry. In order to beguile their master from his boredom, the trio of grotesques stage an impromptu interlude, dominated by Nano, who claims that the dwarf can please a rich man better than the eunuch or the hermaphrodite. The dwarf, explains Nano, is little, and pretty:

> *Else why doe men say to a creature of my shape,*
> *So soone as they see him, it's a pritty little ape?*
> *And, why a pritty ape? but for pleasing imitation*
> *Of greater mens action, in a ridiculous fashion*
> (3.3.11–14)

The first interlude, it may be recalled again, established an identification between folly and the unnatural. The present fragment confirms a further identity between mimicry and deformity, already hinted at in the mountebank scene where Nano appeared as the zany, or mimic, to Volpone's Scoto. At this point one may represent some of the relationships in the play diagramatically as follows:

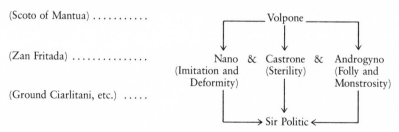

(Scoto of Mantua) . . . .

(Zan Fritada) . . . .

(Ground Ciarlitani, etc.) . . . . .

Volpone

Nano   &   Castrone   &   Androgyno
(Imitation and   (Sterility)   (Folly and
Deformity)   Monstrosity)

Sir Politic

Since Volpone has (presumptively at least) sired both Nano and Androgyno, and since Sir Pol combines the chief attributes of both, one may, with the aid of the diagram, infer what is already emerging plainly in context, that mimicry itself is something monstrous and abnormal. It is unnatural for baboons and apes and parrots to counterfeit human behavior. It is equally unnatural for men to imitate beasts. It argues a perversion of their essential humanity. It is not for nothing, then, that the chief characters of the play fit into one zoological classification or another. As men, they duplicate the habits of beasts; as beasts, they brutishly travesty humanity. They belong to the genus *monster*—half man, half brute—that order of fabulous creatures whose common denominator is their unnaturalness, their lack of adherence to whatever category of being nature has assigned them.

The arrival of Lady Would-be, fuming and fussing over her toilet, and snapping at her servingwomen, provides still a further object-lesson in falsity. Here, as so often in Jonson, face physic symbolizes the painted surface hiding the rotten inside; the cosmetic care of the face signifies the neglect of the soul. It signifies equally an attachment to appearances, an incapacity to look beyond the superficies of life or truth. The powder which Volpone offered to Celia and which Celia did not need, since her beauty was of the platonic sort that revealed the purity of her soul, might with more justice have been given to Lady Would-be, and it is Lady Would-be who deserves the epithet of "lady *vanitie*" (2.5.21) with which Corvino, in his jealous tantrum, has stigmatized Celia.

The scene between Lady Would-be and Volpone serves partly as a burlesque of the parallel scenes in act 1 between Volpone and the other *captatores*. All the essential ingredients of those scenes reappear, but scrambled and topsy-turvy. Once again Volpone feigns sickness, but this time it is in self-defense against the terrible oratory of Lady Would-be. Once again remedies are prescribed, but these are neither Corbaccio's deadly opiate nor his *aurum palpabile* offered as pump-priming, but the fantastic assortment of old wives' restoratives dredged up from Lady Would-be's infernal memory. She rains down the hailstones of her learning on the helpless Volpone, until the archrogue, anticipating the judgment to be rendered on him in act 5, cries out in despair: "Before I fayned diseases, now I haue one" (3.4.62). The whole episode is a rich application of the principle of comic justice. If in the final denouement Volpone suffers the penalty of vice, here he reaps the more ludicrous reward of his own folly. Trapped by Lady Would-be's rhetoric, itself a consequence of his own scheming, he is finally driven to pronounce himself cured. But the talking machine grinds on, and only Mosca's happy notion of exciting her jealousy, as he has previously aroused Corvino's, and for the same purpose, succeeds in getting rid of her. As her contribution to Volpone's coffers, she leaves behind a wrought cap of her own making; this forms a suitably ridiculous contrast to the treasures earlier offered by Corvino, Corbaccio, and Voltore.

The same scene serves as introduction and comic distortion of the scene immediately to follow between Volpone and Celia. Celia's unearthly purity is made to seem even more unearthly by its contrast to Lady Would-be's lecherousness, this latter apparent in the lady's addiction to cosmetics, in her slips of the tongue, and in her barely disguised sexual overtures. Lady Would-be's attempted seduction of Volpone having been thwarted, the stage is set for Volpone's attempted seduction of Celia. Volpone commences his wooing with a characteristic boast: "I, before / I would haue left my practice, for thy loue," he swears, "In varying figures, I would haue contended / With the blue PROTEVS, or the horned *Floud*" (3.7.150–53). Justifiably proud of his powers of disguise, Volpone emphasizes them further by citing a past occasion on which he masqueraded in the ambiguous role of Antinous, Nero's favorite. Embarking on an enumeration of the exotic splendors in store for Celia, he reserves as his final inducement the promise that she will participate, with him, in transmutations without end: "Whil'st we, in changed shapes, act OVIDS tales" (the *Metamorphoses,* of course),

> Thou, like EVROPA now, and I like IOVE,
> Then I like MARS, and thou like ERYCINE,
> So, of the rest, till we haue quite run through
> And weary'd all the fables of the gods.
> Then will I haue thee in more moderne formes,
> Attired like some sprightly dame of *France,*
> Braue *Tuscan* lady, or proud *Spanish* beauty
>   (3.7.221–28)

We have already witnessed, in the first interlude, the metempsychosis of folly and, in the powder offered to Celia in act 2, the transmigrations of vanity. Now, as a climax to his eloquence, Volpone rehearses the metamorphoses of lust. Jonson thus endows his central themes with vertical depth in time as well as horizontal extension in space. Folly, vanity, lust, have been, are, will be. At any given moment their practitioners are legion, and often inter-changeable.

It is at this point that Celia's refusal crystallizes into a repudiation of folly, vanity, and lust combined and that her behavior contrasts most sharply with that of Lady Would-be. The recollection of Lady Would-be lacquering her face and making indecent advances to Volpone brings into sharper focus Celia's sudden horror at her own beauty, and her plea that her face be flayed or smeared with poison, in order to undo the lust she has aroused. If, for Lady Would-be, the cosmetic art is a necessary preliminary to sexual con-quest, its opposite, the disfigurement of the face, becomes for Celia the badge of chastity. Where Lady Would-be strives to adopt Italian vices for her own, Celia's gestures as well as her name demonstrate her alienation from the moral and spiritual province of Venice.

Act 4 carries us back into the open street, where Sir Pol, ignorant of the plot developing at Volpone's house, continues babbling of plots in terms which ordinarily have one meaning for him and another for the audience. After a patronizing recital of "instructions" to Peregrine on methods of deportment in Venice, he confides suddenly that his money-making projects need only the assistance of one trusty henchman in order to be put into instant execution. Evidently he is hinting that Peregrine undertake that as-signment and thus play Mosca to his Volpone. But Peregrine contents himself with inquiring into the particulars of the plots. The most elaborate of these proves to be a way to protect Venice from the plague by using onions as an index to the state of infection on ships entering the harbor. This mad scheme, with its echo of Volpone's claim to have distributed his *oglio* under official patent to all the commonwealths of Christendom, serves chiefly to remind us again of the moral plague prevailing in Venice and of the incomprehension of that fact on the part of those characters who prattle most about disease and cure.

The ensuing scene parodies the episode in act 2 where Corvino discovers his wife in conversation with the mountebank. Just as Corvino interrupts Volpone while the latter is advertising his medicine, so Lady Would-be bursts in on Sir Politic as the knight is dilating on his schemes and projects. As Corvino babbles jealously of lechers and satyrs, so Lady Would-be jabbers of land sirens, lewd harlots, and fricatrices. Corvino beats away the moun-

tebank. Lady Would-be rails at Peregrine. Both harp on "honor," and both
discard that term as soon as it becomes an inconvenience, Corvino when it
becomes an obstacle to his plan of inheritance, Lady Would-be when she
discovers that Peregrine is no harlot in disguise, but a young gentleman. As
for Sir Politic, though he too plays his part in the little impromptu from the
commedia dell'arte, he remains, unlike Volpone, quite oblivious to the fact.
Actually, Sir Pol reenacts not the role of "Signior FLAMINIO," the lover in
disguise—that part, however reluctantly assumed, belongs to Peregrine—but
the female role, the "FRANCISCINA," guarded by a jealous "PANTALONE *di
besogniosi*" (2.3.3–8). The confusion of sexes symbolized in Androgyno, in
the indiscriminate journeyings of the soul of Pythagoras, in Volpone's masquerade as Antinous, in Lady Would-be's error, as well as in the reversed
masculine-feminine roles of Sir Pol and Lady Would-be, contributes its own
kind of abnormality to the deformity of the moral atmosphere chiefly figured
by the metamorphoses of beasts into men. And if one regards Sir Politic's
uxoriousness as a kind of metaphoric emasculation, one may then equate
him with Castrone, as he has already been equated with Nano and Androgyno, to make the pattern of mimicry complete.

The fourth-act trial starts with justice and concludes with a perversion
of it. The monsters begotten by Volpone, the prodigies and portents that
exercised such a hypnotic effect on Sir Pol, now make a lavish and climactic
reappearance in the language of the scene. First they designate their proper
objects. But as Voltore begins to exercise his baleful rhetoric, the parlance
of unnaturalness, appropriate to the guilty, begins to turn against the innocent. Corbaccio disavows his son for "the meere portent of nature"; he is
"an vtter stranger" to his loins, a "Monster of men, swine, goate, wolfe,
parricide" (4.5.108–12). Finally Lady Would-be arrives, the eternal parrot,
to give testimony which virtually clinches the case against Celia:

> Out, thou *chameleon* harlot; now, thine eies
> Vie teares with the *hyaena*
>
> (4.6.2–3)

The beast characters in the play display an unerring faculty for describing
the innocent as beasts. Corvino has already called Celia a crocodile, referring
to that animal's notorious ability to imitate human tears, and Lady Would-
be, though she has her unnatural natural history somewhat confused, invokes
another creature famous for its powers of mimicry, the hyena, as well as the
even more versatile chameleon.

The juxtaposition of the hyena and the chameleon reminds one that
there is a point at which the ideas of metamorphosis and mimicry coalesce.

The chameleon, shifting its colors to blend itself with its environment, indulges in a highly developed form of protective mimicry. Volpone carries the
principle a step further. He goes through his restless series of transformations
not as a shield but in order to prey on his own kind, to satisfy something
in his unnatural nature which demands incessant changing of shape and
form. But knavery and credulity, mimicry and metamorphosis, alike reflect
aspects of one basic folly: the folly of becoming, or trying to become, what
one is not, the cardinal sin of losing one's nature. Only Bonario and Celia,
of all the creatures in the play, never ape others, never change their shapes,
never act contrary to their essential natures. And in the unnatural state of
Venice it is chiefly they, the unchanging ones, who are attacked as hyenas
and chameleons.

Volpone, in short, may be read as a comic restatement of a theme familiar in Shakespeare's plays of the same period, the theme of disorder. Order
figures here not as social balance or political hierarchy, but as a principle of
differentiation in nature whereby each species, each sex, maintains its separate identity. With the loss of clear-cut divisions between man and beast,
between beast and beast, between male and female, all creatures become
monsters. The basic structure of nature is violated. The astronomical portents discussed earlier by Sir Pol and Peregrine in connection with animal
prodigies reflect the upheaval of the cosmos itself following the degeneracy
of man.

But by this time, justice has become as monstrous as its participants,
and the *avocatori* close the session piously intoning their horror at the unnaturalness of Celia and Bonario. Volpone's last and greatest hoax is destined
to set the balance of nature right again. It starts, however, with one more
act of unnaturalness. Volpone, a monster, who therefore occupies no fixed
place in the order of created beings, feigns death and thus symbolically
demonstrates his lack of status. One by one the inheritors file in for the
legacy, only to find that they have been duped by Mosca.

The first to receive her dismissal is Lady Would-be. Having made overtures to both Mosca and Volpone, she is in a position to be summarily
blackmailed. "Goe home," advises Mosca, "and vse the poore sir POL, your
knight, well; / For feare I tell some riddles: go, be melancholique" (5.3.44–
45). Thus the learned lady who knew so many bizarre ways of curing Volpone's melancholy now has the opportunity to treat herself for the same
ailment, and so do her colleagues. The value of this scene consists partly in
its inflicting comic justice on the legacy-hunters before the *avocatori* render
their sterner legal judgments, just as Volpone has already, in Lady Would-
be, met a comic foretaste of the retribution which overtakes him at the

Scrutineo. But since the parrot, for all its shrillness, remains less venal than the crow or vulture, the untrussing of Lady Would-be goes no further. In the realm of the severer truths, vice and folly may appear as different aspects of a similar spiritual malaise. In the realm of poetic justice, however, a distinction continues to be practiced. Vice, which is criminal and attacks others, must suffer public correction, whereas folly, a disease essentially self-destructive, may be dealt with in private and without the assistance of constituted authority. For Lady Would-be it is sufficient that, awakened to some sense of her own folly, she vows to quit Venice and take to sea "for physick."

And so with her preposterous knight, Sir Politic, whom we now encounter for the last time, the victim of a private plot which performs the same service of mortification for him that the final trial scene does for Volpone. The *mercatori* enlisted by Peregrine perform the office of the *avocatori* who pronounce sentence on Volpone, and the divulging of the pathetic notebook, with its scraps from playbooks, becomes the burlesque substitute for the exposure of Volpone's will, in bringing on the disaster. Peregrine, echoing Voltore's suggestion that Volpone be tested on the strappado, warns Sir Pol that his persecutors will put him to the rack. Whereupon the knight remembers an "engine" he has designed against just such emergencies, a tortoise shell. And to the disgust of three hundred years of literary critics he climbs into the ungainly object, playing possum after the fashion of his model, Volpone, who has feigned death in the foregoing scene. The arrival of the merchants brings on the catastrophe:

> MER. 1: What
> Are you, sir? PER: I' am a merchant, that came heere
> To looke vpon this tortoyse. MER. 3: How? MER. 1: S^r. MARKE!
> What beast is this? PER: It is a fish. MER. 2: Come out, here.
> PER: Nay, you may strike him, sir, and tread vpon him:
> Hee'll beare a cart
>
> (5.4.62–67)

Eventually, by stamping and poking, they goad Sir Politic out of his exoskeleton. The scene thus rephrases in a vein of broadest tomfoolery the essential question of the play: "What kind of creatures are these?" Throughout the action one has seen beasts aping men and men imitating beasts on the moral and psychological levels. Here the theme of mimicry reaches its literal climax in an episode of farce, where the most imitative of the characters puts on the physical integument of an animal and the hired pranksters stand about debating its probable zoological classification. The final unshelling of the tortoise, a parallel to the uncasing of the fox in the last scene, arouses further comment from the merchants:

> MER. 1: 'Twere a rare motion, to be seene, in *Fleet-street!*
> MER. 2: I, i'the terme. MER. 1. Or *Smithfield,* in the faire
>   (5.4.77–78)

Sir Politic, thus, so inquisitive about prodigies, has finally become one himself, a specimen fit to be housed among the freaks of Smithfield or amid the half-natural, half-artificial curiosities of Fleet Street. With the knowledge that he is destined to become a victim of the kind of curiosity he himself has exhibited, his disillusionment is complete and his chastisement effected. He and Lady Would-be, the only survivors, in this play, of Jonson's earlier humor characters, are now "out of their humor," purged of their imitative folly by the strong medicine of ridicule.

Public punishment, however, awaits the actors of the main plot. Jonson is not sporting here with human follies like those of the Would-be's, but dealing grimly with inhuman crimes. The names of fabulous monsters, basilisks and chimeras, continue to echo in our ears as the catastrophe approaches, fastening themselves at last onto their proper objects, the conspirators in the game of *captatio*. Voltore's spurious fit spells out in concrete theatrical terms his unnatural status and the lesson pointed by the *avocatori:* "These possesse wealth, as sicke men possesse feuers, / Which, trulyer, may be said to possesse them" (5.12.101–2). The delivery of Volpone's substance to the *Incurabili* places a final and proper valuation on the medicinal powers of gold. The imprisonment of Volpone is specifically designed to give him the opportunity to acquire in reality the diseases he has mimicked and the leisure to ponder the accuracy of his own text: to be a fool born is a disease incurable. Voltore and Corbaccio are henceforth to be secluded from their fellow-men like the unnatural specimens they are, while Corvino's animality is to be the object of a public display more devastating than Sir Politic's brief masquerade as a tortoise.

Thus on successive levels of low comedy and high justice, the monsters of folly and the monsters of vice suffer purgation, exposed as the sort of misshapen marvels they themselves have chattered about so freely. The relative harmlessness of Sir Pol's downfall serves to differentiate his folly from the viciousness of the Venetians, but the many parallels between his catastrophe and theirs warn us that his kind of folly is sufficiently virulent after all, is closely related to graver sins, and, if it persists in imitating them, must ultimately fall under the same condemnation.

If these observations are accurate, it should be clear in what sense the subplot of the Would-be's is relevant to the total structure of *Volpone*. Starting from a contrast between Italian vice and English folly, Jonson personifies the latter in two brainless English travelers, makes their folly consist chiefly in mimicry of Italian vice, and Italian vice itself, in its purest form, consist of the more comprehensive form of mimicry we have termed "metamorphosis," thus bringing the two aspects of evil together into the same moral universe and under a common moral judgment; with the use of the beast fable he binds the two together dramatically, and by the distribution of poetic justice he preserves the distinction between them. Each of the episodes involving the Would-be's, including the much despised incident of the tortoise, thus serves a definite dramatic purpose, and one may conclude, then, that the subplot adds a fresh dimension and a profounder insight without which *Volpone*, though it might be a neater play, would also be a poorer and a thinner one.

EDWARD B. PARTRIDGE

The Allusiveness of Epicoene

Harry Levin claims that Jonson's trick of making his characters say something which frequently has little explicit meaning reaches its logical limit in
Epicoene, "where everything spoken has a high nuisance value and the words
themselves become sheer filagree." There is some truth to this claim, though
not so much as Levin and Alexander Sackton (who elaborated on it in *Rhetoric as a Dramatic Language in Ben Jonson*) make for it. At first glance the
language of *Epicoene* seems remarkably direct and unequivocal; much of it,
of course, remains so after repeated glances. But to think that "everything
spoken" has primarily a nuisance value is likely to make one ignore the subtle
allusiveness of much that is spoken.

Allusive language is one of the slyer ways of throwing discourse into the
parallel engagement of metaphorical language. Allusions suggest another area
of experience—a series of concepts or a set of emotions—which can be seen
juxtaposed, for a moment, to the rest of the discourse. This juxtaposition
of the two worlds—the world of the characters in action and the world
suggested by the allusions—creates some of the comic effect of Jonson's
plays.

We might begin with the allusions to *epicene*. As a substantive, *epicene*
means one who partakes of the characteristics of both sexes. As an adjective,
it carries this meaning and, by transference, also means "adapted to both
sexes." An example of this meaning, according to the *OED,* is Fuller's use
of the word in his *Worthies,* where he described "those Epicoene, and Her-

From *ELH* 22, no. 2 (June 1955). © 1955 by the Johns Hopkins University Press.

maphrodite Convents wherein Monks and Nuns lived together." Further-
more, *epicene* was sometimes used in the seventeenth century to mean
"effeminate," though its use in Jonson's "Epigram on the Court Pucell" does
not seem to carry this meaning, as the *OED* claims it does. The lines are:

> What though with Tribade lust she force a Muse,
>   And in an Epicoene fury can write newes
> Equall with that, which for the best newes goes,
>   As aërie light, and as like wit as those?

"Epicoene" can not properly mean "effeminate" here: a woman does not
do things in an "effeminate" way. It seems rather to carry the meanings
already explained and to imply something unnatural. This suggestion of the
unnatural is emphasized by both "Tribade" and "force," "Tribade" referring
to a woman who practices unnatural vice with other women, and "force"
suggesting a sexual assault. Thus, "Epicoene fury" has more a coloring of
the masculine or the hermaphroditic than of the effeminate. In short, the
main point about all seventeenth century uses of *epicene* is that they suggested the abnormal no-man's-land (and no-woman's-land, too) between the
normal male and the normal female. This meaning is, I think, central to *The
Silent Woman.*

The title, *Epicoene,* refers to much more than the central twist of the
plot in which Morose's wife turns out to be a boy. Nearly everyone in the
play is epicene in some way. Note, for example, Truewit's description of the
epicene women who have lately formed a College: "A new foundation, sir,
here i' the towne, of ladies, that call themselues the Collegiates, an order
betweene courtiers, and country-madames, that liue from their husbands;
and giue entertainement to all the *Wits,* and *Braueries* o' the time, as they
call 'hem: crie downe, or vp, what they like, or dislike in a braine, or a
fashion, with most masculine, or rather *hermaphroditicall* authoritie: . . ."
(1.1.73–80). As Truewit describes these Collegiates, they seem to belong to
some intermediate sex between courtiers and women. Though "courtiers"
then could be used for both sexes, it is generally used in this play to refer
to men. Truewit seems dubious about their exact nature when he tells how
they criticize wit and fashion, at first thinking them "masculine"—that is,
too bold to be feminine—then amending it to "*hermaphroditicall*" apparently because they look like women but act like men. Though "College" was
used loosely for "company," "Collegiates" might have suggested something
unfeminine in an age when only men gathered in colleges and, above all,
only men criticized authoritatively. Jonson emphasizes the educational sense

of the term by alluding to the learning, grammar, honours, and heraldry of their College.

Lady Centaure seems the most clearly epicene of these Collegiates. Characteristically, Jonson suggests her abnormal nature in her name. In the Elizabethan Age "centaur" referred not merely to the fabulous creature with the head, trunk, and arms of a man, joined to the body and legs of a horse, but also, by a figurative extension, to an unnatural hybrid creation or to the intimate union of diverse natures (*OED*). Dekker's use of the word in 1606 reveals this second meaning: "Sixe of these *Centaures* (that are halfe man, halfe beast, and halfe diuell)." In classical literature the centaur is typically goatish, mischievous, and lustful; in so far as it has any single sexual nature, it is male (a female centaur is possible, but extremely rare). A centaur and a satyr may really be the same. In this play Lady Centaure looks like a woman, and in part acts like one, but the masculine side of her nature is implied by Haughty's remark that Centaure "has immortaliz'd her selfe, with taming of her wilde male" (4.3.27–28), apparently by forcing her husband to give her the requisites of a fashionable lady.

All of these Ladies appear so far from the feminine—or what is generally considered the feminine—that Morose, on hearing their loud threats to have him blanketed, cries out, "O, mankind generation!" (5.4.22). I take *mankind* to mean *masculine* or *mannish*, thus disagreeing with Percy Simpson who says that it comes from *mankeen* and means infuriated. Possibly Jonson plays with both meanings, but the primary meaning seems to me to be *masculine*. In two plays written about the time of *Epicoene* Shakespeare used *mankind* to mean *masculine*: see *The Winter's Tale* (2.3.86) and *Coriolanus* (4.2.24). Jonson's comment on the *Coriolanus* passage managed to combine both ideas: "A *mankind* woman is a woman with the roughness of a man, and, in an aggravated sense, a woman ferocious, violent, and eager to shed blood." In Beaumont's *The Woman Hater* (1607), 3.2, the woman hater, running away from a lady who pursues and tries to seduce him, asks, "Are women grown so mankind? Must they be wooing?" In all of these passages, as well as in Morose's exclamation, *mankind* is best understood, I think, to mean primarily *masculine* or *mannish*. The mannishness of these women is suggested by other remarks. For instance: after being solicited by Haughty, Centaure, and Mavis in turn, Dauphine says, "I was neuer so assaulted" (5.2.52). Assaulting the opposite sex is generally thought to be a male privilege. Again: note the comment of the Ladies on Dauphine's neatness. Though "iudiciall in his clothes," he is "not so superlatiuely neat as some. . . . That wear purer linnen than our selues, and professe more neatness then the *french hermaphrodite!*" (4.6.26–31). Neatness is often thought, not always justifiably, to be more characteristic of women than men. The effeminate man has long been associated with a too careful attention to his face and dress, just as the woman who is careless about her neatness seems less feminine. The Ladies thus unconsciously reveal both their own deviation from the feminine and the deviation of their suitors from the masculine. Epicoene adds a remark to this conversation which suggests the inverted sexual customs of their epicene lives. These neat men, according to her, "are the only theeues of our fame: that thinke to take vs with that perfume, or with that lace. . . ." Men have managed sometimes to interest women, sometimes even to "take" them, but customarily they have used other means than perfume and lace. True, we ought to remember that men in Jacobean London did wear lace and use perfume in a way that modern men do not. Yet excessive attention to dress was continually satirized by the dramatists, because it was both irrational and unmanly. The more normal way of attracting women—and as comic as the epicene way—is dramatized in the physical conquest of La Foole and Daw by Dauphine, who is, as a result, besieged by the Ladies. Finally, the sterility of these women makes them less feminine. They have "those excellent receits" to keep from bearing children: "How should we maintayne our youth and beautie, else?" (4.3.57–60).

The "most masculine, or rather *hermaphroditicall* authoritie" of these Ladies Collegiates is best shown by the only one of them whom we see with her husband—Mistress Otter. Perhaps because she is only a "pretender" to their learning, she takes their instruction most seriously. Captain Otter is first mentioned as an "*animal amphibium*" because he has had command on land and sea, but we learn from La Foole that his wife "commands all at home." Clerimont then concludes that "she is Captaine OTTER?" (1.4.26–30). Just before the third act when we first see the Otters, Truewit prepares us for the comic view of their transposed marital relationship. Captain Otter, Truewit says, "is his wifes Subiect, he calls her Princesse, and at such times as these, followes her vp and down the house like a page, with his hat off, partly for heate, partly for reuerence" (2.6.54–57). Modern listeners might not appreciate the full reversal implied in "his wifes Subiect," but anyone who lived before women achieved the legal right to own property and the possession of great financial power (which is the power to subjugate man) must have been aware that the usual relation of husband and wife is reversed, so that she is Captain Otter and he is "like a page."

The first scene in act 3 carries out this reversal. Captain Otter begs to be heard; Mistress Otter rails at him and asks him, "Do I allow you your halfe-crowne a day, to spend, where you will. . . . Who giues you your maintenance, I pray you? who allowes you your horse-meat and man's meat?"

(3.1.36–40). Clerimont, who witnesses this feminine usurpation of the role of the male, observes, "Alas, what a tyrannie, is this poore fellow married too" (3.2.10–11). The ultimate reversal of roles appears in the fourth act scene when, according to the stage direction, Mistress Otter "*falls vpon him and beates him.*"

But more important than the epicene nature of Mistress Otter is the epicene nature of Epicoene herself (or, rather, himself). When first seen, Epicoene is quiet enough to please even Morose. Then, as soon as the wedding is over, complaining loudly, she turns on Morose, who laments, "O immodestie! a manifest woman!" Since "manifest" implies a display so evident that no other proof is needed, Morose seems to be saying that a loud, demanding voice is woman's most characteristic feature. (Morose previously praised Epicoene for not taking pleasure in her tongue "which is a womans chiefest pleasure" [2.5.41–42]). A moment later, Epicoene tells Mute that she will have none of his "vnnaturall dumbnesse in my house; in a family where I gouerne." The marriage is a minute old, and the wife governs. Morose's answer reveals his awareness of their strange marriage and Epicoene's peculiar nature: "She is my Regent already! I haue married a PENTHESILEA, a SEMIRAMIS, sold my liberty to a distaffe" (3.4.54–58). The allusions are revealing. Penthesilea, the daughter of Ares, was the queen of the Amazons who fought in the Trojan war. Semiramis, the wife of Ninus, the mythical founder of the Assyrian empire, ruled for many years after the death of her husband. Like Penthesilea, she was especially renowned in war. Soon after, Morose alludes again to the Amazons, those curiously epicene beings from antiquity, when he cries out, "O *Amazonian* impudence!" (3.5.41). Her impudence seems Amazonian to others than Morose. Truewit, for instance, describes how all the noise and "her masculine, and lowd commanding, and vrging the whole family, makes him thinke he has married a *furie*" (4.1.9–11). When Epicoene is changed from a demure girl to an Amazon, she takes on a new name. Haughty tells her, "I'll call you MOROSE still now, as I call CENTAVRE, and MAVIS" (4.3.14–15). From then until she is revealed to be a boy, she is called by this masculine name. It is only just that, since she has taken over the authoritative power of Morose, she should also take over his name.

Just as Captain Otter becomes epicene as his wife becomes Captain Otter, so Morose loses or is willing to lose his male dominance after Epicoene's "masculine, and lowd commanding." The first sign of a change in Morose comes after he has frightened Mistress Otter with a "huge, long naked weapon."

MOR: Would I could redeeme it with the losse of an eye (nephew)
    a hand, or any other member.
DAV: Mary, god forbid, sir, that you should geld your selfe, to
    anger your wife.
MOR: So it would rid me of her!

(4.4.8–12)

This willingness to become a eunuch so long as it rids him of his epicene
wife prompts him later to plead impotence as a reason for divorce. "I am
no man," he tells the Ladies, "Vtterly vnabled in nature, by reason of *frig-
idity,* to performe the duties, or any the least office of a husband" (5.4.44–
47). When this ruse of declaring himself "no man" fails, he welcomes even
that reflection on virility which the Elizabethans thought the most comic—
being a cuckold. "O, let me worship and adore you," he cries to La Foole
and Daw after they swear that they have lain with Epicoene (5.4.120). Castration, impotence, and being a wittol—all suggest that Morose would even
lose his own maleness to get rid of a wife who at first seemed feminine but
proved epicene.

The epicene natures of the women throw the masculine natures of the
men out of line. When one sex changes, the other is likely to change. Otter's
nature is dislocated by his wife's masculinity, so that the description of him
as "*animal amphibium*" alludes to his divided nature as well as to his amphibious command. Jonson was fond of this sort of word play. In the masque,
Neptune's Triumph, there is "*Amphibion Archy,*" who is described as the
chief "of the *Epicoene* gender, Hees, and Shees." The Broker in *The Staple
of Newes* is called "*Amphibion*" because he is a "creature of two natures"
(2.4.132). The adjective *amphibion* (or *amphibious*) meant having two
modes of existence or being of doubtful nature. Browne's statement—"We
are onely that amphibious piece between a corporall and spiritual essence"
—is the best known example of this use in the seventeenth century. Otter is
an amphibious piece in this play—a being of doubtful nature who looks like
a man, but does not act like one.

Another epicene man is La Foole, who is spoken of first as "a precious
mannikin" (1.3.25)—that is, a little man or a pygmy. When he speaks, he
apparently speaks in an effeminate manner—rapidly and all in one breath.
Talking also characterizes Sir John Daw whom Truewit calls, "The onely
talking sir i' the towne!" (1.2.66). As we have seen already, to Morose
"womans chiefest pleasure" is her tongue. That the audience is apparently
expected to associate women and talking can be inferred from the ironic
subtitle—*The Silent Woman.* Who ever heard of a silent woman? Daw's
barely sensible poem reflects this same assumption:

> *Silence in woman, is like speech in man,*
>   *Deny't who can.*
>
> . . . .
>
>   *Nor, is't a tale,*
> *That female vice should be a vertue male,*
> *Or masculine vice, a female vertue be.*
>   (2.3.123–28)

There is little sense to this in itself, but from the context we gather that, though Daw means it one way, we should take it another way. Daw seems to mean that speech is a defect ("vice" = defect) in a woman just as it is a virtue in a man. "*I know to speake,*" he says in the last line of the poem, "*and shee to hold her peace.*" Silence, which Daw considers woman's crowning virtue, would then be man's great defect. Daw's distinction between the sexes is so extreme and so unsupported by facts that it is comic to most normal people. The normal Elizabethan feeling about silence and women was probably voiced by Zantippa in Peele's *Old Wives' Tale* (731–32): "A woman without a tongue is as a soldier without his weapon." The whole play suggests that both a silent woman and a talkative man are, if anything, inversions of the normal. The tendency of Daw and La Foole to gossip maliciously suggests the inversion of their natures which their actions reveal. Their feminine or at least non-masculine natures are implied also by their lack of courage. One thinks, perhaps erroneously, that men are usually courageous and that women are usually frightened. Helena in *A Midsummer Night's Dream* (3.2.302) says, "I am a right maid for my cowardice." Sir Andrew Aguecheek's fear makes him ridiculous, but Viola's fear seems only normal to the spectator, though it makes her ridiculous to the other characters who do not know that she is really a woman. Similarly, when Daw and La Foole prove themselves so frightened that they allow themselves to be publicly humiliated rather than act on their valiant words, we think of them as somewhat less than the men they appear to be. The Ladies Collegiate are loud, demanding, and aggressive. All, like Centaure, try to tame their wild males. All, in short, are Amazons. Of the men, only Clerimont, Truewit, and Dauphine are not warped by the Amazonian natures of these epicene women.

Yet even these apparently normal men are somewhat ambiguous, sexually. Truewit's first speech in the play suggests the epicene quality of their sexual experience when he remarks that "betweene his mistris abroad, and his engle at home," Clerimont can melt away his time. Since an "engle" was a young boy kept for erotic purposes, Truewit is explaining how Clerimont enjoys the pleasures of both sexes. There had already been an allusion to the homosexual relationship of the Boy and Clerimont in the latter's fourth speech in this first scene. The sexual ambiguity of the characters in this play is nowhere better suggested than in the Boy's remark that the Lady "puts a perruke o' my head; and askes me an' I will weare her gowne; and I say, no: and then she hits me a blow o' the eare, and calls me innocent, and lets me goe" (1.1.16–18). She calls him innocent because he (who is unconsciously feminine in his relationship to Clerimont) refuses to be consciously feminine in his relationship to the aggressive Lady. To be sophisticated (as opposed to innocent) apparently means to be quadri-sexual: a man to both men and women, and a woman to both women and men.

II

This interest in beings who have the characteristics of both sexes suggests that the play is fundamentally concerned with deviations from a norm. Like all of Jonson's major comedies, *Epicoene* explores the question of decorum—here, the decorum of the sexes and the decorum of society. We recognize that most of the characters are epicene because we still have, even in this age of the emancipated woman, a sense of what is normal for the sexes. We may lack Jonson's strong sense of decorum, perhaps because we can not entirely agree with his concept of what is natural. Jonson clearly anticipated that sense of "nature" which became a central dogma in the neoclassic age: that is, the natural is the normal and the universal. Normally, men are brave and aggressive, and women are passive and reserved—or are supposed to be. A cowardly man and an aggressive woman become, in a comedy, ludicrous. Some of Jonson's rigid sense of the decorum of nature has been lost in an age which, like the present one, looks on deviations from nature as pathological—that is, as pitiful. For example, Morose. To many, the spectacle of indolent men torturing a man highly sensitive to noise is closer to sadism than to pure comedy. The reviewer for *The Times* in 1924 thought that, in the Phoenix Society production of the play, Morose was a "tragic figure" tormented by "bounders." But to previous ages such "comedy of affliction" was a social rather than a medical matter. Morose is comic, rather than psychopathic, because he is selfish and vain. When he says, "all discourses, but mine owne, afflict mee, they seeme harsh, impertinent, and irksome" (2.1.4–5), we hear the voice of a proud, not a sick man. Or, rather, Morose's affliction is a disease, but a ridiculous disease. Note that Truewit asks Clerimont, "But is the disease so ridiculous in him, as it is made?" (1.1.148–49). To us no disease seems ridiculous, not even those which are ostensibly the fault of the diseased person—venereal diseases, for instance.

But to the seventeenth century many sicknesses were ridiculous. Bedlam was a comedy, and D'Avenant's diseased nose, the source of countless jibes. The laughter, cruel to us but simply toughminded to earlier ages, apparently came from a sense of decorum so rigid that even the deviations of sickness became ludicrous. No healthy, rational man—the terms overlapped for Jonson—should be so sensitive to noise as Morose. He should be "cured," as Truewit suggests in the last line of the play—that is, brought in line with what Truewit thinks is normal. "Cure" is borrowed from medicine, as the whole theory of the comedy of humours is, and both keep something of their medical sense even when used as Jonson used them; but they are applied to social rather than physical troubles—to hypocrisy, not heart trouble.

One way to observe how Jonson explores the question of what is natural is to note the allusions to deviations from nature—to prodigies and to the strange, the unnatural, and the monstrous. A prodigy to the Elizabethans was something out of the ordinary course of nature, something either abnormal or monstrous. Because Morose is so ridiculously sensitive to noise, Truewit thinks, "There was never such a prodigie heard of " (1.2.3). Morose himself has a contrary view of prodigies. When someone winds a horn outside of his house, he cries out, "What villaine? what prodigie of mankind is that?" (2.1.38–39). Just as Morose thinks that anyone (except himself) who makes noise is a prodigy, so Truewit thinks complete silence is unnatural. To him the silent Morose and Mute are "fishes! *Pythagoreans* all! This is strange" (2.2.3). Pythagoreans were noted for their secrecy as well as for their belief in metempsychosis. Speechless men may look human, but they have the souls of fishes: they are "strange." "Strange" and its equivalents are crucial words to everyone in the play. "Strange sights," according to Truewit, "can be seen daily in these times of masques, plays, Puritan preachings, and mad folk" (2.2.33–36). He then proceeds to tell Morose the "monstrous hazards" that Morose shall run with a wife. Among these hazards is the possibility of marrying a woman who will "antidate" him cuckold by conveying her virginity to a friend. "The like has beene heard of, in nature. 'T is no deuised, impossible thing, sir" (2.2.145–47).

The relationship between Epicoene and Morose appears to others and to themselves as strange, even monstrous. At their first meeting Morose tells her that his behavior, being "rare," may appear strange (2.5.23). Truewit had previously complimented Epicoene on "this rare vertue of your silence" (2.4.91). Epicoene has another idea about silence which appears when she calls Mute down for his "coacted, vnntturall dumbnesse" (3.4.54). Speechlessness apparently seems a deviation from nature to the Ladies Collegiate too because they come to see Epicoene, thinking her a prodigy, but they find her normal—that is, loquacious. Her loquacity, so natural to them, later seems only a "monstrous" impertinency to Morose (4.4.36). Just as she seems a monster to him, so he seems a "prodigious creature" to Mavis when he pleads impotence (5.4.48). The spectators, who stand outside of this created world, measure its prodigies against their own concept of what is normal and natural, and find, presumably, that most of its strange creatures are comic.

Connected with this question of what is natural is another question, a favorite in the seventeenth century—what is the relation of art and nature? This question is brought up early in the opening scene when Clerimont curses Lady Haughty's "peec'd beautie"—pieced, apparently, from her washings, patchings, paintings, and perfumings. Because her artificial beauty offends him, he writes the famous song, "Still to be neat, still to be drest." In this song Clerimont upholds simplicity and nature because, so he thinks, the artifices of powder and perfume may only conceal what is not sweet and not sound. Such pretenses are "*adulteries*"—that is, adulterations or debasings of what should be natural. The natural to him is simple, careless, and free. To be natural a woman must be unpinned, uncorseted, and unadorned. Truewit declares himself to be "clearly o' the other side": he loves "a good dressing, before any beautie o' the world." "Beautie," one gathers, is only nature; "a good dressing" is art. A well dressed woman is "like a delicate garden" to Truewit, apparently because nature in her is trimmed, artificially nurtured, and artfully arranged; its delicacy comes deliberately, not naturally. Art, as he uses it, means the technique of revealing what is naturally attractive and of concealing what is naturally ugly; thus, if a woman has "good legs," she should "wear short clothes." Nor should a lover wish to see his lady make herself up any more than one would ask to see gilders overlaying a base metal with a thin covering of gold; one must not discover "how little serues, with the helpe of art, to adorne a great deale." A lover should only approach his lady when she is a "compleat, and finish'd" work of art.

Because clothes are the most common of all artifices by which the natural is concealed, the relation between art and nature is suggested most clearly in allusions to dress. Clerimont seems swayed from his earlier disdain for the artifices of women when he sees Lady Haughty in all her finery. Truewit assures him that "Women ought to repaire the losses, time and yeeres haue made i' their features, with dressings" (4.1.35–37). In the conversation that follows this observation, art takes on an added dimension: it comes to mean social decorum. Truewit repeats his former point that a woman should artfully conceal her natural limitations. Then the talk slips over into what is socially acceptable when Clerimont ridicules some women whose laughter is rude because it is loud, and Truewit ridicules women whose walk is offensive because it is as huge as that of an ostrich. Characteristically, Truewit says, "I loue measure i' the feet"—"measure" meaning moderation as well as rhythm. Decorous behavior, then, is to the whole person what careful dressing is to the body: an artistic way of repairing the defects of an offensive nature. Even the uncourtly Morose shares the courtly conviction that art can serve and rival nature. He tells Epicoene that he longs to have his wife be the first in all fashions, have her council of tailors, "and then come foorth, varied like Nature, or oftner then she, and better, by the helpe of Art, her aemulous seruant" (2.5.73–75). On a lower social plane Otter reveals that he too is aware of how women can use the artificial to gild or transform the natural. When he is drunk enough to be brave, he begins to curse his wife for being naturally vile. She makes herself endurable only by the most ingenious artifices. "Euery part o' the towne ownes a peece of her," Otter claims. "She takes her selfe asunder still when she goes to bed," and the next day "is put together againe, like a great *German* clocke" (4.2.94–99).

But clothes do not merely artificially conceal nature or repair the losses that the years have made; at times the artistic can take the place of the natural: a person's dress can become the person. Thus, in this play as in other comedies of Jonson, knighthood is thought to be largely a matter of clothes. Clerimont, speaking of Sir John Daw, asks, "Was there euer such a two yards of knighthood, measur'd out by *Time,* to be sold to laughter?" (2.4.151–52). In a bitter arraignment of knighthood Morose implies that the artificial can become the natural when he says that knighthood "shall want clothes, and by reason of that, wit, to foole to lawyers" (2.5.125–26). The most striking reference to the way that dress can change man's nature is Truewit's remark about the disguised Otter and Cutbeard. After he fits them out as a divine and a canon lawyer, he tells Dauphine, "the knaues doe not know themselues, they are so exalted, and alter'd. Preferment changes any man" (5.3.3–5). Dress can so alter what a man is thought to be that his own nature is changed accordingly.

Epicoene, then, is a comedy about nature, normality, and decorum. Its various scenes explore comically and searchingly a number of questions to which, since it is a play, it does not offer any final answers. What is natural and normal for the sexes? What does society expect of men and women? Are women normally gossipy and men normally courageous? What is the relation between the natural and the artificial in social intercourse? But, though the play offers no final answers, it suggests throughout that the various answers dramatized in the physical and verbal action of the play are comic in so far as they violate certain standards of what is masculine and what is feminine, as well as what is natural and what is artificial in dress, behavior, and beauty—standards which, presumably, the spectators bring to the theatre with them.

Comparing Jonson's text with any of the many adaptations of the play may reveal how effective its allusive language is in bringing these standards to the attention of the audience. For instance, George Colman's acting version in 1776. Colman had a good eye for emphasizing the farcical element in the plot, but apparently little feeling for what Jonson's language might suggest. The 1776 acting version is a simpler and, by eighteenth century standards, a more genteel play, but its comedy is thinner and more obvious because Colman (who said in his prologue that Jonson's farce was "somewhat stale") cut out much of the play's allusive language. Though he kept in the speech about the Collegiates who speak with masculine or hermaphroditical authority and Morose's reference to "mankind generation," he generally shifted the emphasis away from the comedy of sexual deviations by cutting out the references to the bi-sexual boy, the Collegiates' living away from their husbands, and Morose's castration, impotence, and cuckolding. The result is what is known as a "cleaner" play, but a tamer and less searching one. In the same way the theme of art versus nature is mangled: the song, "Still to be neat," is kept, though transferred to an earlier passage in the play, but Truewit's first act remarks are cut out, along with most of the crucial references to clothes. In short, for all its deceptive likeness to the play that Jonson wrote in his unrefined age, Colman's version is a far less suggestive comedy about nature, artifice, and not particularly epicene people.

Colman's treatment of *Epicoene* is typical of most adaptations, and prophetic of many modern readings of it. But unless one is aware of the allusiveness of Jonson's language, which adapters like Colman have mangled and which modern readers often disregard, one can not entirely understand Dryden's comment that there is "more art and acuteness of fancy in [*Epicoene*] than in any of Ben Jonson's [plays]."

GEOFFREY HILL

The World's Proportion:
Jonson's Dramatic Poetry
in Sejanus *and* Catiline

> *The worlds proportion disfigured is*
> *That those two legges whereon it doth rely,*
> *Reward and punishment are bent awry.*
> —JOHN DONNE, *The First Anniversary*

Jonson, in his two Roman tragedies, is either a monumental victim of the New Learning, or a brilliant satirist of the contemporary political situation. By an act of secular faith one takes the latter assumption to be true. It is the less respectable choice since, to many, politics is forever loitering about the vestal precincts of Art. There is a tone of hurt suspicion in the voices of the Oxford editors when they discover that *Catiline* is, after all, a dirty book:

> And Jonson's Catiline hardly affects to have any more specious
> aim than to assert the claim of the have-nots against those who
> have—a claim, moreover, here presented in its least persuasive
> form, as the revolt of a needy and debased aristocracy against
> the state at large.

Both Coleridge and Swinburne, however, have intelligent notes on the relationship of these plays to the Jacobean political dilemma. They are at least prepared to accept that Jonson's choice, and treatment, of his themes may have been governed by something other than scholarly perverseness.

From *Jacobean Theatre* (Stratford-upon-Avon Studies 1). © 1960 by Edward Arnold (Publishers) Ltd. St. Martin's Press, 1960.

In both *Sejanus* and *Catiline,* Jonson manages to blend a forthright
dogmatism with an astute trimming. This makes him, in a way, an epitome
of the disturbed decades preceding the outbreak of the Civil War. This was
the time of Selden, the troubled democrat; and of Falkland, the troubled
Royalist; and Jonson knew them both. And, at a period when the tensions
between Court and City were becoming increasingly felt, Jonson abandoned
the public theatres for ten years to become a writer and producer of masques
for royalty and aristocracy. A despiser of the crowd, he yet said "Words are
the Peoples" and captured in his comedies the idioms and inflexions of
common speech. And modern critics have, of course, sufficiently appraised
Jonson's "accurate eye for oddities," his "quick ear for the ordinary turns
of speech." Nevertheless, this very admiration produces its own kind of
danger. To suggest that art, to be significant, must grow from vernacular
roots is so much a contemporary necessity that it becomes, almost, a required
cliché. And to say that, in Jonson,

> the tricks of shysters and crooks, mountebanks, lawyers, news-
> vendors, and monopoly-hunters are transferred to the stage with
> all the relish of one who sees for himself what is under his nose

is to make his satire seem more indulgent than it is. "Relish" and "under
his nose" suggest a slightly myopic gourmet.

Moreover, the recent and thorough evaluation that the comedies have
received from various hands appears to leave a residual implication: that,
compared to the tough contact with life in plays like *The Alchemist* or
Bartholomew Fair, the world of the Roman tragedies is an abstraction, a
retreat into formulas and commonplaces. The cadences and imagery of these
plays are certainly at a remove from those of Busy or Dol Common; but it
could be argued that the "grand commonplaces"—even those that refer back
to Latin originals—are as much part of the seventeenth-century "climate"
as are the idioms of the great comic characters. It seems to be a modern
scholastic fallacy that "living speech" can be heard only in the smoke-room
or in bed; in fact the clichés and equivocations of propaganda or of "public
relations" are also part of the living speech of a society. Character writers
of the seventeenth century used Roman allusions, as modern political car-
toonists employ a kind of visual short-hand, to "tune in" to a required stock
response. It could be argued that the high-pitched invective that runs through
Sejanus and *Catiline* is superb "cartoon" language, with all the serious over-
statement and polemic relevance of that art:

CICERO: What domesticke note
Of private filthinesse, but is burnt in
Into thy life? What close, and secret shame,
But is growne one, with thy knowne infamy?
                              (*Catiline,* 4.316)

The vituperative "filthinesse," "shame," "infamy" could, perhaps, be taken too easily as a mere stage-anger, as an abstraction from the tensions, the "humanity" of real experience. The stresses of Jacobean and Caroline society, culminating in the Civil War, were real enough; yet men declared their living angers, their immediate and pressing problems, in a language comparable to that of *Cataline.* The *Declaration of the County of Dorset, June 1648* was framed in the following terms:

> We demand . . .
> (iv) That our liberties (purchases of our ancestors' blood) may be redeemed from all former infringements and preserved henceforth inviolable; and that our ancient liberties may not lie at the mercy of those that have none, nor be enlarged and repealed by the votes and revotes of those that have taken too much liberty to destroy the subjects'. . . .
> (vii) That we may no longer subjugate our necks to the *boundless lusts* and unlimited power of *beggarly and broken* committees, consisting generally of the tail of the gentry, men of *ruinous fortunes* and despicable estates, whose *insatiable desires* prompt them to continual projects of pilling and stripping us.

The "boundless lusts" and "ruinous fortunes" anathematized in the *Declaration* may be set against Cicero's denunciation of Catiline and his fellows, their "filthinesse," their "shipwrack'd mindes and fortunes" (4.413).

Moreover, Jonson shares with the authors of the *Declaration* a dual attitude towards the name and nature of liberty. The 1648 testament puts liberty in two poses: the first respectable; the second disreputable. "Liberty" in the first case is plainly involved with property and heredity ("purchases of our ancestors' blood"). Opposed to this is a second, destructive "liberty," synonymous with licence ("boundless lusts," "insatiable desires"). In Jonson's moral world, also, a stress and counterstress is evoked from the conflicting connotations of words such as "liberty" or "freedom." In the Roman tragedies "liberty" seems frequently equated with irresponsible power:

CATILINE: Wake, wake brave friends,
And meet the libertie you oft have wish'd for.

Behold, renowne, riches, and glory court you

. . . .

And, being *Consul,* I doubt not t'effect,
All that you wish, if trust not flatter me,
And you'd not rather still be slaves, th[a]n free.
CETHEGUS: Free, free. LONGINUS: 'Tis freedom. CURIUS: Freedom
    we all stand for.

                                                        (1.409)

As parallel to this grotesque shout there is, in *Sejanus,* the "Senates flatterie" of the new favourite Macro; their weak cries of "Liberty, liberty, liberty" as he takes Sejanus's place. The irony here is that the Senators cry out to celebrate the return of that liberty which is a concomitant of property and stability; but we know that "liberty," under Macro, will still be only "licence"—a renewal of "pilling and stripping."

The civic alternatives to such dissolute, destroying forces are "industry," "vigilance" (*Cat.,* 3.33) and a proper reverence for the gods. The Second Chorus in *Catiline* speaks of the need "to make a free, and worthy choice" (2.373); and the good soldier, Petreius, instructs his army in the fundamentals for which it is fighting:

PETREIUS: The quarrell is not, now, of fame, of tribute,

. . . .

but for your owne republique.
For the rais'd temples of th' immortall gods,
For all your fortunes, altars, and your fires,
For the deare soules of your lov'd wives, and children,
Your parents tombes, your rites, lawes, libertie,
And, briefly, for the safety of the world.

                                                        (5.11)

It is clear from this that the word "liberty" regains, in the oratory of Petreius, its respectable associations, being securely anchored next to "lawes" and preceded by the pietist sequence: "gods," "altars," "wives," "children." There is danger in the handling of such deliberately emotive catalogues. At worst, such rhetoric can become a confusion of apparent humility and actual hectoring. William Wordsworth, a late democrat beginning the drift back to conservative orthodoxy, employs a similar imagery in his sonnets of 1802:

altar, sword and pen,
Fireside, the heroic wealth of hall and bower

Wordsworth's invocation is more raucous than Jonson's, being somewhat burdened by the self-imposed romantic role of poet-as-prophet. Jonson, exploiting the dramatic medium, is able to "distance" his orthodox eloquence by projecting it through the mouth of a persona.

Elsewhere, too, the essentially conservative rhetoric is handled with persuasive charm, as in the *Catiline* dedication to the Earl of Pembroke:

> MY LORD: In so thick, and darke an ignorance, as now almost covers the age, I crave leave to stand neare your light: and, by that, to bee read. Posteritie may pay your benefit the honor, & thanks: when it shall know, that you dare, in these Jig-given times, to countenance a legitimate Poeme. I must call it so, against all noise of opinion: from whose crude, and ayrie reports, I appeale, to that great and singular faculty of judgement in your Lordship, able to vindicate truth from error. It is the first (of this race) that ever I dedicated to any person, and had I not thought it the best, it should have beene taught a lesse ambition. Now, it approcheth your censure cheerefully, and with the same assurance, that innocency would appeare before a magistrate.

This is a well-contrived amalgam of religious, political, and literary connotations. The keywords embody dual-associations of order, authority, and harmony in more than one field. "To vindicate truth from error" sounds like Hooker; and "judgement" and "innocency" have theological overtones, even though Jonson's prime application is in secular self-vindication. "Innocency" thus serves to fuse the ideas of divine order and human law. "Censure" is the province of priest and magistrate and satirist; it is also the privilege of master-patron to servant-poet as Jonson suggests. The dedication is not only an extremely bland and suasive piece of self-defence, it is also a testament to conservative legitimist order; within the bounds of such prose, the tenure of kings and magistrates is unquestionably secure. The very "assurance," the intuitive rightness of Jonson's usage, stems from a familiar rhetoric, a vision of order typified by Sir Thomas Wilson:

> I think meete to speake of framing, and placing an Oration in order, that the matter beeing aptly setled and couched together: might better please the hearers, & with more ease be learned of al men. And the rather I am earnest in this behalf, because I knowe that al things stande by order, and without order nothing can be.
>
> [Arte of Rhetorique]

Again, in Jonson's own *Epistle to [Master John] Selden,* the statesman is praised for his "manly elocution," a phrase in which a way of speaking and a way of living become one and the same.

Such evocative vindications of "wholeness" exist, of course, in a social and dramatic context where the unity of ethic and action is a rarity. For the world of Jonson's Roman tragedies is a world "bent awry," distorted chiefly by the perverted lust for private gain at the expense of public good. Against all the evidences of tawdry chaos Jonson poses the orthodoxy of Cicero and Cato: rather as Pope, in the *Epistles to Several Persons,* celebrates the "decency" of agrarian Order in the face of the Whig financiers; and as Yeats sets the "great melody" of Burke against all manifestations of imperial Whiggery.

In both the Roman plays Jonson's vision of moral and civic disorder—though embodied in several forms—is most immediately presented as a reversal of roles in man and woman; as an abdication of power and choice by the former, a usurpation of private and public control by the latter. In *Catiline* the aborted natures of the protagonists is stressed. Sempronia has a very "masculine" wit; she is "a great stateswoman," "a shee-Critick" who can also "play . . . the orator." And, in her conversation with Fulvia she acts and sounds like Brutus in his tent:

> SEMPRONIA: I ha' beene writing all this night (and am
> So very weary) unto all the *tribes,*
> And *centuries,* for their voyces, to helpe Catiline
> In his election. We shall make him *Consul,*
> I hope, amongst us. . . . FULVIA: Who stands beside?
> (Give me some wine, and poulder for my teeth.
> SEMPRONIA: Here's a good pearle in troth! FULVIA: A pretty one.
> SEMPRONIA: A very orient one!) There are competitors.
>
> (2.96)

The derangement is here stressed by the abrupt parenthesis of womanish trivia, chatter about pearls and dentifrice. Sempronia's strength is an errant thing, a matter of coarse presumption and gesturing.

As moral and dramatic corollary to this "roaring girl" is the sharp depiction, throughout the play, of lasciviousness and hysteria in the men of Catiline's party. There is the incident of the homosexual attempt on one of Catiline's pages (1.506–11), an episode which so disturbed Coleridge that he suggested emending it out of existence; he called it "an outrage to probability." This is precisely its point! The nineteenth century preferred a half-remorseful majesty in its great apostates, a power which Jonson is not prepared to depict in the Catiline conspiracy. Catiline is not Captain Ahab. His rebellion *is* an outrage to probability where "probability" is more-or-less synonymous with "Nature" and the "moral law." What Jonson does give, is a dramatic relevance to outrage and abnormality; and where the actions of the protagonists seem most to elude the patterns of reason, that is the point of Jonson's attack. These opponents of Cicero are "men turn'd furies," whose "wishings tast of woman"; into whose mouths Jonson puts a deliberately grotesque hyperbole:

> CETHEGUS. Enquire not. He shall die.
> Shall, was too slowly said. He' is dying. That
> Is, yet, too slow. He' is dead.
>
> (3.663)

In this projection of a world of spiritual and physical disorder the Roman tragedies are close to certain of the comedies. In *Epicoene*, varied strata of imagery and action are explored, to discover intricate evidence of ethical and sexual abnormality, of dangerous (even if trivial) perversion in the private and public functioning of human natures. Sejanus, too, was once

> the noted *pathick* of the time
> . . . .
> And, now, the second face of the whole world.
>
> (1.216–17)

And here the theme of sexual inversion is absorbed into that of broken status, debauched hierarchy. It was by trading his body that Sejanus rose from serving-boy to be potential master of Rome.

In *Catiline*, the play of action and imagery, though less intricate than the machinations of *Epicoene*, has its own manner of involvement. Apart from the "logical" balancing of illogical sexual conditions in men and women, there is a recurring pattern of significant epithets. The conspirators are described (even self-described!) as "needy" and "desperate," "wild," "lost." But they are also shown to be possessed by "sleep" and "sloth" (5.235, 380). At moments of crisis they shout like excited women, or make passes at boys. To be both "wild" and "sleepy," "desperate" yet "slothful" is gross indecorum, even in rebellion's own terms. It is a double inconsistency, a double irony.

In fact Jonson's method, in both the Roman plays, might be termed an anatomy of self-abuse. It is clear that the *Catiline* conspirators are destroyed as much by their own grotesque self-contradictions as by the bourgeois virtue of Cicero. And in both plays a dangerous apathy or rashness on the part of

the body politic is a contributor to the tragedy. Rome, "bothe her owne
spoiler, and owne prey" (*Cat.*, 1.586), is always as much sinning as sinned-
against. Jonson has Sejanus say:

>   All *Rome* hath beene my slave;
> The *Senate* sate an idle looker on,
> And witnesse of my power; when I have blush'd,
> More, to command, th[a]n it to suffer.
>
>   (5.256)

At first sight this might appear an inappropriate hyperbole, since Sejanus is
presented throughout as a blushless villain. It is certainly no sign of regeneration on the part of the evil-doer; but rather a late outcropping of the
morality-technique. Sejanus, though villain, is allowed an "objective" condemnation of the ills of the State, is even, for a moment, permitted a "Ciceronian" touch. Compare:

> CICERO: O *Rome*, in what a sicknesse art thou fall'n!
> How dangerous, and deadly! when thy head
> Is drown'd in sleepe, and all thy body fev'ry!
> No noise, no pulling, no vexation wakes thee,
> Thy *lethargie* is such.
>
>   (*Catiline*, 3.438)

In some respects Jonson has Sejanus fill a dual role. He blends some of the
characteristics of "Scourge"—bringing torment to a corrupt world—with all
the attributes of the *arriviste,* the supposedly amoral disrupter of society's
settled decency. As *Sejanus* progresses, Jonson's moral scathing is directed
more and more against the blushless dereliction of Senate and people; their
abandonment of moral choice. Rome displays the vice of apathy rather than
the virtue of patience. This deliberate duality is again stressed at the end.
Although it would be quite inappropriate to speak of Jonson's "sympathy"
for Sejanus, nevertheless, the drive of the satire is here against society-at-
large rather than against the solitary villain. There is dramatic "pity" for
Sejanus and his children at this point not because, as human-being, Sejanus
deserves it, but because his immediate role as mob-victim makes such treatment necessary.

Jonson's dramatic rhetoric, in these two Roman tragedies, is so constructed as to work on two levels, yet to a single end, a comprehensive moral
effect. The hyperbole of the protagonists is often so excessive as to be a

parable of the spiritual and physical debauchery. At the same time, varied sequences of keywords signal the ethical truth of the action, like spots of bright marker-dye in a greasy flood. In Catiline's wooing of Aurelia, the satiric method is one of profound parody:

> CATILINE: Wherefore frownes my sweet?
> Have I too long beene absent from these lips,
> This cheeke, these eyes? What is my trespasse? Speake.
> AURELIA: It seemes, you know, that can accuse your selfe.
> CATILINE: I will redeeme it.
>
> . . . .
>
> AURELIA: You court me, now. CATILINE: As I would alwayes, Love,
> By this *ambrosiack* kisse, and this of *nectar*.

$$(1.102)$$

Here is an epicene savouring, a ludicrous distinction between flavours in the kisses, each one mincingly appropriated by the demonstrative. It is the absurdity of over-meticulousness. It is the Spenserian-Petrarchan sexual reverence employed in a context which makes its very euphuism obscene. Marvell adapts the method in "To His Coy Mistress":

> Two hundred to adore each Breast

where the point is to satirize the idea of virginity as good bargaining-material. In Marvell, as in Jonson, the perspective requires the utterance of deliberate cliché, but cliché rinsed and restored to function as responsible speech. As the lover in *Amoretti* asks for "pardon" and "grace" from the beloved and fears lest he "offend," so Catiline and his paramour toy with a sacramental idiom ("trespasse," "accuse," "redeeme"). The suggestive rhetoric is finely used. Catiline is made to utter an effective *mélange* of portentousness and off-hand cynicism. We know that he takes himself too seriously and humanity too lightly (his Petrarchan "fidelity" is pasted nicely upon a cynical confession of wife-removal). The total irony of this scene, of course, depends on the fact that this tiny Petrarchan mock-trial is the nearest Catiline ever gets to an understanding of trespass, or of redemption. He and Aurelia utter, unknowingly, a punch-and-judy burlesque of the play's great meanings. It is significant that this evocative scene should be an act of courtship. It is through such sexual attitudinizing and mutual titillation, through such an exposé of the mechanics of allurement, that Jonson presents his broader commentary on the corrupt-world practices of self-seeking and preferment. The forwardness of the female, the decorative word-spinning of the male, are far from being dramatically inconsistent. And though the gaudy Petrarchan is elsewhere seen as a cold destroyer, it is, in fact, the pervading odour of blood that gives a poignant ruthlessness to Catiline's dalliance, his calling Aurelia "sweet."

As in Marvell's *To His Coy Mistress,* or Pope's *Epistle to Dr. Arbuthnot,* Jonson's language is frequently "literary" in the best sense of the term. That is, its method requires that certain words and phrases, by constant repetition in popular literary modes, shall have been reduced to easy, unquestioned connotations. These connotations are then disturbingly scrutinized. Pope's:

> Oblig'd by hunger and Request of friends

requires for its effect the common formula of gentlemanly apologia, on the part of coy amateurs bringing out verse. It is "hunger" that blasts the cliché into a new perspective. Marvell's wit feeds off Suckling's *Against Fruition* as much as it does off Marlowe's *Passionate Shepherd.* Jonson needs the Petrarchan mask even while, in the Catiline-Aurelia scene, he tears it into paper streamers. And, in the following soliloquy from *Sejanus,* Jonson is able to blend the authoritarian tones of Hall-like satire with suggestions of tongue-in-cheek duplicity on the part of the speaker. Sejanus has just concluded his scene of apparently forthright discussion with Tiberius and is alone:

> SEJANUS: Sleepe
> Voluptuous Caesar, and securitie
> Seize on thy stupide powers, and leave them dead
> To publique cares, awake but to thy lusts.
>
> (3.598)

This holds good on two levels. Tiberius *is* voluptuous and does neglect public affairs (though not nearly so much as Sejanus imagines). So far, Sejanus's words may be taken as choric, as in a morality or a satire, setting the scene for the imminent fall of princes. The difference is that Sejanus is gleeful rather than sorrowing or indignant, and that the "prince" whose fall is imminent is not Tiberius. Tiberius is, in fact, far from stupefied, and succeeds in shepherding Sejanus to the slaughter. Hence, Sejanus's choric comment (still true in its essential commentary on an evil prince) becomes also a statement, by implication, of the fatal blindness of hubris, of Sejanus's own recklessness and greed. In the light of what the audience knows but Sejanus does not, the imperatives of the confident puppet-master ("Sleepe, voluptuous Caesar") slide into the subjunctives of a wishful-thinker ("and [may] securitie seize on thy stupide powers").

From a study of such examples one would conclude that Jonson is able to employ ambiguity—of word, phrase or situation—to give what is ultimately a quite unambivalent expression to moral preference or decision. There is, however, a secondary form of ambiguity at work in both plays— more subjective, more cunning even, and with roots in the Janus-like situation of the professional moralist in Jacobean England.

In *Sejanus,* for instance, crucial political implications are guided into a kind of dramatic cul-de-sac, as in the scene where Sabinus is tempted into self-betrayal by Sejanus's hirelings:

> SABINUS: No ill should force the subject undertake
> Against the soveraigne, more than hell should make
> The gods doe wrong. A good man should, and must
> Sit rather downe with losse, than rise unjust.
> Though, when the *Romanes* first did yield themselves
> To one mans power, they did not meane their lives,
> Their fortunes, and their liberties, should be
> His absolute spoile, as purchas'd by the sword.
> LATIARIS: Why we are worse, if to be slaves, and bond
> To Caesars slave, be such, the proud Sejanus!
> He that is all, do's all, gives Caesar leave
> To hide his ulcerous, and anointed face,
> With his balde crowne at *Rhodes.*
>
> (4.163)

The opening of Sabinus's argument is orthodox, reflecting Tudor statecraft as expressed in the Tenth Homily (1547), and anticipating the Canons of 1606 and the Laudian Canons of 1640. James I's considered opinion that "it was unfit for a subject to speak disrespectfully of any "anointed king," "though at hostility with us" [quoted by G. P. Gooch and H. J. Laski, *English Democratic Ideas in the 17th Century*], gives the orthodox viewpoint succinctly enough. Sabinus's acceptance of the official dogmas comes out even in the pithiness of the trotting couplets with which his speech opens. The thought clicks neatly into place together with the rhyme. Then, as a kind of conditional afterthought, Sabinus suggests that very scrutiny of the tenure of kings which he appears to reject at the beginning. The Tudor apologist suddenly begins to speak like a moderate post-Restoration Whig, one to whom: "government exists, not for the governors, but for the benefit of the governed, and its legitimacy is to be judged accordingly." Compare, too, the tone of the opening three lines ("hell," "the gods") with the ironic use of "absolute" to qualify, not "kingship," but "spoile." Dramatically speaking, this argument (absolutist dogma and Whig qualification) is delivered with the appeal of a Lost Cause. Sabinus is innocently speaking his own doom; his "fault" is predetermined, his stage-audience is wholly composed of agents provocateurs and concealed spies, so that his appeals to civic rectitude are sealed off from directly influencing the outcome of the tragedy. It is the theatre-audience or the reader ("invisible" witnesses) who are exposed to the full vision of the noble conservative humiliated and betrayed by exponents of corrupt Power, of cynical *Realpolitik*. And it is arguable that the celebrated line:

> To hide his ulcerous, and anointed face

gains much of its power through a "suspension" (rather than a "union") of opposites. It is at once a well-turned translation of Tacitus's Latin, and an ambiguous metaphor juxtaposing two hostile connotations. These are: "anointed" in the sense of "smeared with (ointment or cosmetic)" and "anointed," meaning "marked with sacramental authority" (compare "The Lord's anointed"). Hence, the phrase pivots Jonson's two most powerful social attitudes—disgust at corruption; and reverence for consecrated power—thus: "Tiberius is corrupt and, what is worse, tries to paint over that corruption"; or "Tiberius is corrupt, nevertheless he is the anointed of the gods." "Face" continues the deliberate ambivalence; it is both physiognomy and "cheek" (one is reminded of the character called "Face" in *The Alchemist*); "bald crown" signifies both "hairless head" (a private impotence) and "stripped authority" (a public impotence). As these words are spoken by Latiaris, the hireling, only in order to trap Sabinus they cannot, therefore, be taken as "active" radicalism. The image is securely bedded down in a web of tangential implication.

This scene in particular makes nonsense of the view of Jonson's "originally non-dramatic nature" [Una Ellis-Fermor, *The Jacobean Drama*]. He so deploys his conservative philosophy as to give it the attraction of Resistance idealism. He commits himself less deeply than, say, Marvell who, in the *Horation Ode on Cromwell's Return from Ireland*, speaks—in his own voice, and without dramatic "distancing"—of Charles's "helpless Right" and of the "bloody hands" of the spectators round the scaffold. And Jonson's dramatic cunning is also in significant contrast to the procedure of Donne, in his *Elegie XVII*:

> The golden laws of nature are repeal'd
> Which our first Fathers in such reverence held;
> Our liberty's revers'd, our Charter's gone,
> And we're made servants to Opinion,

A monster in no certain shape attir'd,
And whose originall is much desir'd,
Formlesse at first, but goeing on it fashions
And doth prescribe manners and laws to nations.
Here love receiv'd immedicable harmes,
And was dispoiled of his daring armes.

. . . .

Only some few strong in themselves and free
Retain the seeds of antient liberty,
Following that part of love although deprest
And make a throne for him within their breast,
In spight of modern censures him avowing
Their Soveraigne, all service him allowing.

The keywords here are like those in Jonson's Roman plays: "Liberty," "free." But it is clear that their significance is far from the "Ciceronian" ideal. Donne's "liberty" is not the state of civic wisdom based on "industry and vigilance," nor is it a concomitant of inherited property. "Strong *in themselves* and free" smells more of the dangerous anarchism that, in *Catiline,* yearns to use the "free sword" (1.230). And the implications of "Our liberty's revers'd" and "retain the seeds of antient liberty" sing out much more sharply and defiantly in Donne's lyric than do the equivalent but "well-buffered" iconoclasms in Jonson. And, at the crux of his argument, Donne, in offering fealty to a Soveraigne clearly not "anointed of the Lord" commits a kind of witty high treason. In his own voice he pays homage to "libertine" nature in terms that Shakespeare preferred to put into the mouth of a branded villain, the bastard Edmund in *Lear.* And, in Jonson, this kind of "freedom" belongs to degenerate conspirators, rather than to Cecil-like "new men" such as Cicero. Both Jonson and Shakespeare, though prepared to give an airing to subversive statements in their work, tend to "contract-out" of direct commitment, whereas Donne pursues, with a cynical faithfulness, the conclusions made inevitable by his accepted premises. It could be argued that such distinctions are the product of the time, distinctions between "revolutionary" ideas circulating in manuscript verses among a small, cultured *élite* and ideas handled in the drama, a medium struggling against official censorship, and always in the blast of public scrutiny and comment. The ambivalence is certainly there. It was noted by Coleridge, when he said of *Sejanus:*

The anachronic mixture in this Arruntius, of the Roman republican, to whom Tiberius must have appeared as much a tyrant as

Sejanus, with his James-and-Charles the First zeal for legitimacy
. . . is amusing.

[in Lectures and Notes on Shakespeare]

In *Catiline,* Jonson's treatment of the "Ciceronian" virtues, and his attitude to the Cicero-Catiline struggle provide a working example of the dramatist's capacity for "suspended" judgement. Sempronia describes Cicero as:

> A meere upstart,
> That has no pedigree, no house, no coate,
> No ensignes of a family? FULVIA: He' has vertue.
> SEMPRONIA: Hang vertue, where there is no bloud: 'tis vice,
> And, in him, sawcinesse. Why should he presume
> To be more learned, or more eloquent,
> Than the nobilitie? or boast any qualitie
> Worthy a noble man, himselfe not noble?
> FULVIA: 'Twas vertue onely, at first, made all men noble.
> SEMPRONIA: I yeeld you, it might, at first, in *Romes* poore age;
> When both her Kings, and *Consuls* held the plough,
> Or garden'd well; But, now, we ha' no need,
> To digge, or loose our sweat for't.

(2.11)

Jonson so places the virtue of old Rome in the mouth of a "modern" degenerate that he gets away with a good deal. To dig or to lose one's sweat honestly at the plough becomes the sweet untainted antithesis to the "sloth," "fatness," "lethargy" of the present. Any scepticism we might have had regarding the tireless virtue of simple poverty is ruled out of court together with Sempronia's gibes. All that she sees as laughable or contemptible we are to receive as serious and worthy. "Rome's *poore* age" is unquestionably Rome's *great* age. Similarly, in *Cynthia's Revels* (1600):

> the ladie Arete, or *vertue,* a poore *Nymph* of Cynthias traine,
> that's scarce able to buy her selfe a gowne

(1.89)

is, in fact, a powerful chastiser of prodigality and corruption. By a connotative slide, therefore, "poor" is made synonymous with "pure."

Jonson is noted for the hard precision of his images; and justly. He builds magnificently so that he may destroy:

> we will eate our mullets,
> Sous'd in high-countrey wines, sup phesants egges,
> And have our cockles, boild in silver shells,
> Our shrimps to swim againe, as when they liv'd,
> In a rare butter, made of dolphins milke,
> Whose creame do's looke like opalls.
>
> (*The Alchemist*, 4.1.156)

The "moral pleasure" here stems from Mammon's lavishing of such imaginative effort on shrimps; and "rare *butter*" is a good, serious joke. Jonson's recreation of the bulk and weight of corruption, of criminal-farcical expenditure, is superb. On the other hand, the persuasive weight of such imagery is sufficient to commit the listener to the acceptance of a good deal of simple and evocative language, as part of Jonson's vision of the Good Life. In the First Chorus of *Catiline*, the pejorative vision of the effeminate men of new Rome (a terse set of epithets: "kemb'd," "bath'd," "rub'd," "trim'd," "sleek'd") works into a passage of much more tenuous verbal "gesturing" when old Rome is evoked:

> Hence comes that wild, and vast expence
> That hath enforc'd *Romes* vertue, thence,
> Which simple poverty first made.
>
> (1.573)

And Fulvia's reply to Sempronia is also a case in point. Her:

> 'Twas vertue onely, at first, made all men noble

is plainly on the right side of the moral fence. "All men" sounds very liberal and fine; so does the easy juxtaposition of "vertue" and "noble." In practice, though, Jonson's social vision is as far from a Leveller's dream as it is from any real faith in a natural aristocracy. Phrases like "all men" make gestures; they do not define or ever truly perform.

Such evasions are to be distinguished from the valid workings of dramatic and rhetorical persuasion. Take, for contrast, this sequence from *Catiline:*

> CHORUS: The voice of Cato is the voice of *Rome*.
> CATO: The voice of *Rome* is the consent of heaven!
> And that hath plac'd thee, Cicero, at the helme.
>
> (3.60)

Here, the anadiplosis, linking Cato's word to the authority of heaven, appears as a legitimate rhetorical parable of the great chain of Being. And, in

this context, the commonplace of ship-of-state (as, elsewhere, the commonplace for body-politic) appears as an authentic, even though limited, statement of civic faith. Jonson *is* pedantic, but his pedantry has little or nothing
in common with the supposedly neurotic crabbedness of the "unworldly"
scholar. He is pedantic as Fulke Greville in his *Life of Sidney* is pedantic:
each is prepared to risk appearing overscrupulous in the attempt to define
true goodness:

> he piercing into mens counsels, and ends, not by their words,
> oathes or complements, all barren in that age, but by fathoming
> their hearts, and powers, by their deeds, and found no wisdome
> where he found no courage, nor courage without wisdome, nor
> either without honesty and truth.

In Jonson, too, the insistent comparison, qualification and paradox—sometimes appearing "in-grown"—is made in the teeth of a barren age. The world
of the Roman plays, like that of many of the comedies, is a world full of
false witness:

> We have wealth,
> Fortune and ease, and then their stock, to spend on,
> Of name, for vertue.
>
> (Catiline, 2.131)

If "name" is a mere commodity, an advertisement without relation to substance or property or ethic, how can "name" alone be trusted? "Name"
must be demonstrated as belonging or not belonging to "thing"; its properties plainly discussed. Hence, in Jonson's dramatic rhetoric, antithetical
pairings are frequent: "inward" opposes "outward"; "justice," "law"; "private gain" is won by "public spoil." In the world of the Roman plays, this
degree of moral scrutiny is painful, but necessary. This is the celebration of
a good man, the dead Germanicus, in *Sejanus:*

> He was a man most like to vertue'; In all,
> And every action, neerer to the gods,
> Than men, in nature; of a body' as faire
> As was his mind; and no lesse reverend
> In face, th[a]n fame: He could so use his state,
> Temp'ring his greatnesse, with his gravitie,
> As it avoyded all selfe-love in him,
> And spight in others.
>
> (1.124)

Here, the heavy antitheses are wrenched across the line, with considerable moral and muscular effort. They do not fall harmoniously within the line-period—and within the limits of their own predetermined world—as do Dryden's fluent couplets to the good man, Barzillai:

> In this short file Barzillai first appears;
> Barzillai, crowned with honour and with years
>
> . . . .
>
> In exile with his godlike prince he mourned
> For him he suffer'd and with him return'd.
> The court he practic'd, not the courtier's art:
> Large was his wealth, but larger was his heart,
> Which well the noblest objects knew to choose,
> The fighting warrior and recording Muse.
>
> (*Absalom and Achitophel,* 817–28)

In terms of Dryden's bland wit, Charles is unquestionably "godlike." This is the very point that Jonson labours to verify in the portrait of Germanicus: "In all / And every action neerer to the gods, / Than men." Jonson's qualifications worry the verse into dogs-teeth of virtuous self-mistrust. If his passage is painfully spiky, Dryden's approaches fatty degeneration. "For him . . . with him," "Large was . . . larger was" are syntactically flabby, embodying the elevated complacency of the thought. The repeated "Barzillai . . . Barzillai" gestures in the general direction of virtue and goodwill. The overall tone of the Barzillai panegyric, it can be argued, has much to do with Dryden's thoroughgoing acceptance of his lot as laureate of the Tory oligarchy. The famously smooth irony of the opening of *Absalom and Achitophel* is, ultimately, an indulgent cherishing irony, making such a smiling, gentlemanly thing of equivocation that only a puritan cit could object.

Jonson's sense of the complexity of Order is very different, both poetically and politically, from Dryden's *practical* political attack and defence. Jonson's awareness can produce both the richly suggestive ambiguities of the Catiline-Aurelia courtship, or Latiaris's speech about Tiberius, and the fine assurance of the Pembroke Dedication. But there are occasions when, it seems, Jonson succumbs to the contradictions of the age, when he is unable, even reluctant, to tie down and tame the airy, "floating" connotations in words such as "noble," or "vertue," or "poverty." The *Catiline* Chorus, for example, speaks of "simple poverty" as though this, and this alone, accounted for the "vertue" of Old Rome. A moral slogan such as this is as blandly shallow as anything produced by Dryden's political partisanship. And in *The New Inn* (1631) there is this, equally emotive, exchange:

NURSE (*who is Lady Frampul disguised*): Is poverty a vice? BEAU-
    FORT. Th' age counts it so.
NURSE: God helpe your Lordship, and your peeres that think so,
If any be: if not, God blesse them all.
And helpe the number o' the vertuous,
If poverty be a crime.

(5.56)

Yet, in *Catiline* it is made explicit that "need" is the reason that so many
flock to the conspirators' support. And Volturtius, a turn-coat and minor
villain, is contemptuously dismissed by Cato without punishment; is even
promised:

> money, thou need'st it.
> 'Twill keep thee honest: want made thee a knave.
>
> (5.299)

Poverty, then, is a virtue only when it is associated with a remote, lyrically
evoked agrarian order, a world so distant that it appears static; or when it
provides a temporary refuge for missing persons of good family. The poverty
that really preoccupies Jonson is the reverse of simple and is far from static;
is, in fact, a prime mover in that constant flux of demand and supply; the
seventeenth-century urban predicament.

    This world of savage indecorum, which, like Tiberius, "acts its tragedies
with a comic face," which to Donne appears "bent awry," is a world that
Jonson struggles to subdue. It may be true that:

> In *Catiline* as in *Sejanus,* Jonson appears wholly inaccessible to
> the attraction of the profound "humanity" and psychology of
> Shakespearian tragedy,

but it is equally true that he is inaccessible to that periodic debauching which
the Shakespearian "humanity" suffered at the hands of, say, John Webster.
There is nothing in Jonson's Roman tragedies to equal the celebrated "syrup"
speech in the Duchess of Malfi's death-scene; and we should at least be
grateful for this. One ought to be sceptical of "timeless moments" in any
art. Jonson redeems what he can:

> It is not manly to take joy, or pride
> In humane errours (we doe all ill things,
> They doe 'hem worst that love 'hem, and dwell there,
> Till the plague comes) The few that have the seeds

Of goodnesse left, will sooner make their way
To a true life, by shame, than punishment.
　　　　　　(*The Devil Is an Ass* 5.8.169)

STEPHEN ORGEL

The Jonsonian Masque and the Limits of Invention

The central problem Jonson faced in the masques was to establish the court dramatically within the symbolic world of his spectacle. This was necessary if the adulation, which from the first had been the function of these shows, was to be more than gratuitous flattery. And it was a problem because, properly, the court could be "glorified" only within the masque section; Jonson, for his own reasons, was primarily concerned with the antimasque. Any real success would have to involve a delicate balance between the two— a balance of a sort we do not ordinarily associate with this "tun of man." But for Jonson the masque was a poem as well as a spectacle, so that on the printed page the move into the world of the court became an assertion of those moral virtues of order and nobility that the court embodied. If the crucial transition at Whitehall was not justified, neither was the poetic as- sertion it represented. It is a remarkable testimony to the integrity of Jonson's imagination that any failure to achieve the necessary unity of form tends to be evident from the quality of the verse in the main masque. *Love Restored* has provided a useful instance: the weak and undefined character of Cupid's poetry implies that something is missing from Jonson's conception of the ideal he is asserting. This is a comparatively simple example. But Jonson had already shown himself capable of producing a type of masque that was more fully imagined and more dramatically realized—and one that was directed as much toward the reader as toward the viewer. Indeed, by 1616, when

From *The Jonsonian Masque.* © 1965 by the President and Fellows of Harvard College. Harvard University Press, 1965.

Jonson presented nineteen masques and entertainments to a reading audience in the first volume of his *Workes,* the success of the masque as literature was clearly of considerable importance.

Taking our cue from the poet, then, let us consider two masques as literary texts—the first, a complex early failure that sets off and illuminates the second, an equally complex success. *Oberon* was composed for the investiture of King James's eldest son, Henry, as Prince of Wales. It was performed on January 1, 1611, with the prince dancing the role of Oberon. In it, Jonson attempts a different kind of dramatic unity from that of *Love Restored,* for *Oberon* is set in an arcadian world large and various enough to contain both antimasque and masque figures.

At the opening of the spectacle,

> *The first face of the* Scene *appeared all obscure, & nothing perceiv'd but a darke Rocke, with trees beyond it; and all wildnesse, that could be presented: Till, at one corner of the cliffe, above the* Horizon, *the* Moone *began to shew, and rising, a* Satyre *was seene (by her light) to put forth his head, and call.*
>
> (1–5)

This stage direction sets the scene for the antimasque world, characteristically obscure and wild. It is a landscape perceived by the light of the moon, whose inconstancy is invoked and embodied by the wanton satyrs. The discord here is moral as well as physical; the antimasque world is a darker one than that of the revels, in which the moon is Cynthia, "Queene and Huntresse, chaste and faire." Sixteen years earlier, a Shakespearean realm of mischief and passion had been discovered by the same light:

> OBERON: Ill met by moonlight, proud Titania.
> TITANIA: What, jealous Oberon! Fairies, skip hence.

But Jonson's Oberon has moved into the masque world, leaving the antimasque to the disorderly creatures of the night.

The satyrs assemble, "leaping, and making antique [antic] action, and gestures." They are presided over by "a Silene," who begins to impose some order upon them. "Chaster language," he urges,

> These are nights
> Solemne, to the shining rites
> Of the *Fayrie* Prince, and Knights.
> (50–53)

This is simply exposition to us, but in performance it would have had the kind of dramatic significance peculiar to the masque form. For *Oberon* was itself part of the "shining rites" by which the prince beneath the mask was declared successor to the throne. This special quality is necessarily lost in a printed version of the masque—and would have been lost, indeed, in any performance given later than the particular season for which the masque was composed. The occasional nature of these shows was both their chief strength and their ultimate weakness.

But the masque as a poem has its own independent virtues. Jonson's text directs the reader's attention to the prince by means of a richly imagined dramatic scene. Although Oberon can have no part in the antimasque, his presence pervades it. In verse full of variety and detail, the satyrs excitedly discuss their expectations of their new ruler, and thereby they anatomize their world:

> SATYRE 4: Will he give us prettie toyes,
>   To beguile the girles withall?
> SATYRE 3: And to make 'hem quickly fall?
> SATYRE 4: Will he build us larger caves?
> SILENUS. Yes, and give you yvorie staves,
>   When you hunt; and better wine:
> SATYRE 1: Then the master of the Vine?
> SATYRE 2: And rich prizes, to be wunne,
>   When we leape, or when we runne?
> SATYRE 1: I, and gild our cloven feet?
> SATYRE 3: Strew our heads with poulders sweet?
> SATYRE 1: Bind our crooked legges in hoopes
>   Made of shells, with silver loopes?
> SATYRE 2: Tie about our tawnie wrists
>   Bracelets of the *Fairie* twists?
> SATYRE 4: And, to spight the coy Nymphes scornes,
>   Hang upon our stubbed hornes,
>   Garlands, ribbands, and fine poesies?
>
>   (84–114)

For all their rowdiness, the satyrs speak in beautifully controlled and varied couplets. The indecorum of their antimasque world is full of humor and grace—qualities that, in theory at least, the advent of a higher good need not destroy. The relationship between the two parts of Jonson's form is seen here less as a conflict than as a progression: the satyrs' anticipation prepares us dramatically for the appearance of Oberon; but also the very purpose of Silenus is to explain to his creatures the values of order and constancy, the social and moral virtues the prince represents. The antimasque thus becomes, both to its characters and to us, an education for the concluding revels.

Silenus is a new sort of figure in the Jonsonian masque, for he comprehends both its worlds. Two years earlier, in *The Masque of Queenes,* an antimasque of witches had been banished by the "sound of loud Musique ... with which not only the Hagges themselves, but theyr Hell, into which they ranne, quite vanished," and evil had been destroyed by the mere imminence of good. In *Oberon,* the shift from antimasque to masque takes place not through a momentary confrontation, but through the gradual ordering of chaos, a creative act. No mere character can bridge the gap between the witches' hell and the queens' heaven. But Silenus possesses "all gravitie, and profound knowledge, of most secret mysteries" (line 50, note c), and he is able to join together the satyrs and the fairy prince. Under his tutelage, the antimasquers renounce old gods and the wild life: "Grandsire, we shall leave to play / With Lyaeus now; and serve / Only OB'RON" (77–79). One wonders how many tipsy spectators in 1611 discerned Bacchus beneath the pedantic pseudonym Lyaeus and realized uncomfortably that Oberon's palace was, unlike Whitehall, dry. The satyrs take the pledge without a whimper, yielding to the promise of better things, and their moral transformation is rewarded by an analogous change in the landscape:

> SILENUS: See, the rocke begins to ope,
> Now you shall enjoy your hope;
> 'Tis about the houre, I know.
> *There the whole* Scene *opened, and within was discover'd the* Frontispice *of a bright and glorious* Palace, *whose gates and walls were transparent.*
>
> (134–40)

We are before the palace of Oberon, the world of the masque. Silenus continues his explanation:

> Looke! Do's not his *Palace* show
> Like another *Skie* of lights?
> Yonder, with him, live the knights,
> Once, the noblest of the earth,
> Quick'ned by a second birth;
> Who for prowesse, and for truth,
> There are crowned with lasting youth:
> And do hold, by *Fates* command,
> Seats of blisse in *Fairie land.*
>
> (143–51)

Even the verse of the antimasque takes on an unfamiliar regularity. But it is not yet time for the masque figures to appear, since Jonson has related both the moral and physical transformations of this world to the orderly changes of nature. The satyrs' revels are to end only with the end of moonlight; in order to "make expectation short," and as a farewell to their presiding deity, they invoke the unchaste moon with a satiric song and an antic dance:

> Now, my cunning lady; Moone,
> Can you leave the side, so soone,
> Of the boy, you keepe so hid?
> Mid-wife Juno sure will say,
> This is not the proper way
>   Of your palenesse to be rid.
> But, perhaps, it is your grace
> To weare sicknesse i' your face,
>   That there might be wagers laid,
>   Still, by fooles, you are a maid.
>
> Come, your changes overthrow
> What your looke would carry so;
> Moone, confesse then, what you are.
> And be wise, and free to use
> Pleasures, that you now doe loose;
>   Let us *Satyres* have a share.
> Though our forms be rough, & rude,
> Yet our acts may be endew'd
>   With more vertue: Every one
>   Cannot be Endymion.
>   (262–82)

Jonson concludes his antimasque with a brilliant parody of two central masque conventions, the masquer's invitation to his lady and the final dance. The song inverts all the courtly values: beneath the moon's masquing costume lie inconstancy and wantonness; her "grace" is deception; she is "wise and free" in being licentious; and her lecherous lovers' "acts" are "endew'd with . . . vertue." But the invocation goes unanswered, for the cock crows and the satyrs bow in reverence before the long awaited revelation:

> SILENUS: Stay, the cheerefull *Chanticleere*
>   Tells you, that the time is neere:
>   See, the gates alreadie spread!
>   Every *Satyre* bow his head.

> *There the whole palace open'd, and the nation of* Faies *were dis-*
> *cover'd, some with instruments, some bearing lights; others sing-*
> *ing; and within a farre off in perspective, the knights masquers*
> *sitting in their severall sieges: At the further end of all, Oberon,*
> *in a chariot, which to a lowd triumphant musique began to move*
> *forward, drawne by two white beares, and on either side guarded*
> *by three* Sylvanes, *with one going in front.*
>
> (286–98)

Within the palace is the world of the masque, at once characterized by triumphant music and pageantry. The dramatic figures, the satyrs of the antimasque, have now become the audience for a symbolic spectacle. Its significance is explained by Silenus and an attendant sylvan, who prepare us for the songs and dances that are to conclude the entertainment and that, to the spectator at Whitehall, were the longest and most important part of the presentation. But, to a reader, such theatrical elements of the work exist only through their literary counterparts; harmony, order, courtliness, grace—the values expressed by music and dance—must be established by Jonson's poetry. So while the characterizations, descriptions, everything that gave substance to the ideal world and its prince, served to justify the revels in performance, they essentially replace the revels when the masque becomes a poem.

Silenus, speaking of Oberon to the satyrs, had described him as a principle of natural beauty and perfection:

> *Satyres,* he doth fill with grace,
>   Every season, ev'ry place;
>   Beautie dwels, but in his face
>
>   . . . .
>
>   He is lovelier, then in May
>   Is the Spring, and there can stay,
>   As little, as he can decay.
>
> (62–73)

It is worth remarking on the fact that the first real difficulty we encounter in the verse arises when Jonson attempts to represent his principle of order. The image of the prince, lovelier than spring, is abstract and conventional to the point of meaninglessness; but it is the sudden obscurity and awkwardness of the poetry that are most striking. The Oxford editors' gloss on "stay As little"—"must advance to further beauty"—is obviously correct. Yet it is surprising that the embodiment of universal order should be defined in verse of so much indirection, so little clarity and ease. Significantly, we come upon precisely the same difficulties again when we reach the ideal world of the masque section.

The opening song establishes a milieu for Oberon's progress toward the ideal. The Platonic ascent becomes a principle of physics and a characteristic of the entire universe:

> Melt earth to sea, sea flow to ayre,
>   And ayre flie into fire,
> Whilst we, in tunes, to ARTHURS chayre
>   Beare OBERONS desire;
>   (300–303)

Nature that framed us of four elements doth teach the prince to have an aspiring mind—to ascend not only the Platonic ladder but also "Arthurs chayre," the throne of hereditary British monarchs. Here is the crucial moment in the masque, for at this point Jonson must move back into the court; the heir of "the nation of Faies" must also become the new Prince of Wales. I quote the whole transition:

> Whilst we, in tunes, to ARTHURS chayre
>   Bear OBERONS desire;
> Then which there nothing can be higher,
>   Save JAMES, to whom it flyes:
> But he the wonder is of tongues, of eares, of eyes.
>   (302–6)

The clumsiness of the third and fourth lines, the mysterious "But" of the fifth, reflect the awkwardness of the transition. Dramatically, the problem is to identify King James with the father of the fairy prince, the incarnation of King Arthur. This is more difficult to effect within the masque than the identification of Prince Henry with Oberon, because James was not a masquer whereas the prince was in fact both Oberon and himself.

The sudden presentation of King James as the object of the prince's aspiration is like the breach of decorum that had disturbed Jonson in his *Masque of Queenes,* where Queen Anne had taken her place among such figures as Penthesilea, Artemisia, Berenice, and Zenobia. The poet had felt compelled to defend himself from a "possible Objection" by an appeal to the timelessness of Fame and the "all-daring Power of Poetry" (lines 670 ff). The objection itself, is of course, trifling and hardly worth such an energetic reply. But obviously Jonson was attempting to deal with the same basic problem: how was the sovereign to be praised *within* the masque?

Now the mention of "Arthurs chayre" would have prepared a court audience or a contemporary reader for a reference to King James, certainly more than it does a modern reader. It was part of the Tudor propaganda program to claim descent from King Arthur, and indeed Jonson several times employs a well-known anagram of the period:

> EVAN: . . . yow meane his Madestees Anagrams of *Charles James Stuart.*
>
> JENKIN: I, that is *Claimes Arthurs Seate,* which is as much as to say, your Madestee s'ud be the first King of gread Prittan, and sit in Cadier Arthur, which is Arthurs Chaire, as by Gots blessing you doe.

So the allusion to the king at this point in the masque was not a surprise. But this transition from Arthur to James is one that has nothing to do with the *action* of the masque, which would require the king to appear in the symbolic character that has been established for him. The dramatic movement has taken us inward and upward toward the source of light and order, but at the crucial point in the masque this movement has been violated. The masque, in order to be relevant to the real world it symbolizes, must recognize that there is a power higher even than Oberon. Indeed, around the concept of this ultimate power, the object of the prince's aspiration, Jonson has created his masque world. What we end up with, however, is King James, who is not at the center of the masque world, but outside it.

To satisfy the requirements of the production at Whitehall, Jonson had to find a means of including the king in the masque without investing him with properties that, as a spectator, he could not sustain. What goes wrong in *Oberon* is that we are suddenly required to see James enthroned in all his physicality among "bright Faies, and Elves," creatures of no substance "formes, so bright and aery." Thus described, the unfortunate monarch may remind us of Bottom. Conversely, Jonson's problem was to establish Oberon within the world of the court, to bring the masque figure back into Whitehall so that he might serve as a representation of Prince Henry. Until this has been accomplished, praise rendered to Oberon is irrelevant to the prince beneath the mask, and praise rendered to King James is irrelevant to the world the masque has created. This is precisely where *Oberon* fails.

To the reader, therefore, the panegyric of the masque section has the sound of hollow flattery:

> His meditations, to his height, are even:
> And all their issue is a kin to heaven.

> He is a god, o're kings; yet stoupes he then
> Neerest a man, when he doth governe men.
>   (342–45)

There is no synthesis of this praise of the temporal monarch with the following adulation of the ultimate power of the arcadian universe:

> 'Tis he, that stayes the time from turning old,
> And keepes the age up in a head of gold.
> That in his own true circle, still doth runne;
> And holds his course, as certayne as the sunne.
> He makes it ever day, and ever spring,
> Where he doth shine, and quickens every thing
> Like a new nature: so, that true to call
> Him, by his title, is to say, Hee's all.
>   (350–57)

The hyperbolic illusion and the real facts have not come together in a moment of revelation; on the contrary, lacking the commanding presence of the king's person or the spectacular effects of the stage production, we feel only that somebody looks ridiculous, that something is being overstated. Nor are the finest moments in the verse dictated by the dramatic movement of the masque. By requiring us to take its extravagance literally, the verse tends only to undercut the delicate balance between the court world and the symbolic fiction that describes it:

> To whose sole power and magick they doe give
> The honor of their being; that they live
> Sustayn'd in forme, fame, and felicitie,
> From rage of fortune, or the feare to die.
>   (331–34)

Of course, an hour or two of dancing might have given the contemporary spectator sufficient evidence of the fairy knights' substantiality to counteract the disintegrating effects of this sort of hyperbole; and in any case, the necessary illusions were being maintained by the art of Inigo Jones. But neither of these, strictly speaking, was relevant to Jonson's problem, and he had yet found no literary substitute for them. In the masque-poem, Oberon's revels came as a distinct anticlimax.

Of the group of masques Jonson prepared under King James, *Neptunes Triumph for the Returne of Albion* seems to me one of the most successful in dealing with the problems outlined above. It was prepared for Twelfth

Night 1624 and celebrated the return of Prince Charles and the Duke of
Buckingham from their trip to Spain, where they had attempted to arrange
a marriage between the prince and the sister of Philip IV. The project had
been understandably unpopular with everyone except the old king and
Charles's friends, and the unsuccessful outcome of the negotiations had been
a cause for great public rejoicing at the prince's homecoming in October
1623. The masque barely touches on the match, which would have been a
sore point, but makes much of the "safe" return of the emissaries. It was
never performed, owing to a disagreement over precedence between the Spanish and the French ambassadors; but it was rehearsed up to the last moment,
with Charles and Buckingham as the principal masquers.

Like *Love Restored, Neptunes Triumph* opens in the banqueting room
at Whitehall; it takes place both literally and figuratively in the court of King
James. "All, that is discovered of a *Scene,* are two erected Pillars, dedicated
to *Neptune.* . . . The *Poet* entring on the *Stage,*" to distribute handbills of
the argument of the masque, "is cald to by the *Master-Cooke.*" The antimasque consists of a discussion between these two of the spectacle the poet
has contrived for the evening's entertainment.

The cook demands a description of the coming masque: "Sir, this is my
roome, and region too, the banquetting-house! And in matter of feast, and
solemnitie, nothing is to be presented here, but with my acquaintance, and
allowance to it" (24–27). He proceeds to compare his function with that of
the poet. "A good *Poet,*" he points out, "differs nothing at all from a *Master-*
Cooke. Eithers Art is the wisedome of the Mind. . . . I am by my place, to
know how to please the palates of the ghests; so, you are to know the palate
of the times: study the severall tastes." And, surprisingly enough, it is the
cook, not the poet, who begins to sound most like the Jonson who was King
James's masque writer. The poet complains with the voice of one who chafes
under the necessity of writing to order: "That were a heavy and hard taske,
to satisfie *Expectation,* who is so severe an exactresse of duties; ever a
tyrannous mistresse: and most times a pressing enemie" (54–56). But the
cook urges that the problem must be dealt with, and it is relevant, as the
ensuing dialogue shows, not only to the court masque writer, but to any
creative artist:

> COOKE: She is a powerfull great Lady, Sir, at all times, and must
>   be satisfied: So must her sister, Madam *Curiositie,* who hath
>   as daintie a palate as she, and these will expect.
> POET: But, what if they expect more than they understand?
> COOKE: That's all one, Mr. *Poet,* you are bound to satisfie them.

> For, there is a palate of the Understanding, as well as of the
> Senses. The Taste is taken with good relishes, the Sight with
> faire objects, the Hearing with delicate sounds, the Smelling
> with pure sents, the Feeling with soft and plump bodies, but
> the Understanding with all these: for all which you must
> begin at the Kitchin. There, the *Art* of *Poetry* was learnd,
> and found out, or no where: and the same day, with the *Art*
> of *Cookery.*
>
> (58–73)

The cook is insisting that an appeal to the mind properly involves an appeal
to all the senses as well, that poetry cannot be intellectualized, that every
resource at the poet's command is to be explored in order to reach the
spectator's understanding. Above all, to Jonson, the audience must be made
to do more than view the spectacle—they must see the significance of the
symbolic figures and of the central device on which the masque depends.

As it continues, this scene between the cook and the poet becomes a
dramatic presentation of what Jonson had attempted to achieve through his
development of the masque form. Structurally, the function of the Jonsonian
antimasque was to set up a world of particularity, which was organically
related, and at the same time in contrast, to the symbolic world of the
masque. In other words, the antimasque set up a problem for which the
masque was a solution. In a very real sense, then, for Jonson it was the
antimasque that served to give meaning to the masque, to explain it, to make
the audience understand. It is not all surprising that the poet of *Neptunes
Triumph,* who has so much trouble with audiences who "expect more than
they understand," disapproves strongly of antimasques:

> COOKE: But where's your *Antimasque* now, all this while?
>   I hearken after them.
> POET: Faith, we have none.
> COOKE: None?
> POET: None, I assure you, neither doe I thinke them
>   A worthy part of presentation,
>   Being things so *heterogene,* to all devise,
>   Meere *By-workes,* and at best *Out-landish* nothings.
> COOKE: O, you are all the heaven awrie, Sir!
>   For blood of *Poetry,* running in your veines,
>   Make not yourselfe so ignorantly simple.
>
> (213–27)

And it is the cook, finally, who provides the antimasque, both the burlesque dances that immediately precede the main masque and indeed this whole discussion forming the first half of the spectacle. We have already seen how seven years later Jonson, writing to the taste of King Charles, was to omit his own antimasque from *Loves Triumph Through Callipolis* for one of Inigo Jones's devising. So the old poet, deprived of his world of particulars, finds it necessary to prefix a note to that masque entitled explicitly, "To make the Spectators Understanders," which serves to explain the theory on which the masque has been contrived.

Logically, then, the antimasque is the place where the poet of *Neptunes Triumph* sets forth the argument of his masque. We are still in the Banqueting House at Whitehall, and what the poet reads for the cook's approval is an allegorical triumph for the return of Prince Charles to England. The Spanish journey ("through *Celtiberia*") is described: the prince becomes Albion; his father, Neptune; Buckingham (Master of the King's Horse) becomes Hippius, Neptune's "powerfull MANAGER of *Horse*"; Sir Francis Cottington (*Charles's private secretary*), "*Proteus*, Father of disguise"—Clarendon was to remark of Cottington, "his greatest fault was that he could dissemble." Gradually through the poet's device, we begin to see the court as a mythical realm, and the machines of the masque as examples of Neptune's power and symbols of his grace. The antimasque dialogue prepares us for the transformation scene and serves in a very direct way to make us "understanders":

> COOKE.   How do you present 'hem?
> In a fine Iland, say you?
>
> POET: Yes, a *Delos:*
> Such as when faire *Latona* fell in travaile,
> Great *Neptune* made emergent.
>
>   . . . .
>
> COOKE: Ha' you nothing,
> But a bare Island?
>
> POET: Yes, we have a tree too,
> Which we doe call the Tree of *Harmonie,*
> And is the same with what we read, the *Sunne*
> Brought forth in the *Indian Musicana* first,
> And thus it growes. The goodly bole, being got
> To certaine cubits height, from every side
> The boughes decline, which taking roote afresh,
> Spring up new boles, & those spring new, & newer,
> Till the whole tree become a *Porticus,*

> Or arched Arbour, able to receive
> A numerous troupe, such as our *Albion,*
> And the Companions of his journey are.
> And this they sit in.
> COOKE: Your prime *Masquers?*
> POET: Yes.
>   (177–211)

However elaborate its symbols, the allegory is nevertheless directly concerned with actual and familiar facts; this, indeed, is its point and chief strength. It is a remarkably inclusive representation of the event that would have been the main topic of conversation in the court for the past three months. Even the delay between the prince's landing in October and the Twelfth-Night masque is dealt with:

> COOKE: But, why not this, till now?
> POET: —It was not time,
>   To mixe this Musick with the vulgars chime.
>   Stay, till th'abortive, and extemporall dinne
>   Of balladry, were understood a sinne,
>   *Minerva* cry'd.
>   (159–65)

There is irony here, for the unsuccessful poet who disdains antimasques "is not to be identified with Jonson," as the Oxford editors point out. "Jonson himself," they continue, "far from jealously secluding the Poet's courtly music from the 'vulgar's chime' . . . was interweaving the Poet's elegant academic strain with the most genially Epicurean of all his Antimasque-roles—the humours of his 'brother poet,' the Cook."

Herford and Simpson's introduction to *Neptunes Triumph* is excellent, but neither they nor any other commentators appear to have noticed that the relationship between the cook's antimasque and the poet's masque is an organic one. The Oxford editors remark, "The plan of treating Antimasque and Main Masque as rival shows presented by two antagonists of corresponding character was perhaps the most effective of all devices for connecting them." The two sections are more than "rival shows," however; they are complementary and fully embody the Jonsonian concepts of antimasque and masque. The device the poet reads turns the event it deals with into an allegory, takes it into the world of symbolic deities so that it becomes more than the occasion of Prince Charles's return. It is finally a kind of mythical truth, embracing, by the end of the masque, the whole state. By contrast, the

cook's antimasque—"a dish out of the kitchen . . . a *metaphoricall* dish!"—
presents not truth, but rumor and falsehood. Its dancers emerge from a great
stewing pot, dressed as meats of various kinds, appealing in the most obvious
way not to "a palate of the Understanding" but to the sensual appetite. These
figures represent, as the cook carefully points out, a segment of the court;
they are the people who "relish nothing but *di stato*," who gossip endlessly
about the business of state,

> Know all things the wrong way, talk of the affaires,
> The clouds, the cortines, and the mysteries
> That are afoot, and, from what hands they have 'hem
> (The master of the Elephant, or the Camels)
> What correspondences are held; the Posts
> That go, & come, and know, almost, their minutes,
> All but their businesse: Therein they are fishes.
> But ha' their garlick, as the *Proverb* says,
> They are our *Quest of enquiry*, after newes.
>
> (245–55)

The "relish" with which these figures spread false reports of court affairs is
enough to stamp them as gluttons; and their characterization through two
forgotten proverbs as fish and garlic easily relegates them to the cook's
stewing pot. In this masque, the antimasquers are those who "know all things
the wrong way," and the deformity of their minds is embodied in the person
of the real court figure who is identified as their leader. He has already been
allegorized by the poet in his summary of his masque as "The Sea-Monster
Archy" (172), the circulator of "tales and stories" that formed part of
"th'abortive, and extemporall dinne" at Albion's return three months earlier.
Archy is Archibald Armstrong, the court dwarf, who had accompanied the
prince to Spain; he leads the antimasquers as the chief promulgator of false
tales, and his dancers embody whatever in the court world threatens the
truths of the poet's allegory.

But the threat need not be destroyed. Antimasque and masque have a
genial relationship in this work, and the cook's invention can be accepted
in the spirit of play and assimilated with ease into the larger world of the
poet's creation. "Brother Poet," the cook urges, "Though the serious part /
Be yours, yet, envie not the *Cooke* his art." And the poet replies, "Not I.
Nam lusus ipse Triumphus amat"—even a triumph likes fun, and the main
masque serves less as a rival show than as the high point of the evening's
entertainment.

The striking quality of the opening of the main masque is that it manages to allegorize the audience and setting along with the event. We are no longer in the Banqueting House at Whitehall, but in Neptune's court, watching the landing of Albion and his train. They come on their floating island; and when "the Island hath joynd it selfe with the shore . . . *Proteus, Portunus, and Saron,* come forth, and goe up singing to the State, while the Masquers take time to Land" (ll. 361–65). The problem in *Oberon* of incorporating King James in the masque has been solved here; not only is the king addressed as Neptune, but the whole court becomes involved in the transformation. So, when the masquers are ready to take their dancing partners from the spectators, "*Proteus, Portunus, Saron,* goe up to the Ladies with this Song":

> PRO: Come, noble *Nymphs,* and doe not hide
> The joyes, for which you so provide:
> SAR: If not to mingle with the men,
> What doe you here? Go home agen.
> POR: Your dressings doe confesse,
> By what we see, so curious parts
> Of *Pallas,* and *Arachnes* arts,
> That you could meane no lesse.
> PRO: Why doe you weare the Silkewormes toyles;
> Or glory in the shellfish spoyles?
> Or strive to shew the graines of ore
> That you have gatherd on the shore,
> Whereof to make a stocke
> To graft the greener Emerald on,
> Or any better-water'd stone?
> SAR: Or Ruby of the rocke?
> PRO: Why do you smell of Amber-gris,
> Of which was formed *Neptunes* Neice,
> The Queene of Love; unlesse you can,
> Like Sea-borne *Venus,* love a man?
> SAR: Try, put your selves unto't.
> CHOR: Your lookes, your smiles, and thoughts that meete,
> *Ambrosian* hands, and silver feete,
> Doe promise you will do't.

> (472–503)

This is a poem about artifice and leads, indeed, to that most complex work of art, the choreography of the revels. But as the three singers examine the nymphs' "arts," it becomes clear that all parts of the natural world, organic and inorganic, terrestrial and aquatic, have contributed to the perfection of this beauty. The verse has an urgency that speeds its lyrical movement. At times it even displays an undercurrent of violence—the toiling silkworms are slaves; the despoiled shellfish, a conquered nation. Images are piled up almost greedily, and not a moment's pause is permitted in the catalogue of riches. As one singer ends, another takes up the theme, and sharp-eyed Saron even adds a gem that Proteus has neglected to mention.

Whitehall has become Neptune's court, and what the sea gods urge is that it is not enough for the audience to be passive observers. In effect, the masque has ceased to be a spectacle and has managed to make its audience integral to its action. Nor has the transition from masque world to court been left to the verse to accomplish, as in *Oberon*; here the synthesis is inherent in the very structure of the work. Just as the failure of *Oberon* had been reflected at the crucial moment in the awkwardness of its poetry, so the success of *Neptunes Triumph* may be measured by the extraordinary grace of the song just quoted. When, shortly afterward, the cook reenters with a second antimasque of sailors, we find that these dances are no longer threats to the world of the masque, but are now a part of it. The transformation scene is complete.

Among Jonson's masques, there seem to me few successes quite so brilliant as *Neptunes Triumph,* though an examination of several others, notably *Mercurie Vindicated* (1616) and the unfortunate *Pleasure Reconcild to Vertue* (1618), would reveal many of the same qualities. But here we might look briefly at one other, in which the problem of establishing the court within the masque world has been solved in a unique way. *The Gypsies Metamorphos'd* (1621) is particularly interesting because, as I have remarked, it is substantially all antimasque. It was commissioned by Buckingham as part of the entertainment for King James's visit to Burley-on-the-Hill, the duke's country seat. The device calls for a band of gypsies to tell the fortunes of members of the assembled court. The parts of the gypsies were taken by courtiers, with Buckingham in the leading role. The great interest provoked by the masque must have been generated partly by the aptness of the fortunes, but mainly by the rowdy good humor that was so much to the king's taste. There is in the masque no real plot, but only the central contrivance of the fortune telling: the antimasque world needs to employ no symbolic fable in order to be relevant to the world of the court. Hence the fortunes are quite specific in their allusions to particular qualities of the individual courtiers. Reference is made, for example, to the king's dislike of tobacco and pork; and the Countess of Buckingham, the mother of two of the masquers, is reminded that "Two of Your sonnes are *Gypsyes* too" (513). All the courtiers are addressed directly and in their own persons. James has been established within the masque by letting him, in effect, represent himself.

We shall respect Jonson's achievement all the more if we examine the masques provided by his rivals under King James. Francis Beaumont, for example, in his *Masque of Gray's Inn and the Inner Temple* (1613), prepared for the wedding of King James's daughter with the Elector Palatine, ignores the problem of relating the audience to the masque world. Aside from the reference embodied in the device—"Jupiter and Juno willing to doe honour to the Mariage of the two famous Rivers Thamesis and Rhene, imploy their Messengers severally, Mercurie and Iris for that purpose"—Beaumont treats his production merely as a spectacular private entertainment with none of the special relevance Jonson attempted to give his masques.

Daniel, whom Jonson had replaced in 1605 as court masquemaker, is aggressively self-effacing about the value and function of his productions. "Whosoever strives to shew most wit about these Pun[c]tillos of Dreames and shews," he writes, "are sure sicke of a disease they cannot hide, and would faine have the world to thinke them very deeply learned in all misteries whatsoever. . . . *Ludit istis animus, nonproficit.*" "The mind plays here and does not profit." And, in fact, Daniel's masques were primarily opportunities for his designer to exercise his scenic ingenuity. Daniel made no attempt to achieve the dramatic coherence of the Jonsonian masque, and both *The Vision of the Twelve Goddesses* (1604) and *Tethys' Festival* (1610) are little more than pageantry.

Campion's *Lord Hay's Masque* (1607) does deal directly with the court and attains something like the unity of the best Jonsonian masques. But the difference in quality between this work and the masque as Jonson conceived it lies precisely in the fact that Campion evidently considered blatant flattery indispensable to the form. One example will sufficiently illustrate the point:

> The God of Peace hath blest our land
>
> . . . .
>
> We throgh his most loving grace
> A King and kingly seed beholde,
> Like a son with lesser stars
> Or carefull shepheard to his fold.

The hollowness of these alternative epithets for the king is revealed when we try to imagine a masque device whereby James *could* be represented by both the sun and a shepherd at the same time. Campion uses the two images because they are the stock-in-trade of the masque writer: the court is either a pastoral world or the universe. But in *Lord Hay's Masque,* they serve no dramatic or symbolic purpose. We have seen that Jonson's success was in part the result of his ability to use conventions in a functional way. After 1588, for example, to compare England with Neptune's realm was hardly uncommon. But in *Neptunes Triumph,* calling the king a monarch of the seas is not simply hyperbole, for the epithet is inherent in the very device of the masque. It is just this integrity that all three of Campion's court productions lack.

Finally, looking ahead, I should note that, with the possible exception of Chapman, the only contemporary masque writer to conceive of the form in Jonsonian terms appears to have been Milton. *Comus* is frequently adduced as the death blow of the masque, yet in many respects it applied Jonson's technique with a success the earlier poet himself rarely attained. That Milton was constantly aware of his work as a real masque—as a symbolic representation of the milieu in and for which it was created, as a production wherein, when the lords and ladies became masquers, the real world became indistinguishable from the world of the masque—is obvious from the frequency and complexity with which references to his audience, the Earl of Bridgewater and his family and court, are woven into the fabric of the piece. To take only the most striking example, the attendant spirit at the end of his long prologue says that he will disguise himself as "a swain"

> That to the service of this house belongs,
> Who with his soft pipe and smooth dittied song
> Well knows to still the wild winds when they roar,
> And hush the waving woods.

The swain intended is Henry Lawes, the musician of *Comus,* who had obtained the commission for the young poet to write the masque. The spirit compares Lawes to Orpheus in verse that takes on new vividness and strength; but the part of the spirit is, in the production at Ludlow Castle, being played by Lawes himself. What Milton presents, then, is the Lawes of the real world becoming for a time the Lawes of the masque world. The question of flattery is not relevant here, for the disguise—as in Henry VIII's revels, over a century earlier—expresses a basic truth. To Milton, as to Jonson, the function of the court masque is the making of viable myths, whereby courtiers take on the character of heroes, kings of gods, events of symbols. That the myths should be, however incompletely, meaningful for us, too, is the special triumph of the Jonsonian masque.

What I have said should, I think, enable us to view Jonson's masques with some sense of what Jonson was trying to achieve and, therefore, with some sense of what constituted a success in this form. We should be wary, then, of generalizations about "the bondage of tasteless flattery which even the doughtiest of Jacobean poets complacently endured." As for the bondage, the important thing is not that it was there, but that Jonson was able to use it creatively—where Campion, for one, was not. Fetters to a great poet become strengths: "Nuns fret not at their convent's narrow room." And Jonson can hardly be called complacent, when the development of his masques shows a continual, and ultimately successful, effort to establish the praise of the court organically within the masque, where it was valid.

I have withheld a consideration of Jonson's critical comments on the masque until now, since I feel that an understanding of what he was trying to achieve is more likely to be gained by examining what he actually did. But it is certainly relevant that Jonson did theorize about the nature of the masque form. Such remarks appear in various dedications, prefatory notes, and footnotes to the printed versions. In the preface to *Hymenaei*, he speaks of the masque as symbolic poetry. The statement is worth quoting in full:

> It is a noble and just advantage, that the things subjected to *understanding* have of those which are objected to *sense*, that the one sort are but momentarie, and meerely taking; the other impressing, and lasting: Else the glorie of all these *solemnities* had perish'd like a blaze, and gone out, in the *beholders* eyes. So short-liv'd are the *bodies* of all things, in comparison of their *soules*. And, though *bodies* oft-times have the ill-luck to be sensually preferr'd, they find afterwards, the good fortune (when *soules* live) to be utterly forgotten. This it is hath made the most royall *Princes*, and greatest *persons* (who are commonly the *personators* of these *actions*) not onely studious of riches, and magnificence in the outward celebration, or shew; (which rightly becomes them but) curious after the most high, and heartie *inventions*, to furnish the inward parts: (and those grounded upon *antiquitie*, and solide *learnings*) which, though their *voyce* be taught to sound to present occasions, their *sense*, or doth, or should always lay hold on more remov'd *mysteries*. And, howsoever some may squemishly crie out, that all endevor of *learning*, and *sharpnesse* in these transitorie *devices* especially, where it steps beyond their little, or (let me not wrong 'hem) no braine at all, is superfluous; I am contented, these fastidious *stomachs* should leave my full tables,

and enjoy at home, their cleane emptie trenchers, fittest for such
ayrie tastes: where perhaps a few *Italian* herbs, pick'd up, and
made into a *sallade,* may find sweeter acceptance, than all, the
most nourishing, and sound meates of the world.

$$(1-28)$$

In part, this seems to be an answer to Daniel's preface to *The Vision of the
Twelve Goddesses,* in which he insists on the insubstantiality of such spectacles. But Jonson goes further—he asserts that the masque may be a self-
sufficient work of art, for which poetry supplies the essential quality. Jonson
is the cook of *Neptunes Triumph,* as well as its poet; he claims that his
masques are "full tables," "the most nourishing, and sound meates of the
world." He treats his spectacles as poems, and it is therefore relevant to note,
as the Oxford editors do, that "He lays down the theory of 'these devices'
in the terms which Aristotle applies to the drama." It is perhaps even more
important to remark that Jonson was almost alone among contemporary
writers in making such claims for the masque. Only Chapman (who, Jonson
told Drummond, alone "next himself . . . could make a Mask") replied to
critics of his one court production with a Jonsonian remark: "Every vulgarly-
esteemed upstart dares break the dreadful dignity of ancient and authentical
poesie."

    In 1610, Daniel was obviously attacking Jonson's conception of the
form when he wrote in the preface to *Tethys' Festival:* "And for these figures
of mine, if they come not drawn in all proportions to the life of antiquity
(from whose tyrannie, I see no reason why we may not emancipate our
inventions, and be as free as they, to use our owne images) yet I know them
such as were proper to the business, and discharged those parts for which
they served, with as good correspondencie, as our appointed limitations
would permit." Daniel thinks of the requirements of the form as "appointed
limitations" and uses them to excuse whatever his critics may find lacking
in his text: the masque (he says in effect) is, after all, not a literary form.
But those same limitations became first Jonson's tools and then incidental
elements in a much larger structure. So Jonson would hold precisely that his
rival's figures were *not* "proper to the business." And we must recognize
Jonson's claims because in great measure he substantiated them. He explicitly and continuously worked against the attitude Daniel represented, an
attitude that another masquemaker worked into *The Maid's Tragedy:*

> LYSIPPUS: Strato, thou hast some skill in poetry; what think'st
>   thou of the masque? Will it be well?
> STRATO: As well as masques can be.

LYS.: As masques can be?

STRA.: Yes; they must commend their king, and speak in praise
of the assembly, bless the bride and bridegroom in the person
of some god; they're tied to the rules of flattery.

Strato's opinion, indeed, appears to have been almost universal. Bacon
himself, who (Beaumont tells us) was responsible for the extravagant production of *The Masque of Gray's Inn and the Inner Temple*, remarks of
masques and triumphs, "These Things are but Toyes, to come amongst such
Serious Observations." The statement is made in an essay of 1625. The Lord
Chancellor would have seen a good many of Jonson's masques by then, but
he does not appear to have agreed that, "though their *voyce* be taught to
sound to present occasions, their *sense*, or doth, or should alwayes lay hold
on more remov'd *mysteries*."

Just as it is clear that Jonson alone conceived of the masque as literature,
so it is equally clear that this was his primary concern for it. This much is
evident from the mere fact that he included his masques in the 1616 edition
of his works. Nevertheless, there is a curious uncertainty in his theorizing,
as if he did not know quite where to begin to establish his new literary form.
In the learned footnotes and prefaces we sense that Jonson somehow felt a
need to vindicate his attempt to treat the masques as significant didactic
poetry. He explodes straw men:

The twelvth, and worthy *Soveraigne* of all I make *Bel-anna,* Royall
Queene of the *Ocean;* of whose dignity, and person the whole
scope of the *Invention* doth speake throughout. . . . But, here, I
discerne a possible Objection, arising agaynst mee, to which I
must turne: As, *How I can bring* Persons, *of so different* Ages,
*to appeare, properly, together? Or, Why (which is more unna-
turall) . . . I joyne the living, with the dead?* I answere to both
these, at once, Nothing is more proper; Nothing more naturall:
For these all live; and together, in theyr *Fame;* And so I present
them. Besides, if I would fly to the all-daring Power of *Poetry,*
Where could I not take Sanctuary? or in whose *Poëme?* For other
objections, let the lookes and noses of Judges hover thick; so they
bring the braines: or if they do not, I care not. When I suffer'd
it to goe abroad, I departed with my right: And now, so secure
an Interpreter I am of my chance, that neither praise, nor dispraise
shal affect me.

(*Queenes,* lines 655 ff)

He justifies at length the simplest dramatic effects:

> [If the witches had explained their purpose] eyther before, or
> other-wise, it had not bene so naturall. For, to have made them-
> selves theyr owne decipherers, and each one to have told, upon
> theyr entrance, *what they were, and whether they would,* had
> bene a most piteous hearing, and utterly unworthy any quality of
> a *Poeme;* wherein a *Writer* should alwayes trust somewhat to the
> capacity of the *Spectator.*
>
> (Queenes, lines 100 ff.)

He takes refuge in barely relevant pedantry:

> That they [the four humors] were personated in men, hath (al-
> readie) come under some *Grammaticall* exception. But there is
> more then *Grammar* to release it. For, besides that *Humores* and
> *Affectus* are both *Masculine in Genere,* not one of the *Specialls,*
> but in some Language is knowne by a *masculine* word.
>
> (Hymenaei, note to line 112)

But ultimately he speaks of the masque in the specifically moral terms he
applies elsewhere to the best poetry:

> all Repraesentations, especially those of this nature in court, pub-
> lique Spectacles, eyther have bene, or ought to be the mirrors of
> mans life, whose ends, for the excellence of their exhibiters (as
> being the donatives, of great Princes, to their people) ought al-
> wayes to carry a mixture of profit, with them, no lesse then
> delight.
>
> (Loves Triumph, lines 1 ff.)

This expresses the same humanistic conviction as the preface to *Volpone.*
Jonson is quite explicit, and if we take him literally we shall treat the masques
very seriously indeed.

I have [elsewhere] already mentioned E. W. Talbert's valuable article
["The Interpretation of Jonson's Courtly Spectacles"], which suggests that
we view Jonson's masques as Renaissance ethical-didactic poems: "The voice
of Jonson's courtly spectacle, I submit, is that of the panegyric *laudando
praecipere;* the sense, that of precepts *de regimine principum* enlarged by
the ethical-poetical *credo* of a staunch Renaissance humanist." There is a
good deal of validity in this, though the application of Jonson's remarks may
be carried too far. For often, examining the masques themselves, we find the
symbolic and didactic elements of the masque world a mere perfunctory

epilogue to the antimasque. We have seen, for example, that *laudando prae-cipere* will not at all describe *Oberon,* in which the panegyric and the dramatic elements of the masque work in direct opposition. It is necessary to temper all of Jonson's critical statements with a knowledge of the works in which they appear; the one quoted last above is prefixed to the late *Loves Triumph Through Callipolis* (1631), which has no antimasque. For the masque world alone, the description it offers is apt enough. Yet in attempting to characterize the Jonsonian masque, of course, we can hardly ignore the antimasque.

A brief but admirable statement of the masque's place in its social and courtly context has been given by Jonas A. Barish. The form, he observes,

> represents a society not so much aspiring after as joyfully contemplating its own well-being, the possession of the blessings it considers itself to have achieved. The compliments to the king . . . are one expression of this self-congratulation on the part of the community. To eulogize the king is to congratulate the society, of which the king is figurehead, for the communal virtues symbolized in him. To the extent that the actuality falls short of the ideal, the masque may be taken as a kind of mimetic magic on a sophisticated level, the attempt to secure social health and tranquillity for the realm by miming it in front of its chief figure. The frequency of prayer as a rhetorical mode in the masques is hence not accidental.
>
> [in *Ben Jonson and the Language of Prose Comedy*]

As it is here summarized, the function of the court masque remained essentially unchanged from its earliest beginnings. Its form, by contrast, seems to be almost infinitely mutable. It is, admittedly, an especially difficult one to define, largely because it involved so many disparate elements. Certainly to the contemporary audience, dancing and spectacle were important attractions of the masque; and what often seems to us a gratuitous addition to a lively antimasque would not have appeared so in seventeenth-century Whitehall. But Jonson was writing for two audiences, treating the nonliterary requirements of his form as literary ones, external demands as organic ones. Therefore, if sometimes the main masque with its revels seems perfunctory, this is not merely a mechanical failure in transcribing the spectacle for the reader. It is a structural flaw within the masque itself, such as we have found in *Love Restored* and *Oberon.* . . .

We must read and judge the masques as we read the rest of Jonson's poetry and drama. No matter how much we may use a knowledge of the exigencies of production and the demands of Jonson's position in our effort to understand how and why he should have developed the form as he did, we must be aware at all times that these exigencies were poetic problems to him. What he achieved at his best was a synthesis of the world he wrote for and the world he created.

WILLIAM BLISSETT

The Venter Tripartite in The Alchemist

In *The Alchemist* of Ben Jonson, the cheaters making up the
"venter tripartite" are the old enemies of mankind—The World,
the Flesh, and the Devil—put in a realistic London setting and
attired like men and women of the time. Dol is obviously the
Flesh in appearance and behavior. Subtle, engaged in nefarious
arts and often associated with loud noises and evil smells, is a
secularized Devil. The third role, that of the World, is less readily
recognized. At first Sir Epicure Mammon promises to fill it, but
he proves too gullible and libidinous. In a morality play, his role
would be that of Carnal Imagination. The smooth, adroit dissem-
bler, Face, moves increasingly into the center of the plot until,
ending the venter tripartite, he proves the Devil is an ass. The
conclusion of the play is as bland as that of *Volpone* was severe.
The householder Lovewit gains riches and a young wife and con-
dones the actions of his unjust steward. The respectable worldling
even more than the disreputable is the winner in this world.

The "judging spectator" of the two most generally esteemed and most
similar of Ben Jonson's comedies is required to be extraordinarily agile when,
at the end of *Volpone* and of *The Alchemist*, the playwright makes equal

From *Studies in English Literature 1500–1900* 8, no. 2 (Spring 1968). © 1968 by
William Blissett. William Marsh Rice University, 1968.

claims for his nod of assent and pleasure. The laws of Venice are applied so stringently to Volpone, Mosca, and the other delinquents as to lead some to say that the play verges on tragedy; whereas the hubbub at the end of *The Alchemist* verges on farce: comparable dupes lose only cash and other metal moveables and, of the cheaters, two escape without gain or loss and the third appears to profit himself and is the undoubted agent of another's profit.

In mitigation of the harsh outcome of *Volpone* it may be argued that, since the law has been not only contravened but invoked by the contraveners, judicial consequences must be expected; further, that the animal characterization of the base persons makes their punishment quite unlike any judgment of souls and hence still appropriate to comedy, while Celia and Bonario are deliberately under-characterized so as to preclude any expectation that they will shine forth—and demand to be paired off—at the end; and further, that Volpone's springing up yet once more to speak the epilogue prevents the shock of the sentence from lingering: he will retire to the wings, not to the Incurabili. To all these considerations must be added the words of the playwright in his dedication to the two universities:

> And though my *catastrophe* may, in the strict rigour of *comick* law, meet with censure, as turning back to my promises: J desire the learned, and charitable critick to haue so much faith in me, to thinke it was done off industrie: For, with what ease J could have varied it, neerer his scale (but that I feare to boast my owne faculty) J could here insert. But my speciall ayme being to put the snaffle in their mouths, that crie out, we neuer punish vice in our *enterludes,* &c. I tooke the more liberty; though not without some lines of example, drawne euen in the ancients themselues, the goings out of whose *comoedies* are not alwaies ioyfull, but oft-times, the bawdes, the seruants, the riuals, yea, and the masters are mulcted: and fitly, it being the office of a *comick-Poet,* to imitate iustice, and instruct to life, as well as puritie of language, or stirre vp gentle affections.

But this very claim to "imitate justice" in *Volpone* makes more acute the problem of *The Alchemist*. For two centuries Jonson was deemed pre-eminent in the possession and exercise of "judgment," yet he devised a play in which, to be sure, fools are shown to be the fools they are and made to pay the price of their folly, but in which the law appears to be broken with impunity and a certain kind of wrong-doer is commended by a late-introduced "straight" character who seems to embody not only the good humor but the good sense of the audience.

Of course, it is no new thing for a playwright to work within a certain pattern and yet suddenly, on occasion, to reverse it. The festive outcome of Shakespearean comedy in the 1590's, with its wedding music and dance, is such a pattern, but *Love's Labour's Lost* gains its piquancy and distinction by contravening expectation and, through the application of a sort of comic anti-matter, suddenly disappearing, along with its baffled audience, "you, that way: we, this way." But *The Alchemist* does not give the impression of simply taking a holiday from the judicious world, as *Bartholomew Fair* does. Festivity at the end of *Love's Labour's Lost* is dissolved and dispelled, but *The Alchemist* still invites, still requires judgment.

Perhaps the way into the play will eventually issue into a way out. Three players enter, and two are characterized at once. It would be a sad actress indeed who could not by makeup, style of speech, and appropriate bumps and grinds, build her role to substantial fullness before the name of Dol Common is spoken or she is claimed by her companions as "our republic." In such a case, *déformation professionnelle* is usually quite pronounced, and, the moral condition of the character being a *donnée*, she is from the beginning analogous to a figure in a morality play, whether or not individualizing traits such as a humorous disposition or a quick wit or a heart of gold are subsequently filled in.

Naturally, we look first at Dol Common, and our summing-up is instantaneous and, as it falls out, never altered. But we listen first to a thin, noisy, foul-spoken man whom we recognize from his threadbare and starveling appearance to be the alchemist of the play's title. An immediate question arises: why is the playwright at pains to make him so noisy that the quiet-voiced third member of the group must frequently and apprehensively beg him to lower his voice?

> FAC.: You might talk softlier, rascall.
> SVB.: No, you *scarabe*,
> Ill thunder you, in peeces. I will teach you
> How to beware, to tempt a *furie*'againe
> That carries tempest in his hand, and voice.
>   (1.1.59–62)

In terms of realistic detail, the initial answer is that the Alchemist is somewhat deaf, but why this detail? The real answer, I think, is bound up with the Alchemist's astounding first line—"Thy worst. I fart at thee." The theaters of the world must wait nearly three centuries for Pére Ubu to match it for audacity and emphasis. It will certainly make any audience sit up; it establishes the thorough bass of the play's style and decorum; it precludes the possibility of the play's magic being benevolent, theurgic, highbrow. But put noise and stink together in a context of necromancy and the black arts—and keep them together, for the climax of the play's action is a loud explosion, and the air is not cleared until the plague has lifted and the Alchemist has departed—and there is enough evidence to associate this closely-observed Jacobean charlatan with the morality prototype. Jonson himself is to give us the master-clue in *The Staple of News:* in one of the choric episodes one chattering playgoing woman says to another, who hopes to see a devil on the stage: "That was the old way, Gossip, when *Iniquity* came in like *Hokos Pokos*, in a *Iuglers* ierkin, with false skirts, like the *Knaue* of *Clubs!* but now they are attir'd like men and women o' the time, the *Vices,* male and female!"

In the first scene of *The Alchemist,* then, three characters enter into a plot or business agreement or "venter tripartite" to waylay various specimens of humanity, and one is at once recognizable as a figure of the Flesh, the second as a figure of the Devil. The third, Jeremy the Housekeeper, known as Face, is much less strongly characterized at the outset, but this again is appropriate, for who has as clear a conception of the World as of the more alluring or fascinating enemies of the soul?

Morality characterization is largely based on the old phrase "*nomina-numina*"—the name is the nature or spirit of the thing named. To name Dol Common is to know her, and the subsequent variations on her name are merely the arpeggios of concupiscence. The name "Subtle" must detain us longer. First actually named by Sir Epicure Mammon early in the second act, the Alchemist has been called Sirrah, rogue, whelp, slave, mongrel, doctor dog by Face; sovereign—and stinkard—by Dol; and doctor by Dapper and Drugger. Subtle may have been intended by the humanist playwright as a satiric jab at scholasticism and its Doctor Subtilis; but a perusal of the various forms of the word current in the Renaissance encourages a reference at once wider and more to our purpose. Two of the basic meanings of "subtle" are "rarefied" or "penetrating" and "skilful" or "crafty." The *Oxford English Dictionary* gives (1398) "The ayre and brethe drawen in by the mouth is amended and puryd, and made subtyll therein," and (1617) "The subtileness of the Ayre." Shakespeare seems to draw on both meanings, directly and as transferred epithet, in Juliet's exclamation: "What if it be a poison which the friar / Subtly hath minister'd to have me dead?" (4.3.25). Usually he employs the second: "Am I politic, am I subtle, am I a Machiavel?" (3.1.103) and, very memorably, Richard of Gloucester's "As I am subtle, false, and treacherous" (1.1.37). This last-quoted line, by one who is determined to prove a villain, should serve as a reminder that the word is regularly used in a context of spiritual malice. "He's the devil," says a Volscian soldier of Coriolanus. "Bolder," replies Aufidius, "though not so subtle" (1.10.17).

The Devil is subtle: he is devious, and he is prince of the powers of the air. Caxton (1471) says, "He chaunged hymself in guyse of a serpent this is to vnderstand in subtyllesse and in malice," and Coverdale's translation of Genesis 3.1 is to fix the word in subsequent translations (and in *Paradise Lost*): "The serpent was sotyller then all the beastes of the felde." The same word carries over from the devil to the devilish arts. Caxton (c. 1489) writes of one who was "the subtillest nygromancer that ever was in the world," and *The Institution of a Christian Man* (1537) warns against "charmes, wytche-craftes, or any other false artes subtiles and inuented by the dyuell." Very close to the time of the play, in 1603, Archbishop Samuel Harsnet declared against "Egregious Popish Impostures" by attacking "our subtiliated, sublimated new spirits of the Sorbon."

But it is not necessary to go beyond the works of Ben Jonson himself to see how closely packed is the parcel of associations. The Prologue to *The Devil Is an Ass* says, "Though you presume SATAN a subtill thing, / And may haue heard hee's worne in a thumbe-ring. . ." (5–6), and clearly he is drawing on both senses. Both senses also come into play when a senior devil says to a junior who is assuming a dead man's body, "And, looke, how farre your subtilty can worke / Thorough those organs, with that body" (1.1.144–45). Without in this instance using the word "subtle" Jonson explicitly assigns alchemy to the domain of the Devil when Manly asks Wittipol why Fitz-Dottrell loves the Devil so:

> O Sr! for hidden treasure,
> Hee hopes to finde: and has propos'd himselfe
> So infinite a Masse, as to recouer,
> He cares not what he parts with, of the present,
> To his men of Art, who are the race, may coyne him,
> Promise gold-mountaines, and the couetous
> Are still most prodigall!
>
> (1.5.16–22)

In *The Alchemist* itself, Kastril asks Face, "But do's he teach / Liuing, by the wits, too?" and Face replies, "Any thing, what euer, / You cannot thinke that subtiltie but he reads it. / He made me a Captain. I was a starke pimpe" (3.4.41–44). The comic irony of this passage depends on our knowing that Subtle is a rogue without supernatural powers, and yet it draws sustenance from the covert association with the devil, as does Surly's threat "to find / The subtilties of this darke *labyrinth*" (2.3.308). We come to realize that this dark labyrinth has "Fortune's privy lodging" at its center. Alchemy (like chemistry, which is still jocularly called "stinks") was a smelly business with its concoctions and menstrues; around the Devil too clung a cloud of brimstone. Dol calls her quarrelling associates "you abominable pair of stinkards" and Face later calls Subtle "you smoaky persecutor of nature!"—both phrases calling to mind the evil-smelling perversities of the Devil and of the alchemist. Ananias speaks better than he knows at the end of the play when he and Tribulation Wholesome beat at the door:

> Come forth, you seed of sulphure, sonnes of fire,
> Your stench, it is broke forth: abomination
> Is in the house.
>
> (5.3.44–46)

The poet that "writ so subtly of the fart" is Ben Jonson.

Before the third member of this infernal trinity can be more fully characterized, the clients begin to arrive, and he must busy himself in a Mosca-like role as Subtle's agent in the complications of the intrigue. (The Devil is very busy, as Latimer used to say, and those who renounce him must renounce "all his works.") This intrigue consists in the cozening of a realistically conceived sampling of the citizenry of contemporary London. The two small-timers move easily within the power of the cozeners: as their names tell us, Dapper's life is circumscribed within clothes that cut a flashy figure, and Drugger's within the bounds of his trade. The engine of deception turns over in low gear as Sir Epicure Mammon pauses at the door of the house before making one of the superb entrances of drama.

With such a name, it might be expected that Sir Epicure Mammon would step in to fill the incompletely sketched third role, except for two insurmountable reservations. One is that Jeremy, who has been acquitting himself with great dispatch as Captain Face, now adds to himself a second disguise as Lungs, and begins to occupy the central position as the manipulator not only of the dupes but of Dol and Subtle, who act on his cues and shift their shapes less daringly and dangerously than he does. Dol appears and disappears fleetingly through most of the play, and Subtle, after his canting virtuoso pieces in the debates with Surly and Ananias, retires to busy himself with the magisterium behind scenes. "Face" may be defined as "command of countenance, especially with reference to freedom from indication of shame; a bold front; impudence, effrontery, 'cheek.'" "Lungs," realistically appropriate to the plier of the bellows, is also where deep lies come from. Face, then, is in rapid process of growing into this third role, and that is one reason for the exclusion of Sir Epicure as a candidate for it; the other is that Sir Epicure simply will not do as an embodiment of the World.

For all his "pomps and vanities," Sir Epicure Mammon bears about as much resemblance to Mammon, god of worldlings, as he does to Epicurus, the high-minded and frugal philosopher of refined pleasure: the name is a double travesty. One cannot listen to and share the sensual excitement of his great speeches without realizing that such glorious tumidity is not a property of the calculating World. A real worldling, like Shaw's Sir Andrew Undershaft, employs a very different rhetoric. Sir Andrew, reverting to explicit morality, could indeed play the World, but Sir Epicure would then play Carnal Imagination. That he is carnal in the sense of spiritually undiscerning is proved by his dealing with sorcery yet supposing all the while the sorcerer to be devout. Surly shares this delusion with him, but Mammon goes further in self-deception:

> SVR.: Why, I haue heard, he must be *homo frugi,*
> A pious, holy, and religious man,
> One free from mortall sinne, a very virgin.
> MAM.: That makes it, sir, he is so. But I buy it.
>   (1.2.97–100)

That he is carnal in the sense of being given to fleshly motions is amply shown by his dealings with Dol. As for imagination, the connotations of which in the Renaissance are usually pejorative, Mammon is (if one may allude to one great phrase) scattered in the imagination of his heart, for he is (to gather in another) of imagination all compact. Something of a lunatic ("He has, this month, talk'd, as he were possess'd" [1.4.16]), he is more of a lover and poet in Theseus's self-deluding sense, as is demonstrated in the fourth act. At its inception he addresses himself: "Now, EPICVRE, / Heighten thy selfe, talke to her, all in gold" (4.1.24–25). At the height of the excitement he is still cockering up his genius, though ostensibly addressing Dol:

> and then renew
> Our youth, and strength, with drinking the *elixir,*
> And so enjoy a perpetuitie
> Of life, and lust.
>   (4.1.163–66)

And at the end he exclaims, "O my voluptuous mind! I am iustly punish'd" (4.5.74).

Acid resentment and unctuous hypocrisy are both sins of the World, but vinegary Ananias and oily Tribulation belong to a simpler order of satire not immediately relevant to our discussion. That leaves the role of World to Face—unless Surly cares to claim it. He does. But the cards are stacked and the dice loaded against the petty gamester in the big game. "You are incredulous," observes Mammon, and Surly replies:

> Faith, I haue a humor,
> I would not willingly be gull'd. Your *stone*
> Cannot transmute me.
>
> (2.1.77–79)

Later, Mammon explains to the Alchemist,

> This gent'man, you must beare withall.
> I told you, he had no faith. SVR: And little hope, sir,
> But, much less charitie, should I gull my selfe.
>
> (2.2.122–24)

Perhaps a little faith and hope and charity might be just the thing to prevail against the World, the Flesh, and the Devil (but that would be another play); all Surly can see is

> That *Alchemie* is a pretty kind of game,
> Somewhat like tricks o'the cards, to cheat a man,
> With charming.
>
> (2.3.180–82)

The name Pertinax means obstinate, and Surly means surly: at no point must director or actor allow the audience a moment of sympathy or fellow-feeling with this spoil-sport. His must be the cheerless position of being "nobody's fool," and as this world goes we greatly prefer the slimmer and more ingratiating out-and-out-rogue. We are depressed when he thinks he has deserved and won Dame Pliant, exhilarated when his machinations are foiled by Face, and Kastril roars at him the unroarable "pimp!" and "trig!" No, when it comes to the true spirit of this world, Face is your only man.

Or so it seems while the venter tripartite is in operation. But no sooner has the difficulty with Surly been dispatched than the ever-present but forgotten eventuality occurs: Lovewit the master has returned to the city and is in the neighborhood. "Yes, and I dwindled with it," says Subtle when asked if he has heard the hubbub at the door. "Dwindled" is the word: Subtle flourishes only in the bad air of the plague; he is a pest in time of pestilence; rid of one, rid of the other. "Dwindled" we know him to be, but "a little exalted / In the good passage of our stock-affaires" he still declares himself as he kisses Dol, the "fly" and "Queen of Faery" of this malodorous Lord of the Flies, the "fine flitter-mouse" of this threadbare prince of the powers of the air. He has yet one more scheme that may retrieve everything even this late in the day:

> Soone at night, my DOLLY,
> When we are shipt, and all our goods aboord,
> East-ward for *Ratcliffe;* we will turne our course
> To *Brainford,* westward, if thou saist the word:
> And take our leaues of this ore-weaning raskall,
> This peremptorie FACE.
>
> (5.4.74–79)

It is not to be. Face stands possessed of the keys of the trunks, and, as far as this play is concerned, we shall see that possession is the whole of the law. He turns the tables finally on his confederates:

> The right is, my master
> Knowes all, has pardon'd me, and he will keepe 'hem.
> Doctor, 'tis true (you looke) for all your figures:
> I sent for him, indeed. Wherefore, good partners,
> Both hee, and shee, be satisfied: for, here
> Determines the *indenture tripartite,*
> Twixt SVBTLE, DOL, and FACE.
>
> (5.4.126–32)

"Some knock," says the stage-direction. "Harke you, thunder," says Face. It is the devil's own racket, and Subtle exclaims from the heart, "You are a precious fiend!" and Dol, with similar propriety, "Poxe vpon you, rogue." Face is all smug expansiveness:

> SVBTLE,
> Let's know where you set vp next; I'll send you
> A customer, now and then, for old acquaintance:
> What new course ha' you?
>
> (5.4.143–46)

Subtle in reply clinches the allusion to his morality-role:

> Rogue, I'll hang my selfe:
> That I may walke a greater diuell, then thou,
> And haunt thee i'the flock-bed, and the buttery.
>
> (5.4.146–48)

This is certainly an adumbration of the title and theme of *The Devil Is an Ass:* the clever worlding will outdevil the poor devil every time.

But it is not quite the point and not quite the end of this play. We must reckon at last with the respectable man of the world. This master, in a tangential and crooked reference to a parable already sufficiently puzzling, commends his unjust steward because he has done wisely, for the children of darkness are in their generation wiser than the children of light. "The world will love his own," is a proverb-like phrase in an Elizabethan play. Among the children of darkness (and who, in this play, is not a child of darkness?) one must be wisest or shrewdest of all, and it is Lovewit. Lovewit breaks no law, indeed offers to return any misappropriated property to whoever undertakes to prove his title to it; meanwhile, he keeps all goods and chattels, including "puss my suster" (for what she is worth); and he has the pleasure of being a good fellow, freely forgiving all those who have amused and enriched him.

To this the "judging spectator" must nod his head in assent: yes, the World is like that. Lovewit? You have to hand it to him. And as for Face, let's give him a hand.

THOMAS M. GREENE

Ben Jonson and the Centered Self

The dual image of circle and center is an organizing principle of all Ben Jonson's work. The circle (suggesting perfection, harmony, equilibrium in cosmos, society, household, soul) is doubled by the center (suggesting governor, king, house, inner self). Both images are represented as achieved ideals in the masques; in most of Jonson's other works, the circle appears to be broken, and the center, if there is one, is associated with solitary and upright independence. Dwelling symbolically at home emerges as an important value in the poems, but the home in the plays generally figures as an inadequate fortress open to invasion and adultery. The poems and comedies contrast the self-reliant centered self with characters who are or seek to be metaphysically volatile, who would shift, disguise, transform, and multiply themselves. This will to multiply the Protean self is the basic subject of Volpone, *almost all of whose characters seek their own metamorphosis, and whose villains are finally punished with confinement. The rogues and gulls of* The Alchemist *share a common desire to be "sublimed." But* Bartholomew Fair *reveals a greater tolerance of the world's changeful variety.*

I

"Deest quod duceret orbem" reads the motto of Ben Jonson's famous *impresa* with the broken compass. After the fashion of *imprese*, it contains a kind of transparent enigma, to be solved in this case by the reading of its author's canon. For the *orbis*—circle, sphere, symbol of harmony and per-

From *Studies in English Literature 1500–1900* 10, no. 2 (Spring 1970). © 1970 by Thomas M. Greene. William Marsh Rice University, 1970.

fection—becomes familiar to the student of Jonson as one of his great unifying images. In a sense, almost everything Jonson wrote attempts in one way or another to complete the broken circle, or expose the ugliness of its incompletion. We have had a study of the circle in the European imagination, [George Poulet's *Les Métamorphoses du cercle*,] and another of the circle in seventeenth-century England, [Marjorie Nicholson's *The Breaking of the Circle*,] both valuable explorations of this image's evocative range. But as both studies teach us, even geometric images can be plastic—must be so, insofar as they are animated by the imagination, and their cultural contexts can never fully define their suggestiveness. One criterion of the major artist is the process by which traditional symbols acquire in his work an individual resonance even as they illuminate retrospectively their tradition.

In the case of an artist like Jonson, the imagery of circularity is one means of intuiting, beneath the turbulent richness and vehement variety of his work, its underlying coherence. But it is also a token of his massive artistic independence. In Jonson, the associations of the circle—as metaphysical, political, and moral ideal, as proportion and equilibrium, as cosmos, realm, society, estate, marriage, harmonious soul—are doubled by the associations of a center—governor, participant, house, inner self, identity, or, when the outer circle is broken, as lonely critic and self-reliant solitary. Center and circle become symbols, not only of harmony and completeness but of stability, repose, fixation, duration, and the incompleted circle, uncentered and misshapen, comes to symbolize a flux or a mobility, grotesquely or dazzlingly fluid. Most of the works in Jonson's large canon—including the tragedies and comedies, verse and prose—can be categorized broadly in their relation to an implicit or explicit center. That is to say, one can describe an image or character or situation as durable, as center-oriented and centripetal (I shall use these terms as more or less synonymous) or one can describe them as moving free, as disoriented and centrifugal, in quest of transformation. To sketch these categories is to seem to suggest absolute poles, ethically positive and negative. But although much of Jonson's writing encourages that suggestion, it does not lack its tensions, its ambivalences, its subtle shifts of emphasis. If the categories are not themselves transformed, they show up as altered under the varying artistic light.

The great storehouse of Jonson's centripetal images is the series of masques which assert, almost by definition, the existence of an order. The succession of anti-masque to masque, of crudity and disorder to beauty and order, demonstrates over and over the basic harmony of the cosmos and the realm. If the charm of the anti-masque, in its picturesque gaucherie, exceeded for some spectators the more solemn appeal of what followed, this frivolous superiority did not affect the authorized affirmations of the conclusion. In *The Masque of Beauty,* the allegorical figure Perfectio appears on the stage "In a vesture of pure Golde, a wreath of Gold upon her head. About her bodie the Zodiacke, with the Signes: In her hand a Compasse of golde, drawing a circle" and in a marginal note Jonson explains of the zodiac: "Both that, and the Compasse are known ensigns of perfection." These circles of perfection determine the choreography of many masques and, so to speak, the poetic choreography of many more, adding concentric denotations to the limpid verbal patterns.

The circles of the masques have reference first of all to the central figure of the king, literally seated in the center of the hall and directly facing the stage area. The king, associated repeatedly with the sun, is himself a symbolic orb—fixed, life-giving, dependable:

> That in his owne true circle, still doth runne;
> And holds his course, as certayne as the sunne,
> *(The Masque of Beauty)*

a source of radiance and order:

> Now looke and see in yonder throne,
> How all those beames are cast from one.
>   This is that Orbe so bright,
> Has kept your wonder so awake;
> Whence you as from a mirrour take
>   The Suns reflected light.
> Read him as you would doe the booke
> Of all perfection, and but looke
>   What his proportions be;
> No measure that is thence contriv'd,
> Or any motion thence deriv'd,
>   But is pure harmonie.
> *(The Masque of Beauty)*

The king's presence opposite the masquing stage (where the actors can point and bow to him) represents a kind of metaphysical principle which the dancers attempt to embody. Thus Reason will address the dancers of *Hymenaei:*

> Thanke his grace
> That hath so glorified the place:
> And as, in circle, you depart
> Link'd hand in hand; So, heart in heart,

> May all those bodies still remayne
> Whom he (with so much sacred payne)
> No lesse hath bound within his realmes
> Then they are with the Oceans streames.

Here the orb of the king's presence and the circles of the dance are associated with the community of the realm, the island encircled by Ocean.

The occasion for this particular masque was a court wedding, and Jonson employs the choreographic circle to symbolize most obviously the band of matrimony. At the climax of the final dance, the masquers form a circle, from the center of which Reason explicates the symbolism:

> Here stay, and let your sports be crown'd:
> The perfect'st figure is the round.
> Nor fell you in it by adventer,
> When Reason was your guide, and center.
> This, this that beauteous Ceston is
> Of lovers many-colour'd blisse.
> Come Hymen, make an inner ring,
> And let the sacrificers sing.
>
> (*Hymenaei*)

But the masque does not limit the significance of its intricate symmetries to its occasion. The last quotation suggests that the harmony of marriage depends upon that inner principle of restraint and equilibrium embodied by the figure named Reason. Earlier in the performance, an immense sphere has been discovered on stage, "a microcosme or globe (figuring Man)," whose passions and humors Reason succeeds in subduing. The ideal circle of perfection thus makes its claims upon the human soul, as upon king, realm, marriage, dance, cosmos, and principle.

The concept of an inner moral equilibrium also informs most of Jonson's verse, but there the achievement of circular harmony is considerably more precarious. The facile affirmations of the masques are intended for spectacle rather than drama, but in the verse (as in the drama) the effort to close the circle is restored to the bitter clash of the historical world. In the epigrams, epistles, and encomiastic tributes, the judgment is shrewder, the voice caustic, the moral combat uncertain. The brilliant sarcasm of the destructive pieces legitimizes the integrity of the compliments; taken together, they demonstrate the finesse of an observer neither sycophantic nor misanthropic, on whom nothing is lost, capable of fervid as well as witty discriminations. From most of the poems, we hear less asserted of the larger spheres of perfection, metaphysical or political, and more of the stable, if beleaguered, human center.

Several of the personal tributes in *The Forrest* come to rest at their conclusions upon an image of rooted stability, typically situated in an actual residence, a house or estate, a dwelling—with all the accreted meaning Jonson brings to the verb. Thus the compliment to Sir Robert Wroth:

> Thy peace is made; and, when man's state is well,
> 'Tis better, if he there can dwell

and again the closing lines of "To Penshurst":

> Now, Penshurst, they that will proportion thee
> With other edifices, when they see
> Those proud, ambitious heaps, and nothing else,
> May say, their lords have built, but thy lord dwells.

Both of these poems come to suggest that the act of dwelling at home with dignity, style, and integrity, as their respective subjects are said to do, involves a kind of inner homing, a capacity to come to rest within. Thus the reader is not quite sure where to find the literal meaning when he reaches the last quatrain of the poem which follows the two just quoted. This poem, entitled "To the World. A Farewell for a Gentlewoman, Vertuous and Noble," concludes as follows:

> Nor for my peace will I goe farre,
> As wanderers doe, that still doe rome,
> But make my strengths, such as they are,
> Here in my bosome, and at home.

To make one's strengths at home may mean to lead a retired life, but it means as well to find that home in one's own bosom. Jonson will praise the same centered strength when he addresses an individual who is outwardly quite unlike the gentlewoman—the polymath John Selden:

> you that have beene
> Ever at home: yet, have all Countries seene:
> And like a Compasse keeping one foot still
> Upon your Center, doe your Circle fill
> Of generall knowledge.
> ("To the World")

Virtually all the heroes and heroines (the terms are not misapplied) of the verse seem to possess this quality of fixed stability.

The grandiose spherical perfections of the masques are not, to be sure, altogether missing from the lyrics. The marriage of England and Scotland under James is celebrated in imagery reminiscent of the more stylized genre:

> The world the temple was, the priest a king,
> The spoused paire two realmes, the sea the ring,
>
> > ("On the Union")

as well as the visionary ideal of poetry:

> I saw a Beauty from the Sea to rise,
> That all Earth look'd on, and that earth, all Eyes!
> It cast a beame as when the chear-full Sun
> Is fayre got up, and day some houres begun!
> And fill'd an Orbe as circulat, as heaven!
>
> > ("The Vision of Ben Jonson, on the
> > Muses of His Friend M. Drayton")

But on the whole the circles of the lyric verse shrink toward their center, toward the Stoic individual soul, self-contained, balanced, at peace with itself even in isolation.

> He that is round within himselfe, and streight,
> Need seeke no other strength, no other height;
> Fortune upon him breakes her selfe, if ill,
> And what would hurt his vertue makes it still.
>
> . . . .
>
> Be always to thy gather'd selfe the same.
>
> > ("To Sir Thomas Rawe")

This intuition of the *gathered* self, whatever its antecedents in the Roman moralists, is profoundly Jonsonian, more personal and more spontaneous than the inclusive ideals of cosmos and realm. It is of a piece with the emotional reserve which Edmund Wilson misrepresents as coldness. It is by definition exclusive:

> Well, with mine owne fraile Pitcher, what to doe
> I have decreed; keepe it from waves, and presse;
> Lest it be justled, crack'd, made nought, or lesse:
> Live to that point I will, for which I am man.
> And dwell as in my Center, as I can.
>
> > ("The Underwood")

As Jonson aged and watched the centrifugal forces in his society acquire increasing power, this sense of the beleaguered central self became more insistent and more poignant. This is certainly the sense of the moving poem from which I have just quoted ("To One That Asked to Be Sealed of the Tribe of Ben") as it is of *The New Inne,* one of the so-called "dotages," where the ultimate victory of the valiant man is "Out of the tumult of so many errors, / To feel, with contemplation, mine own quiet." What depths of mastered suffering are betrayed by the proud serenity of this arrogant and beautiful phrase!

From the beginning the verse portrays with vivid scorn the ugliness of the uncentered, ungathered selves, whose disorientation always seems related to some principle of discontinuity. The self which is not at home paints, feigns, invents, gossips, *alters* its manner and passion as whim or necessity dictates. The dramatic life of the satirical poems and passages lies in their confrontations. They may confront simply the disoriented self in its whirling flux with the poet's alert and steady eye—and then we wait for the whip-lash phrase which stings and tells. Or they may confront the social frenzy with some centered figure who holds out:

> You . . . keepe an even, and unalter'd gaite;
> Not looking by, or back (like those, that waite
> Times, and occasions, to start forth, and seeme)
> Which though the turning world may dis-esteeme,
> Because that studies spectacles, and showes,
> And after varyed, as fresh objects goes,
> Giddie with change, and therefore cannot see
> Right, the right way: yet must your comfort bee
> Your conscience, and not wonder, if none askes
> For truthes complexion, where they all weare maskes.
>
>   ("The Forrest," XIII)

In the verse as in the masques, the circular values of virtue tend in their constancy to be transcribed by nouns and adjectives:

> Her Sweetnesse, Softnesse, her fair Curtesie,
> Her wary guards, her wise simplicitie,
> Were like a ring of Vertues, 'bout her set
> And pietie the Center, where all met.
>
> All offices were done
> By him, so ample, full, and round,
> In weight, in measure, number, sound,

> As though his age imperfect might appeare,
> His life was of Humanitie the Spheare—
> ("The Underwood," LXXXIII)

but the hideous antics of vice, because variable, must depend on a livelier
poetry of verbs:

> Be at their Visits, see 'hem squemish, sick
>
> . . . .
> And then, leape mad on a neat Pickardill;
> As if a Brize were gotten i' their tayle,
> And firke, and jerke, and for the Coach-man raile
>
> . . . .
> And laugh, and measure thighes, then squeak, spring, itch,
> Doe all the tricks of a saut Lady Bitch.
> ("The Underwood," XV)

Jonson seems to see his centered figures moving perpetually through this
purgatory of the Protean, still at rest when active, just as the vicious are
unstable even when torpid. He reports on the one hand the paradox of Sir
Voluptuous Beast married, who metamorphoses his innocent wife into the
serial objects of his past desire: "In varied shapes, which for his lust shee
takes." The married lecher is still in a sense adulterous. But Jonson registers
too the opposing paradox of a William Roe, who will return from a voyage
with his "first thoughts":

> There, may all thy ends,
> As the beginnings here, prove purely sweet,
> And perfect in a circle always meet.
> So, when we, blest with thy returne, shall see
> Thy selfe, with thy first thoughts, brought home by thee,
> We each to other may this voyce enspire;
> This is that good Aeneas, past through fire,
> Through seas, stormes, tempests: and imbarqu'd for hell,
> Came back untouch'd. This man hath travail'd well.
> ("To William Roe")

He travels well who in a sense never travels (or travails) at all, who circum-
scribes hell with his courage and whose mind knows no exile, keeping one
foot still upon his center, compass-like, and lives through tempest, here in
his bosom and at home.

II

The equilibrated energy of the centered self is most amply demonstrated by Jonson's *Timber*. The stress in that work falls on the faculty of judgment, and in fact it demonstrates this faculty at work, choosing among authors and passages, discriminating conduct and style.

> Opinion is a light, vain, crude, and imperfet thing, settled in the imagination, but never arriving at the understanding, there to obtain the tincture of reason.

The passages gathered in *Timber* are exercises of the reasonable understanding. A sentence like the one quoted seems to place the imagination in an outer layer of consciousness, where the centrifugal "opinion" can momentarily alight. The understanding is further within, at the psychic center of gravity, impervious to the flights of the butterfly-caprice. All of *Timber*, whether or not "original" in the vulgar sense, seems to issue from this center of gravity.

The shrewd and sane judgment of the prose is unwittingly parodied in *Catiline* by the figure of Cicero, a ponderous center of Roman gravity indeed. In *Sejanus*, the tenacious indignation of the upright Lucius Arruntius is more recognizably human, but his unrelieved railing falls short of the composure of the gathered self. This ideal seems rather to be approached by the minor character Lepidus, whose moral strategy amidst the dangerous political disintegration remains home-centered:

> the plaine, and passive fortitude,
> To suffer, and be silent; never stretch
> These armes, against the torrent; live at home,
> With my owne thoughts, and innocence about me,
> Not tempting the wolves jawes: these are my artes.

Lepidus is slightly ambiguous because his decision figuratively to "live at home" contrasts with the zealous sense of political responsibility which motivates Arruntius and the other Germanicans. Lepidus is represented as naive, but it is the Germanicans who are destroyed. In the "violent change, and whirle" of Tiberian Rome, all patterns of centripetal order are gone; even Fortune's wheel seems in the closing speeches to lead only downward, and the single remaining sphere is the adulterous liaison of Livia and Sejanus:

> Then Livia triumphs in her proper spheare,
> When shee, and her Sejanus shall divide
> The name of Caesar.

. . . .
And the scarce-seene Tiberius borrowes all
His little light from us, whose folded armes
Shall make one perfect orbe.

The comedies as well—far less distant from Jonson's tragedies than is the
case with Shakespeare—are mainly concerned with a centrifugal world, and
again in them the circles are often ironic. Thus, in *The Staple of News,* the
servants of Lady Pecunia all need to be bribed, without exception or competition, by the visitor who would reach their mistress:

We know our places here, wee mingle not
One in anothers sphere, but all more orderly,
In our owne orbes; yet wee are all Concentricks.

And in *Poetaster,* the banished Ovid laments his exile with an ironic lack of
centered self-reliance:

Banisht the court? Let me be banisht life;
Since the chiefe end of life is there concluded

. . . .
And as her sacred spheare doth comprehend
Ten thousand times so much, as so much place
In any part of all the empire else;
So every body, mooving in her sphaere,
Containes ten thousand times as much in him,
As any other, her choice orbe excludes.

In the comedies, moreover, where the embodiments of a moral judgment
appear only fitfully, it is much harder to locate a sense of a center. Perhaps
the closest dramatic equivalent to the gathered self, living "at home," is the
literal house, putative center of bourgeois dramatic existence. The weakness
of the house as refuge or protective fortress seems to mirror the weakness
of a centerless society.

Weak Jonson's houses certainly are, when it is necessary to exclude the
potential marauder. There is in fact a recurrent pattern of domestic invasion,
beginning with *The Case Is Altered,* where the miser Jaques de Prie is obsessed with fear that an intruder will break in to pilfer his hidden gold. His
fears are indeed realized, and we learn as well that he has himself pilfered
both his gold and his daughter from a former master. In *Sejanus,* it is Agrip-
pina's house which is invaded by a pair of the tyrant's spies and an *agent
provocateur,* to trap fatally the outspoken Sabinus. In *Catiline,* where the

hope for political order is a little less desperate, Cicero succeeds in thwarting the conspirators' plot to murder him at home. But his escape is narrow. His luck is better than the hapless Morose's (of *Epicoene*), caricature of the centered self, whose hatred of noise leads him to "devise a roome, with double walls, and treble seelings; the windores close shut, and calk'd; and there he lives by candlelight." It is Morose's special torment to be visited on his wedding day by a houseful of young city sparks, posturing fools, and pretentious women of fashion. "The sea breaks in upon me!" he cries at the high tide of the invasion. His double walls are of no avail. That Morose's humor does indeed represent a deliberate caricature of the centered self is made clear by one of his speeches:

> My father, in my education, was wont to advise mee, that I should always collect, and contayne my mind, not suffring it to flow loosely; that I should looke to what things were necessary to the carriage of my life, and what not: embracing the one, and es- chewing the other. In short that I should endeare myself to rest, and avoid turmoile: which now is growne to be another nature to me.
>
> (*The Silent Woman*)

Here we follow the process which wrenches the norm into the grotesque. And the cost is the frustration of barriers against the world which are always inadequate.

This pattern of domestic invasion has to be noticed, I think, when one considers those other comedies where a husband tries, more or less unsuc- cessfully, to protect his wife from adulterous advances. The fear of cuckoldry on the part of Kitely (in *Every Man in His Humor*) is unjustified but none- theless acute. Corvino's fear (in *Volpone*) is equally acute until the commer- cial element intrudes. Fitzdottrell's intermittent anxiety (in *The Devil Is an Ass*) over his wife is abundantly justified by the wiles of her suitor, and perhaps one is justified in adding to the list the plots of the witch Maudlin (in *The Sad Shepherd*) to undermine Robin Hood's marriage by assuming the form of Marian. Still another variant is the staged incursion of the dis- guised Surly (in *The Alchemist*) to make off with Dame Pliant. The obvious *fabliau* comedy of these episodes has to be included in the broader pattern of domestic invasion. The havoc caused by the various invasions measures the defenselessness of characters who depend for their protection on bricks and mortar. The mischief in *The Alchemist* occurs because the master of the house is literally away from home. In other plays the absence is figurative rather than actual, but the mischief is approximately equal.

In the disoriented world of Jonson's comedies, the most nearly successful characters seem to be the chameleons, the Shifts and Brainworms and Faces who refuse to be centered, who are comfortable with the metamorphoses society invites. A kind of witty complicity emerges occasionally from Jonson's treatment of his disguisers, to suggest that he was taken by their arts in spite of himself. Thus Carlo Buffone describes the transformations of Puntaruolo (in *Every Man out of His Humor*) with a sarcasm very nearly lyrical:

> These be our nimble-spirited Catsos, that have their evasions at pleasure . . . no sooner started, but they'll leap from one thing to another, like a squirrel, heigh: dance! and do tricks in their discourse, from fire to water, from water to air, from air to earth, as if their tongues did but e'en lick the four elements over, and away.

So Picklock (in *The Devil Is an Ass*) will proudly describe his Protean changeability:

> Tut, I am Vertumnus,
> On every change, or chance, upon occasion,
> A true Chamaelion, I can color for't.
> I move upon my axell, like a turne-pike,
> Fit my face to the parties, and become,
> Streight, one of them.

We are of course meant to see this pride as ironically misplaced, but such is not the case of Brainworm in *Every Man in His Humor,* whose skill in manipulating disguises seems to win justified approbation. Thus when at the conclusion Brainworm exclaims "This has been the day of my metamorphosis," he is rather admired than scolded. The human value of his whirlwind role-changing seems to counterbalance the more familiar value of the elder Knowell's advice to his nephew: "I'd ha' you sober, and contayne yourself." Perhaps this early play betrays a genuine tension in Jonson's moral sympathies which the "authorized" morality of the verse and later plays tends to becloud. There is indeed scattered evidence to suggest a strain of half-repressed envy for the homeless and centrifugal spirit. *Volpone* seems to me the greatest, though not the only work, to deal with that strain and make it into art.

III

The subject of *Volpone* is Protean man, man without core and principle and substance. It is an anatomy of metamorphosis, the exaltations and nightmares of our psychic discontinuities. It is one of the greatest essays we possess on the ontology of selfhood. For *Volpone* asks us to consider the infinite, exhilarating, and vicious freedom to alter the self at will once the ideal of moral constancy has been abandoned. If you do not choose to be, then, by an irresistible logic, you choose to change, and in view of the world we are called upon to inhabit, perhaps the more frequently one changes, the better. Machiavelli wrote: "He is happy whose mode of procedure accords with the needs of the times. . . . If one could change one's nature with time and circumstances, fortune would never change." Volpone demonstrates the ultimate hectic development of Machiavelli's shifty pragmatism, and raises it from a political maxim to a moral, even a metaphysical state of being.

This metaphysical dimension is introduced almost at the outset, in the cynical show performed by Volpone's dwarf and hermaphrodite. The history of Androgyno's transformation through history by means of metempsychosis, a process which exposes his soul to all the most debasing conditions of human and even bestial existence—this history announces and parodies the series of disguises and transformations assumed by the citizens of Jonson's fictive Venice. Androgyno's soul was once contained in the body of Pythagoras, "that juggler divine," and went on, "fast and loose," to enter other bodies. The human jugglers of the play themselves operate on the basis of a fast and loose soul.

The will to multiply the self animates the long speech by Volpone which appears at the exact middle of the play and which gives that will what might be called its classic statement. The speech is ostensibly intended to advance the seduction of Celia, but as Volpone is progressively carried away by his fantasy, his intoxication has less and less to do with the bewildered woman he seems to address. What his speech really betrays is his secret heart's desire:

> Whil'st, we, in changed shapes, act Ovids tales,
> Thou, like Europa now, and I like Jove,
> Then I like Mars, and thou like Erycine,
> So, of the rest, till we have quite run through
> And weary'd all the fables of the gods.
> Then will I have thee in more moderne formes,
> Attired like some sprightly dame of France,

> Brave Tuscan lady, or proud Spanish beauty;
> Sometimes, unto the Persian Sophies wife;
> Or the grand-Signiors mistresse; and, for change,
> To one of our most art-full courtizans,
> Or some quick Negro, or cold Russian;
> And I will meet thee, in as many shapes:
> Where we may, so, trans-fuse our wandring soules,
> Out at our lippes, and score up summes of pleasures.

The passion behind this extraordinary speech involves more than the histrionic art; it aims at the perpetual transformation of the self. Thus the various disguises which Volpone assumes—invalid, mountebank, corpse, *commendatore*—have to be regarded as tentative experiments toward that multiplication, to the point that the very term *disguise* comes to seem inadequate.

The role of corpse is that least suited to the many-selved man, and the stroke is suggestive which imbues Volpone with a fear of paralysis. His worst moment before the end comes when he must lie immobile in court to counterfeit a dying invalid:

> I ne're was in dislike with my disguise,
> Till this fled moment; here, 'twas good, in private,
> But, in your publike, *Cave,* whil'st I breathe.
> 'Fore god, my left legge 'gan to have the crampe;
> And I apprehended, straight, some power had strooke me
> With a dead palsey: well, I must be merry,
> And shake it off.

It is no accident that the language of this soliloquy is echoed in Volpone's sentence:

> Since the most was gotten by imposture,
> By feigning lame, gout, palsy, and such diseases,
> Thou art to lie in prison, crampt with irons,
> Till thou bee'st sicke and lame indeed.

This terrible punishment contains the profundity of a Dantesque *contrapasso*. The sinful thirst for perpetual metamorphosis calls for the immobility of bed and chain.

Volpone's passion for transforming himself is shared, imitated, fragmented, and complemented by most of the remaining characters. It is shared most conspicuously by his parasite Mosca, whose disguises are even more supple, more volatile, more responsive to the pressure of events, and in the worldly sense, more practical:

> But your fine, elegant rascall, that can rise,
> And stoope (almost together) like an arrow;
> Shoot through the aire, as nimbly as a starre;
> Turne short, as doth a swallow; and be here,
> And there, and here, and yonder, all at once;
> Present to any humour, all occasion;
> And change a visor, swifter, then a thought!
> This is the creature, had the art borne with him.

Thus runs Mosca's accurate self-appraisal, whose delight in his art must have been shared by his creator, but remains tinged nonetheless by the irony of a pitiless judgment. The irony extends *a fortiori* to the play with deception which occupies the two deceivers' victims. The rhetoric of Mosca's auto-congratulation is anticipated by his praise of the legal profession, and by extension of Voltore:

> I, oft, have heard him say, how he admir'd
> Men of your large profession that could speake
> To every cause, and things mere contraries,
> Till they were hoarse againe, yet all be law;
> That, with most quick agilitie, could turne,
> And re-turne; make knots, and undoe them;
> Give forked counsell.

Voltore's quick agility to turn and return sounds like the volatility of a Mosca, a fly, a swallow who will turn short and be here and there and yonder all at once. Only a little slower to turn is Corvino, whose savage anger for his wife's (allegedly) compromising appearance at her window succeeds in an instant to the decision to prostitute her. Even the feeble Corbaccio, so frightening in his murderous senility, attempts to disguise the poison he proffers as a medicinal opiate, just as he disguises from himself the truth of his condition:

> faines himselfe
> Yonger, by scores of yeeres, flatters his age,
> With confident belying it.

But the funniest example of discontinuity is Lady Wouldbe, whom Volpone calls "perpetual motion." The comedy of her inspired scene at his bedside stems from his frustration in damning the tide of her conversation.

Each of his anguished attempts to silence her provides a channel to a new topic, until he recognizes his helplessness before her infinite variety. The lady indeed produces a therapeutic philosophy to justify this trick of her mind and tongue to ramify without end:

> And, as we find our passions doe rebell,
> Encounter 'hem with reason; or divert 'hem,
> By giving scope unto some other humour
> Of lesser danger: as, in politique bodies,
> There's nothing, more, doth over-whelme the judgement,
> And clouds the understanding, then too much
> Settling, and fixing, and (as't were) subsiding
> Upon one object.

The lady's notion is that sticking to the subject is positively dangerous to the indisposed soul. Her speech provides a rationale, at her own trivial verbal level, for the perpetual motion which the more sinister Venetians also embody in their fashion. There is a special joke here for the student of Jonson, for what is this "settling and fixing, and, as 'twere, subsiding" of the judgment but that very gathering of the self which we know the playwright to have admired above all? It was an audacious and delightful thought to insert this allusion to the play's missing center into the incoherent chatter of an absurd blue-stocking.

The disguises and role-playing of the main plot are repeated in the subplot chiefly by the character of Peregrine, who in act 5 poses successively as a newsbearer and merchant, while giving out that the real Peregrine is actually a spy. But the more interesting character for our purposes is Sir Politic Wouldbe. We know from the verse that Jonson admired only those travelers who, in a symbolic sense, remained at home—as the Englishman Sir Pol conspicuously refuses to do. His opening lines, with their fatuous cosmopolitanism, already damn him: "Sir, to a wise man, all the world's his soile. / It is not Italie, nor France, nor Europe, / That must bound me, if my fates call me forth." His rootlessness, his homelessness, in the Jonsonian sense, are underscored again by the Polonius wisdom of his travel philosophy:

> And then, for your religion, professe none;
> But wonder, at the diversitie of all;
> And, for your part, protest, were there no other
> But simply the lawes o' th' land, you could contest you.

> Nic: Machiavel, and monsieur Bodine, both,
> Were of this minde.

Sir Politic's cultural relativism is his own equivalent to Volpone's fantasy of Protean eroticism, to Mosca's calculated visor-changing, to Lady Wouldbe's theory of diversion. He is an eternal traveler in the deepest sense, with his chameleon's willingness to do as the Romans and take on the moral coloring of his surroundings. His tongue repeats what its owner hears, like the tongue of the parrot his name suggests. The tortoise shell in which he finally hides suggests a creature without a stable home base, and this is indeed the symbolic interpretation Sir Pol himself makes of his own exile: "And I, to shunne, this place, and clime for ever; / Creeping, with house, on backe."

Set against all these figures of transiency stands the figure of Celia, who represents—more effectively than her associate Bonario—whatever principle of constancy the play contains. In her chief dramatic scene, her role is simply to hold firm under pressure, and she fulfills it. She is the one important character who is immobile and centripetal, and Jonson underlines this distinction by framing her drama in terms of immurement. We first hear of her as guarded and imprisoned by her fearful husband, and this imprisonment is intensified after she drops her handkerchief to Scoto-Volpone.

> I'le chalke a line: o're which, if thou but chance
> To set thy desp'rate foot; more hell, more horror,
> More wilde remorceless rage shall seize on thee,
> Then on a conjurer, that, had heedlesse left
> His circles safetie, ere his devill was laid.

Celia must remain at the center of a circle drawn by her husband, who fails to recognize the greater strength of her own inner centrality. This recognition is implicitly reached by the judges who, at the play's end, deliver her from her immurement and return her, a free agent, to her father's house. This enfranchisement contrasts not only with the forced paralysis of Volpone, but with the other sentences as well: Mosca is to live "perpetual prisoner" in the galleys, Corbaccio will be confined to a monastery, and Corvino pilloried. So many ways of denying the febrile thirst for transformation.

Throughout the play, the basic instrument of transformation was to have been gold. It is wrong, I think, to consider wealth as the ultimate goal of *Volpone*'s various scoundrels. Wealth is rather the great transformer, the means of metamorphosis:

> Why, your gold . . . transformes
> The most deformed, and restores 'hem lovely,

As't were the strange poeticall girdle. Jove
Could not invent, t' himselfe, a shroud more subtile,
To passe Acrisius guardes. It is the thing
Makes all the world her grace, her youth, her beauty.

The cruel lesson of the play is that gold fails to confer that infinite mobility
its lovers covet, but rather reduces them to the status of fixed, sub-human
grotesques. To multiply the self is to reduce the self—to fox, crow, fly,
vulture, and tortoise. That art which turns back on nature by denying natural
constancies ruins both nature and itself.

The very opening lines of *Volpone* invoke a pair of alternative circles.

Good morning to the day; and, next, my gold:
Open the shrine, that I may see my saint.
Haile the worlds soule, and mine.

. . . .

That, lying here, amongst my other hoords,
Shew'st like a flame, by night, or like the day
Strooke out of chaos, when all darkenesse fled
Unto the center. O, thou sonne of Sol,
(But brighter then thy father) let me kisse,
With adoration, thee.

The gold piece, an illusory sun, occupies the place of king, soul, *anima
mundi,* God. The travesty of worship is augmented by the scriptural misquotation. On the day of creation, according to scripture, darkness did not
fly to the center but to the outer chaos beyond the firmament. Volpone's
blunder gives away his basic misapprehension. His moral strategy depends
on centrifugal assumptions, on the labyrinthine flux of a world without
order. But he betrays in fact merely the benighted darkness of his own center.

IV

The issue at stake in Jonson's comedies was not irrelevant to the crisis
of what might be termed Renaissance anthropology. I have argued elsewhere
that the sixteenth century witnessed the climax of a many-sided debate over
the flexibility of the human self. The high Renaissance on the continent
appeared intermittently to promise both a lateral mobility, a wider choice of
roles and experience, and a vertical mobility, an opening toward something
like transcendence of the human condition. To abridge summarily a very
complex history, one can say that the vertical mobility came to be recognized
as chimerical, but that the lateral mobility was permanently and progressively

conquered for the modern world. In England, more tardy and conservative than the continent, these new perspectives were regarded more cautiously, but they did not fail gradually to be recognized. Shakespeare, in comedies and tragedies alike, punishes the character who is stubbornly immobile, to reward the character who adapts and shifts. But Jonson's drama, more truly conservative, reflects as we have seen the horror of a self too often shifted, a self which risks the loss of an inner poise. It reflects this horror even as it portrays, more brilliantly than Shakespeare, the whirlwind virtuosos of such multiplication. *Volpone* portrays virtuosos of basically lateral transformations. His other supreme artists, the scoundrels of *The Alchemist,* tend to play rather with vertical transformation—or, to use the play's own jargon, with "sublimation."

The sublimation presents itself ostensibly to the various characters—the trio of rogues included—as basically financial, but, just as in *Volpone,* gold becomes a counter and a metaphor for an ulterior good which varies with the individual. They all want to be raised—socially, sexually, religiously, metaphysically; they all hunger for the transmuting miracle of their respective alchemies. The one apparent exception is Surly, who announces explicitly his uniqueness: "Your stone cannot transmute me." No one of the other major characters possesses the judgment to say that, and it is of ironic significance that Surly himself will return two acts later transmuted by disguise. Once in the house, his righteous anger modulates into cupidity for Dame Pliant's fortune, and he demonstrates that he is in fact no more impervious to the stone than are the objects of his contempt. No Ciceros and no Celias here; the impulse to sublimation is well nigh universal.

Like trickster, like victim—both share the same dreams upon the stone. This of course is the meaning of the opening quarrel, which shows each mountebank furious at the other's ingratitude for having been raised to his new social elevation—a raising that is phrased even here in alchemical hocus-pocus. Face has been "translated" by Subtle, who has

> Rais'd thee from broomes, and dust, and watring pots,
> Sublim'd thee, and exalted thee, and fix'd thee
> I' the third region, call'd our state of grace.
> Wrought thee to spirit, to quintessence, with paines
> Would twise have won me the philosophers worke.

So Subtle, in Face's version, has thanks to him acquired a new incarnation.

> Why! who
> Am I, my mungrill? Who am I?

shouts Face at the outset, and the mongrel magician snarls:

> I'll tell you,
> Since you know not your selfe

But Subtle can only tell him who he has been, and what he is now, and Doll can remind them both pleadingly what they may hope to become.

Thus their hopes to be translated through their art reach across the gulf of deception to join the quainter dreams of their clients. The scale of ambition runs from the banal fantasies of a Drugger through the Puritans' quest to "raise their discipline" to the stupendous images of Epicure Mammon. In the sexual apotheoses of Mammon, like Volpone's, the self is endlessly renewable and his partner more variable than nature herself:

> Wee'll . . . with these
> Delicate meats, set our selves high for pleasure,
> And take us downe againe, and then renew
> Our youth, and strength, with drinking the elixir,
> And so enjoy a perpetuitie
> Of life, and lust. And, thou shalt ha' thy wardrobe,
> Richer than Natures, still, to change thy selfe,
> And vary oftener, for thy pride, then shee:
> Or Art, her wise, and almost-equall servant.

Nature indeed is the victim of all those people who choose to alter and transcend their condition; they all want, in Mammon's memorable phrase, to "firke nature up, in her owne center."

The literal center of the action, the house of Lovewit, is, until the fifth act, a usurped and thus a displaced center. The centrifugal displacement is suggested metaphorically in Mammon's opening lines:

> Come on, sir, Now you set your foot on shore
> In Novo Orbe; here's the rich Peru,
> And there within, sir, are the golden mines,
> Great Salomon's Ophir!

Exoticism equals eroticism, and both lead away from home. The moral center of the play is also elusive, since Lovewit, when he returns, acquires a kind of complicity along with a wife and fortune. The officers of justice, unlike those of *Volpone*, remain permanently deceived. The closest approximation to a moral resolution appears in Face's valedictory to the audience:

> I put myselfe
> On you, that are my country; and this Pelfe,

> Which I have got, if you do quit me, rests
> To feast you often, and invite new ghests.

Country here means "jury," but it also means *mes semblables, mes frères.* Face is asking the spectators to show their tolerant forgiveness of his shenanigans by their applause. Jonson's appreciation of the artist-scoundrel qualifies his disapproval of the centrifugal self, a little to the detriment of artistic coherence.

Bartholomew Fair, the last of Jonson's three master comedies, leads all of its bourgeois characters out of their houses to baptise them in the tonic and muddy waters of errant humanity. Away from the protective custody of their routine comforts, they wander, lose themselves, mistake the fair's disguises, pass through the ordeals it has prepared for them, and reach the chastening conclusion: "Remember you are but Adam, Flesh, and blood!" In the midst of these comic ordeals, the identity of lost home and lost selfhood is very strong, strongest of all in the mouth of Cokes the fool:

> Dost thou know where I dwell, I pray thee? . . . Frend, doe you know who I am? or where I lye? I doe not my selfe, I'll be sworne. Doe but carry me home, and I'le please thee, I ha' money enough there, I ha' lost my selfe, and my cloake, and my hat.

In the end Cokes will go to his dwelling, at the home of his kinsman the justice, but the justice will bring, so to speak, the fair home with him. He will invite, that is to say, all the rowdy and disreputable denizens of the fair to dinner, in a spirit that mingles festivity with reproof:

> JUSTICE: I invite you home, with mee to my house, to supper: I will have none feare to go along, for my intents are *Ad correctionem, non ad destructionem; ad aedificandum, non ad diruendum.* So lead on.
>
> COKES: Yes, and bring the Actors along, wee'll ha' the rest o' the Play at home.

Bartholomew Fair ends with this word "home," like the "Farewell of the Vertuous Gentle-woman." But the home of the comedy is inclusive, and we glimpse—at least in this one work of mellow license—a Jonson less jealous of the centered self's prerogatives, more warmly and less ambiguously tolerant of the histrionic personality.

Perhaps there is meaning to be read in the openness of Jonson's last dramatic home—the bower of Robin Hood and Marian in *The Sad Shepherd.* In this charming, unfinished work of his old age, the last incarnation of the

Protean figure, the witch Maudlin, is unambiguously repellent, but the dwelling itself is virtually unprotected by physical walls. It depends for its strength on the circular affection of man and woman: "Marian, and the gentle Robinhood, / Who are the Crowne, and Ghirland of the Wood." Here, in less ritualistic symbols than the wedding masques', Jonson reaches out to find the completion of his orb in the mutuality of conjugal love. "Where should I be, but in my Robins armes. / The Sphere which I delight in, so to move?"

Many late poems, as we have seen, represent a lonely shrinking inward to a harder and isolated core. But we can perhaps discern a contrary impulse reflected in the motto of the aging Jonson's *ex libris: Tanquam explorator.* Was Eliot thinking of that moving phrase when he wrote in *Little Gidding:* "Old men ought to be explorers"? In *The Sad Shepherd,* at any rate, there is a fresh urge to venture out. To be sure, the quality of an *explorator,* for Jonson, involved less of a Sir Politic Wouldbe than a William Roe, whose ends always meet his beginnings. But we can be grateful that his intuition of the centered self continued to leave room for an exuberant if discriminating curiosity. The compass, keeping still one foot upon its center, never ceased to swing its other foot wide in firm and unwearied arcs.

WILLIAM KERRIGAN

Ben Jonson Full of Shame and Scorn

Ben Jonson appears in modern criticism as a "public" writer whose most characteristic poems reveal his enduring satisfaction in the virtues of a "social world." He is our sane poet, a genius of intelligent conviviality, the light assumed by the shadow of our Donne. Repeatedly contrasting these two great figures in order to assure a coherent history of seventeenth-century poetry, we have tended to slight or ignore the abiding melancholy of Jonson. He observed in a well-known passage from [*Timber, or*] *Discoveries:*

> What a deale of cold business doth a man mis-spend the better part of life in! in scattering *complements,* tendring *visits,* gathering and venting *newes,* following *Feasts* and *Playes,* making a little winter-love in a darke corner.

This from the public man who scattered so many compliments in his poetry, who visited his friends and wrote about those visits, who praised the festive life and who was, indeed, a professional follower of plays—"a deale of cold business," Ben Jonson concluded. His social comedies are hardly celebrations of the pleasures of social life. When writing for the public stage he seems to have felt little attraction for the festive comedy of Shakespeare: the laughter inspired by his sharp-toothed drama is the judgmental laughter of moral scorn. Though he virtually created, in England, the festive spectacle of the court masque, one of his contributions to the development of this form was

From *Studies in Literary Imagination* 6, no. 1 (April 1973). © 1973 by the Department of English, Georgia State University.

111

an antimasque setting asocial energies against the harmony celebrated by the masque itself. Moreover, he adopted a philosophy calculated above all to lend both dignity and fortitude to a man in pain.

Jonson's debt to the sixteenth-century revival of classical Stoicism has been documented extensively. But there has been scant realization of how much several of his finest poems depend upon an historical irony created by this Christian appropriation. Surely, the assumptions about fate and destiny in the classical texts posed no significant obstacles for the neo-Stoic. Lipsius, for instance, was able in a few nimble pages of his *De Constantia* to translate fate into providence, necessity into the will of God, and emerge with a fully Christian notion of patience: patience was simply due respect for the authority of God. As Joseph Hall [in *Heaven vpon Earth and Characters of the Vertues and Vices*] said with a succinctness born of fierce piety, no good Christian could abjure his patience and complain of ill fortune without standing guilty of outright blasphemy: "I must therefore either blaspheme God in my heart, detracting from his infinite justice, wisdome, power, mercy, which all shall stand inviolable, when millions of such wormes as I am, are gone to dust; or else confesse that I ought to be patient." God ordered all time and patience was the loving, willing submission to this divine procession. But the new endorsement of patience, unremarkable though it may seem, was nothing less than a revolution in the history of virtue. The identical value had been built upon an antithetical premise.

Montaigne, with the air of a man speaking about matters seldom mentioned before a Christian audience, began his essay on "A Custom of the Island of Cea" by suggesting that the defiant heroism of classical statesmen and philosophers, their claims to be without fear of death, "evidently have a ring of something beyond patiently waiting for the end when death comes to us." The great men of antiquity might declare their willingness to endure all calamities because, should life become truly intolerable, they allowed themselves to triumph over ill fortune through the noble act of suicide. In philosophers such as Epictetus, Aurelius, and Seneca, it was this fundamental liberty which underlay, like a first postulate, the psychology of Stoic patience. Calmly one suffered, imperturbable with the knowledge that, finally, fortune was under one's control. Seneca put this speech into the mouth of god:

> Despise poverty; no man lives as poor as he was born: despise pain; either it will cease or you will cease: despise death; it either ends you or takes you elsewhere: despise fortune; I have given her no weapon that can reach the mind. Above all, I have taken care that no one should hold you captive against your will: the

way of escape lies open before you: if you do not choose to fight, you may fly. For this reason, of all those matters which I have deemed essential for you, I have made nothing easier than to die.

[*De Providentia*]

Given the possibility of suicide, all suffering was ultimately voluntary. The wise man of the Stoics lived always with the freedom of self-homicide to sustain him in adversity. He was obliged to endure no pain beyond the tolerable, no outrage beyond his capacity to suffer honorably. Life could never humiliate him, for any vein in his body was a path to absolute tranquillity.

Seneca realized that a philosophy which denied the right of voluntary death would also upset the psychological disposition necessary to his Stoicism. With that door shut, life would become a prison. The right not to endure made life endurable:

Thou shalt find some, yea even those who have made profession of Philosophie, that will denie that any man ought to violate or shorten his life, and that maintayne it for a foule offence, for a man to murther himselfe, and that it were better to expect the end which Nature hath determined. But hee that speaketh thus, seeth not that he cutteth off the way of libertie. The eternall Law hath done nothing better, than to give us one onely entrance into life, and divers issues. . . . This is one thing, wherein we cannot complain of life, she retaineth no man.

[*Epistulae* LXX]

Believer in just such a philosophy, Montaigne the Christian scorned these classical meditations as "ridiculous." Robert Burton [in *The Anatomy of Melancholy*], after recounting the pagan arguments for suicide, dismissed them as "profane Stoical Paradoxes . . . impious, abominable, and upon a wrong ground." The heroic suicides of antiquity were "martyrs to a foolish philosophy."

The *locus classicus* for the Christian repudiation of suicide is to be found in the *De Civitate Dei* of Augustine, who carefully distinguished martyrdom from pagan suicide. Self-homicide contradicted the sixth commandment; weakness drove men to this sad end, not greatness of soul; Job who suffered was greater than Cato who did not; to die of one's own volition for the sake of avoiding sin was in fact to commit the most terrible sin; and finally, the Stoic ritual of wise death reversed the primary instinct of self-preservation, "the first and strongest demand of nature." Lactantius [in *Institutes* III], repeating these arguments, added that the Christian God was Lord of life and death, neither of which a man could cause through the agency of his own will. Consequently, "if any violence is offered to us, we must endure it with equanimity." Presenting all these arguments, Aquinas managed to strengthen the case. Suicide was the one unpardonable sin, for by definition the act could not allow for repentance. Its ethical context involving more than an individual and God, suicide diminished the community and was therefore a civil crime. The discussion of suicide in the *Summa* occurs within the larger discussion of civil justice. "No man," Aquinas wrote, "is judge of himself." Suicides were denied hallowed burial and their estates confiscated by the government. With the full weight of authority—philosophical, ecclesiastical, and civil—Christianity deprived its patient followers of the essential liberty of the patient Stoics.

The classical Stoic was patient because he reserved the freedom to kill himself. The Christian, imprisoned in the time of God, was patient precisely because he had been denied that liberty. Hall was especially rigorous about this matter. In *Heaven upon Earth* ill fortunes become "Crosses" and the Christian must carry his destined burdens, exacting though they be, with righteous merriment. Suicides, "like unto those fondly impatient fishes, that leap out of the pan into the flame, have leapt out of this private hell that is in themselves, into the common pit." Whereas Seneca praised his god for having made dying so easy in order to permit suicide, Hall noted that his God had made dying so dreadful an ordeal in order to discourage suicide.

In the opening passage of *Biathanatos* Donne confessed that "whensoever any affliction assailes me, mee thinks I have the keyes of my prison in mine own hand, and no remedy presents it selfe so soone to my heart, as mine own sword." The most fascinating and most dangerous sections of this book, hardly so heretical as has sometimes been assumed, present a history of the suicidal impulse, contending that classical suicides expressed fundamentally the same psychological disposition as Christian martyrs. Donne agreed with the Fathers that suicide could not be self-interested, committed for the sake of avoiding sin or shame or mere tedium: suicide might be lawful only when done solely for the glory of God. But who could know what had transpired within the secret soul of a martyr? Donne recognized that the martyrdom of Apollonia, "as well as any other, might have been calumniated to have been done, out of wearinesse of life, or fear of relapse, or hast to heaven, or ambition of Martyrdome." He argued his paradox as tactfully as possible, hoping not to overthrow orthodox opinion, but to confound the smug certitude of many Christians and promote a more charitable response toward self-homicide. Still, however tentative, his arguments seem an obvious rebellion against the Christian sense of patience in all adversity. Donne's

Christian could suffer with the thought of being able, conceivably, to escape his suffering without incurring damnation: the psychology of patience has been shifted back toward its classical form.

But certainly most serious Christians of the time did not harbor such thoughts without remaining conscious of their inherent sinfulness. What Donne permitted himself, Jonson denied himself, and the consequence of this refusal is the subject of his great epigram "To Heaven." The epigram, along with the handful of theological poems, the epitaphs, and several of the formal odes and love elegies, occupies the melancholy "darke corner" of his lyric poetry. Though perhaps unique among his works in subject matter, it is a central text for understanding Jonson, more revealing, even, than the epitaphs for his son and daughter. It is the richest statement he left about the implications of the "deale of cold business" in this life.

"To Heaven" is also a more elaborate and difficult poem than Jonson has usually been credited with. A prayer about the nature of prayer, the epigram moves through five units of four lines each and concludes with a resolution concerning future prayers in the last six lines:

> GOod, and great GOD, can I not thinke of thee,
>   But it must, straight, my melancholy bee?
> Is it interpreted in me disease,
>   That, laden with my sinnes, I seeke for ease?
> O, be though witnesse, that the reynes dost know,
>   And hearts of all, if I be sad for show,
> And iudge me after: if I dare pretend
>   To ought but grace, or ayme at other end.
> As thou art all, so be thou all to mee,
>   First, midst, and last, conuerted one, and three;
> My faith, my hope, my loue: and in this state,
>   My iudge, my witnesse, and my aduocate.
> Where haue I beene this while exil'd from thee?
>   And whither rap'd, now thou but stoup'st to mee?
> Dwell, dwell here still: O, being euery-where,
>   How can I doubt to finde thee euer, here?
> I know my state, both full of shame, and scorne,
>   Conceiv'd in sinne, and vnto labour borne,
> Standing with feare, and must with horror fall,
>   And destin'd vnto iudgement, after all.
> I feele my griefes too, and there scarce is ground,
>   Vpon my flesh ⟨t⟩ 'inflict another wound.

> Yet dare I not complaine, or wish for death
>   With holy PAVL, lest it be thought the breath
> Of discontent; or that these prayers bee
>   For werinesse of life, not loue of thee.

The two initial questions are, as we first encounter them, somewhat obscure in tone and context. Insofar as Jonson protests against prevalent misconceptions of his melancholy and his disease, they would appear to be rhetorical, belligerently rhetorical. Yet his denial of these judgments is mitigated by the curious play on "ease" and "disease." While he asserts his innocence, Jonson also concedes his guilt, since any man searching for "ease" must be in a state of "dis-ease." The first unit of this poem informed by legal metaphors may generate a tone either of spirited defense or tacit admission and we have, at this point, no context within which this doubleness is intelligible.

But most puzzling, who has perpetrated the misconceptions to which these questions object? Demanding in its privacy, the closed dialogue with God makes little attempt to orient earthly readers toward the points at issue between speaker and audience. Swinburne believed that Jonson, having been accused of melancholy by other people, was here taking his case before the heavenly court: "the meaning is not—'Can I not think of God without its making me melancholy?' but 'Can I not think of God without its being imputed or set down by others to a fit of dejection?'" Herford and the Simpsons approved this reading, citing Swinburne as the inspiration for a quaint biographical fantasy: "it is plain that he had . . . moods of rapt absorption in divine things, or of shuddering self-abasement. Sometimes these thoughts fell upon him in company, and then the jesters of the Mermaid would rally him on his 'melancholy.'" George Burke Johnston also accepted the gloss in his edition of 1954 and this probably mistaken, certainly limited reading has never, to my knowledge, been questioned. As the poem contains no overt reference to imperceptive friends, the burden of proof really lies with Swinburne and his followers. They have offered none.

The interpretation receives some confirmation from two phrases in the poem, "sad for show" in line 6 and "lest it be thought" in line 24. The first would seem to clarify "melancholy" and "disease," suggesting that Jonson has been accused of affecting discontent in his spiritual affairs. But why must his accusers comprise only false friends, much less "the jesters of the Mermaid"? The second phrase clearly means "lest it be thought by you, Lord"— unless we are to suppose that Jonson would rearrange his devotions, refuse the prayer of Paul, in order to appease the misconceptions of his friends. If he would do so, then why would he solicit vindication from heaven? Why not simply modify the outward show of his devotion "lest it be thought" what it is not, his "melancholy" and his "disease"? The reason for addressing God is his belief that the thoughts, interpretations, and judgments of the world cannot survive divine scrutiny. Is it likely, then, that he would vow at the end of the poem to act within the bounds of devotional behavior proscribed by the imperceptive accusers of this world?

The relationship of Jonson to God, not Jonson to his companions, is the subject of this epigram. Though we may doubt whether he has been charged by his friends, we can know for certain that he has been found guilty by God: for some while he has been "exil'd from thee." Swinburne's misreading conceals the conceptual daring of the poem, for the two alternatives he chooses between exclude the most natural interpretation. The lines mean, "Can I not think of you, Lord, without the world, and certainly you, judging my thoughts as melancholy, interpreting my prayers as diseased?" Throughout "To Heaven" Jonson, defending himself against an imputed crime of the spirit, considers the misjudgment of heaven. The situation assumed by the epigram resembles one Jonson defined in the closing words of a letter to John Donne. Some false rumor has been whispered about the town: "I desire to be left to mine own innocence which shall acquit me, or Heaven shall be guilty." As we will see, Jonson has been punished—and wrongly, he insists—for the crime of speaking righteous prayers with impure motives.

This man is not "sad for show." He maintains that he has just reasons to seek for ease. Defending the motives of past and present prayers, Jonson appeals to the unerring omniscience of God, a "witnesse" who searches the "reynes" and "hearts" of all His fallen sons (Ps. 7:9; Jer. 11:20, 20:12; Rev. 2:23). He reinvokes both the pledge of David and the divine promise tendered Jeremiah:

> Examine me, O Lord, and prove me; try my reins and my heart.
>
> (Ps. 26:2)

> I the Lord search the heart, I try the reins, even to give every man according to his ways, and according to the fruit of his doings.
>
> (Jer. 17:10)

Though God and the world have agreed about his "disease," Jonson requires a full hearing for this case of conscience. God must be "all" to him, a "state" of grace which he desires but has not yet achieved. To this time, Jonson feels, God has been only his "judge." Now he asks God to waive the sentence, permitting him to engage the other aspects of the triple Godhead: "O, be thou witnesse." He hopes as well for an "advocate" to stand parallel to the "love" of his own psychological trinity ("My faith, my hope, my love"). In this spiritual trial God, it would seem, is being called as a witness against Himself. And the God who is in fact "iudge . . . witnesse, and . . . advocate" may testify against His own judgment, such paradoxical adjudication having made possible the Atonement. Aiming only at grace, Jonson would "dare pretend" to no other end, as later in the poem he would "dare . . . not complaine." Yet the tone seems dangerously close to outrage at divine injustice. A quarrelsome Jonson invites, demands that God keep His promise to Jeremiah and give a man his due in spiritual examination. The reader must, like God, judge him "after."

The next series of questions creates an implicit pun on the word "state." Jonson has been "exil'd" from God, driven from the "state" of all-filling grace. "Rap'd," he has suffered a kind of negative rapture which has, instead of seizing him from this world and into heaven, like the rapture of Paul, impelled him away from heaven and into the second "state" of line 17— "my state," the earthly state "full of shame, and scorne." In his exile God "but stoup'st" to Jonson, treating him as unworthy of divine attention. We do not know, at this point in the poem, why God should act "now" as one whose dignity were being compromised in attending to the prayers of Ben Jonson. But surely the reasons for this slight and for the exile itself concern the "melancholy" and "disease" of the opening questions. Jonson has been stooped to, his prayers left unanswered as if unheard: God has not been "all" to him. The most plausible inference is that Jonson, in the judgment of heaven, does not know how to pray, how to think of God and seek for ease, understanding neither what is required by heaven nor what is best for himself. For this injustice, though he dare "not complaine," Jonson seeks redress. The tone, once again, would seem to belie his assertion of innocence. There is a sense of accusation, the hurt of a man deeply insulted: "And whither rap'd, now thou but stoup'st to mee?" How dare God treat him so? The question barely restrains an exclamation.

Then the prayer turns gentle, as if in apology for these emotions and in tacit recognition of his "dis-ease." "Dwell, dwell here still" is the exhortation of a man aiming only at grace. But having offered this prayer, Jonson immediately realizes that his wish should not have to be articulated. It is a moment of logical and psychological revelation: "Oh, being euery-where / How can I doubt to finde thee euer, here?" His plea for God to dwell here "still"—meaning "always" and standing parallel to "ever, here"—has assumed that God was not, is not now, here. "How can I doubt" in the next line implies "I do doubt, but should not have to doubt." His prayer, then, has assumed the impossible. At the center of the poem Jonson confronts the

necessarily paradoxical existence of an exile from heaven. For if God is everywhere and Jonson is indeed absent from God, then he must be nowhere:
"Where haue I beene this while exil'd from thee?" This is no scholastic
quibble. Capable of describing the Trinity with masterful concision and accuracy, Jonson knows full well where God must be—everywhere. Yet he
recognizes a tragic discontinuity between knowledge by theological precept
and knowledge by direct experience. God is all, but is not all to him. God
is everywhere, but is not here with him. Tested against his own experience,
the axioms of orthodox theology collapse. This crisis of divinity becomes,
inevitably, a crisis of self-knowledge: the difference between two ways of
knowing God dissolves into the difference between two ways of knowing
Ben Jonson. For either Jonson knows himself and God is unjustly absent, or
Jonson does not know himself and God is justly absent. Brilliantly, the tone
of the poem is contrived to generate both these possibilities. The querulous
despair of "To Heaven" reveals both Jonson's conception of himself (unjustly
accused) and God's conception of Jonson (unjustly accusing).

Having defined God, Jonson proposes a definition of himself:

> I know my state, both full of shame, and scorne,
>   Conceiu'd in sinne, and unto labour borne,
> Standing with feare, and must with horror fall,
>   And destin'd vnto iudgement, after all.
>
> (17–20)

"*Language* most shewes a man." Having defined himself, Jonson has defined
his poem. The man is "both full of shame, and scorne," and so is the
language of this epigram to God. Its tone, obscure on first reading, is precisely that, a union of humility and presumption fashioned with impeccable
control:

> GOod, and great GOD, can I not thinke of thee,
>   But it must, straight, my melancholy bee?
>
> (1–2)

Acknowledging the primacy of God, the question is humble, deferential,
ashamed. The words "must, straight" fix the absolute authority of divine
judgment. But Jonson dares to question God and these same words may
chide the haste and intransigence of divine judgment.

> Is it interpreted in me disease,
>   That, laden with my sinnes, I seeke for ease?
>
> (3–4)

"Here is no true disease," the question implies. But the speaker is admittedly "laden with sinnes" and, by logical inference, in a state of "disease." Such contrasting innuendoes proceed through the entire poem, shame predominant in the question of line 13, scorn in the question of line 14, shame once more in the prayer and question of lines 15–16. At line 20 the two emotions join remarkably: "And destin'd vnto iudgement, after all." Having earlier in the poem requested God to judge him "after," here Jonson remarks that the truly final judgment belongs to heaven. The phrase "after all" may be read as a flat statement of fact: after all the trials of this life a fallen man must appear before the court of God. But, gathering in a single climactic word the complete list of earthly sorrows, this phrase seems to bear an unmistakable hint of admonition, a sense of the bitter lot of fallen man. He must bear "all" and more than "all": for after all this, a life begun in sin and lived in fear, a death died in horror, he is still destined to be judged. The phrase "after all" is itself "both full of shame, and scorne."

The next lines appear to evoke the image of a tortured martyr and, in this context, distantly recall the Augustinian belief that even suffering martyrs have no justification for ending their lives:

> I feele my griefes too, and there scarce is ground,
> Upon my flesh t⟨o⟩ 'inflict another wound.
>
> (21–22)

The lines are extraordinarily moving once we consider the implications of "too." For what has been added to the description of his "state" in the previous four lines? The new element cannot be "griefes," those having been amply represented already. As the metrical and syntactical parallelism suggests, the essential difference is between "I know" and "I feele." Jonson wants God to understand in no uncertain terms that before Him is a man who appreciates the difference between knowing and feeling his state. Suggestive of the previous distinction between knowing God by theology and by experience, the power of this contrast between two kinds of self-knowledge resides in the rarest nuances of language. The definition of feeling as opposed to knowing turns on a question of literary taste. Lines 17–20 give off a faint air of summary. The passage is almost cliché, almost a recitation got by rote from the common pulpit of Renaissance England. Emphasizing the difference between "I know" and "I feele," Jonson indicates in the subtlest way his poet's knowledge that this language may have seemed impersonal and unfelt to the discriminate ear of God. But, feeling his "state," he can "scarce" tolerate another affliction. "Ground" puns on the legal term.

In the relationship of this man to God, defendant to judge, there is no just cause for further punishment or continued exile:

> Yet dare I not complaine, or wish for death
>   With holy PAVL, lest it be thought the breath
> Of discontent; or that these prayers bee
>   For wearinesse of life, not loue of thee.
>
> (23–26)

Somehow he will endure, regardless of the verdict. And he will endeavor, as always, to love his judge.

It is only now that the beginning of the poem is fully comprehensible. God has stooped to Jonson and exiled him from heaven because, in His judgment, a melancholy and discontented Jonson has wished for death. Death is the "ease" which, again in the judgment of God, Jonson has desired. Such prayers are blasphemous accusations in disguise, for to love God the Christian Stoic must also love his life, however miserable, however wearisome. At the conclusion of the poem Jonson once again declares his innocence: he would not dare wish release from the miseries of life ordained by God and inseparable from the fallen state. But in another sense the passage should be read as a concession to divine justice and to the self-knowledge implicit in that justice.

Paul prayed for death in Rom. 7:24, Phi. 1:23, and 1 Cor: 5:1. Donne considered these passages in *Biathanatos* and recommended the commentary of Calvin:

> though it be [*a sinne to offer my selfe even to martyrdome, only for wearinesse of life*] [*Or to wish death simply for Impocencie, Anger, Shame, Povertie, or Misfortune;*] yea to wish heaven meerely for mine own happiness; yet certainly *S. Paul* had some allowable reasons, *to desire to be dissolved, and be with Christ.* And Calvin by telling us upon what reason, and to what end he wished this, instructs us how we may wish the same. He sayes, Paul desired not death, for deaths sake, for that were against the sense of Nature, but he wished it, to be with Christ.

Pagans committed suicide for the sake of *taedium vitae* or, as Donne and Jonson both translate, "wearinesse of life." Calvin instructed Christians that they might pray for death not "for the sake of losing any thing, but as having regard to a better life." Why then should Jonson refuse to speak the righteous prayer of the Apostle? Surely he does not imagine Paul to have prayed from weariness of life. Calvin was unequivocal on this point; Paul deliberated "in a spirit of content." However, Calvin warned the reader of Rom. 7:24–25 of the peculiar sins associated with the prayer for death, restricting its propriety as narrowly as possible. Jonson might well have had the passage before him:

> Paul, by his own example, stimulates them to anxious groaning, and bids them, as long as they sojourn on earth, to desire death, as the only true remedy to their evils; and this is the right object in desiring death. Despair does indeed drive the profane often to such a wish; but they strangely desire death, because they are weary of the present life, and not because they loathe their iniquity. But it must be added, that though the faithful level at the true mark, they are not yet carried away by an unbridled desire in wishing for death, but submit themselves to the will of God, to whom it behooves us both to live and to die; hence they clamor not with displeasure against God, but humbly deposit their anxieties in his bosom; for they do not so dwell on the thoughts of their misery, but that being mindful of grace received, they blend their grief with joy, as we find in what follows.
>
> He then immediately subjoined this thanksgiving, lest any should think that in his complaint he perversely murmured against God; for we know how easy even in legitimate grief is the transition to discontent and impatience.

The faithful "level at the true mark" as Jonson promises to "ayme" at grace alone. Paul himself, despite "legitimate grief," felt it necessary to qualify his prayer "lest any should think" he spoke from "discontent and impatience." He also dared not complain. But Jonson, more careful still, vows not even to offer this dangerous prayer "lest it be thought the breath / Of discontent." Calvin understood that the Pauline prayer for death could be spoken with impunity only by those certain of their spiritual composure, certain of what their motives were not. Jonson, knowing his state and feeling his griefs, cannot be certain. If "GOod, and great GOD" has been right all along about his melancholy and his disease, then his hypothetical prayer for death would in fact be offered from *taedium vitae*, not "love of thee." He dare not pray with Paul because he might wish death for all the profane reasons defined by Calvin: the man scarcely has flesh for another wound. So he denies himself the privilege of this prayer and he resolves to exercise Christian patience, explicitly purging his devotions of any taint of Senecan patience. The end of the poem is appropriately both a vindication and a confession.

In his seeming absence from God, Jonson plays his own advocate in

"To Heaven." He addresses God with magnificent tact, advocating himself with such delicacy that his accusations are qualified by his concessions, his scorn balanced against his shame. He prays only for grace and only from love. The ease he seeks for is to dwell with God "here" in this life. The breath of discontent in the prayers of this good man dissolves into that love of God which is coincident with love of life. Though he may wish to wish for death, Jonson defines prayer in such a way that he cannot express this desire and, by implication, has not in the past expressed this desire. What has been judged a melancholy discontent by God and resulted in his exile is really the hard knowledge of our true state on earth—our origin, our labor, our destiny—and the feeling which accompanies this knowledge. Despairing, Jonson is not "sad for show." His address to heaven is almost, but not quite a complaint. His motive is almost, but not quite, weariness of life. His search for ease is "dis-ease" but not "disease." The poise of tone is simply exquisite: "How can I doubt to finde thee euer, here?" The brilliant question doubts even as it asserts that doubt is inconceivable. As God is absent from "here" even though He cannot be absent from "here," as God is not "all" even though He must by definition be "all," so Jonson defends himself even though he dare not complain. "To Heaven" displays one of the most complex and moving relationships with God in the history of devotional verse. Though unique among his poems in its direct exploration of this relationship, great poems are necessarily unique. It is central to Jonson as, say, "The Extasie" is central to Donne, "The Sacrifice" to Herbert, "The Garden" to Marvell. "I know my state, both full of shame, and scorne" is one of those lines of radiant self-awareness into which and out of which the entire work of a poet seems to flow. Any reader of Jonson should know and should feel the power of this self-definition, so spacious and yet so concise, remembering the quick scorn for unnamed or renamed figures in the epigrams, the elaborate humility of the poems of praise, the odes to himself where shame and scorn stand poised, as they do here, in the fine balance of his tone. But the stylistic mastery of "To Haven" extends beyond tone.

His chosen *impresa* was a broken compass which, having begun to trace a circle, remains forever unable to complete the partial figure. God, Jonson maintains, is "First, midst, and last." Imitating this form, the first and last lines of the epigram end with the word "thee," and the rhyme words of lines 1 and 2 are repeated in reverse order at lines 25 and 26. This circular link of beginning and end, "thee" and "bee" doubling back on themselves, implies a hidden question and its definitive answer: "Thee bee?" "Bee thee." God is also "midst," though Jonson has cause to doubt His presence "here." So, in the middle two lines of the poem, we find the same rhyme we find first and last, yet each word is punctuated by a doubting question mark—"thee? mee?" Ample, full, and round, the art of Jonson transfigures the physical body of the poem, creating a rich emblem of his subject. The shaping of the verse indicates how the "state" of this life is held within the "state" of heaven. Beginning with "GOod and Great GOD," the poem returns to "thee" in the final line: God, the pattern suggests, can be known without doubt when considered "first" as creator and "last" as judge. He undoubtedly occupies these positions at the boundaries of each individual life, at the boundaries of time itself, and at the boundaries of this poem. But in the "midst," in the sweep of time, in the mortal state, our relationship with God is complicated by our separation from Him. To one wishing to be sealed of the Tribe of Ben he wrote:

> Well, with mine owne fraile Pitcher, what to doe
> I have decreed; keep it from waves, and presse;
>   Lest it be justled, crack'd, made nought, or lesse:
> Live to that point I will; for which I am man,
>   And dwell as in my Center, as I can,
> Still looking to, and ever loving heaven.
>   ("An Epistle Answering to One That Asked
>   to Be Sealed of the Tribe of Ben," 56–61)

The author of "To Heaven" places the word "mee" and thus himself "midst," within his emblematic center, "looking to, and ever loving heaven." Aristotle had theorized about a linear art and Jonson endorsed the classical form in *Discoveries:* the "*Whole* . . . and perfect" poem "hath a *beginning, a mid'st,* and an *end.*" But the God of "To Heaven," Alpha and Omega, bends the classical structure into an appropriate Christian circle. Only the center is in doubt. Both Jonson and God desire concentricity—a state in which both of them reside "here." Who is to make the gesture of submission and move to touch the other? The two rhyme words at the center of the poem summarize all its tensions. Shall Jonson insist scornfully on his own sense of justice or kneel ashamed before the justice of God? Can he doubt the divine presence? Does he pray from weariness of himself or love of God? Is it disease to seek for ease? Who possesses the more accurate knowledge of Ben Jonson? Mee? Thee? These issues hold the center of the deft circle of "To Heaven."

However circular his art, the legless compass of his device represents an epitome of frustration—incompleted action and unrealized intent. The ode

"To the Immortall Memorie, and Friendship of that Noble Paire, Sir Lucius Cary, and Sir H. Morison" indicates that the root of this frustration pierces beyond a sense of sin or self-imposed failure or mere inadequacy to strike the very condition of being alive. Here Jonson measures his "lines of life" against the exemplary circles of the "Brave Infant" and Henry Morison:

> Goe now, and tell out dayes summ'd up with feares,
> And make them yeares;
> Produce thy masse of miseries on the Stage,
> To swell thine age;
> Repeat of things a throng,
> To shew thou hast beene long,
> Not liv'd; for Life doth her great actions spell,
> By what was done and wrought
> In season, and so brought
> To light: her measures are, how well
> Each syllab'e answer'd, and was form'd, how faire;
> These make the lines of life, and that's her ayre.
>
> (53–64)

Ethics and aesthetics inseparable, the passage moves from considering art as life—literary productions judged morally as actions—to considering life as art. The standard assumed by this two-handed vocabulary is the familiar one of the necessary syncopation between time and action, all things best performed in due season. His life the "Sphere" of "Humanitie" (50), Morison fulfilled the offices appropriate to his age, "most a vertuous Sonne" (47). But Jonson has disfigured that circle in which virtue answers season, his days "summ'd" not like the "summ'd" circle of the Brave Infant (9), but added one to the other, a monotonous accumulation of "feares." He has been long and only long, redundant, the geometry of his life resembling the meaninglessly repetitive circles of the "Stirrer" (30). As in "To Heaven," the form of the ode becomes elaborately emblematic of its moral assumptions and of the life, the art of its creator. The pattern allows Jonson to "stand," an act associated with the model of rectitude left by Morison (43–45). At one point he sets his own name moving with the wheeling stanzas, "*Jonson*" appearing triumphantly as the first word of the Stand (85). But the same form which permits him to stand, balancing syllable against syllable, also requires him to repeat himself, circling about the same arguments and the same metrical patterns. The triple stanzas of the Pindaric ode stand and turn, finish and begin again, winding their way through this lengthy poem. These

are truly the "lines of life," a phrase placed at the mathematical center of
the ode, at the center of its central line (64). Jonson submits to a formal
design which licenses him to stand only at the expense of repeating "of
things a throng." The design of life, to which he also submitted, was not
dissimilar in its demands.

Any man who perceives in his own life and in the lives of others an
acute disjunction between time lived and action accomplished confronts, I
suppose, two possible modes of repairing this disharmony or, better, two
modes of disposing his emotions to fit the contours of the situation perceived.
One is the response of virtually everyone who encounters this problem. It is
healthy, traditional, obvious: the man may emphasize the failure of the actor
and suggest his reformation on the assumption that the seasons of life, being
either neutral or given, cannot be blamed. The other is, for most of us, a
hypothetical response only: he may instead blame the demands of time, the
natural shape of life, assuming that the moral sloth of the actor is, given the
vicissitudes of human nature, constant and irremediable. He may, that is,
wish he had been allotted less time for waste and inactivity. Now Jonson
surely condemns the wasteful Stirrer who, "For three of his foure-score . . .
did no good" (32), as he surely condemns his own failures of accomplishment. But this poem places a surprising emphasis on the degeneration inherent in the full time of a normal life.

Writing in his mid-fifties, Jonson argues that "life may perfect bee" only
in "short measures" (74). He exalts a friendship made perfect by early death.
The brief life of Morison, the sudden bloom and fall of the "Lillie of a Day"
(69), delete the long hours which have deformed the lives of other men. They
provide no time for misshapen repetitions, failures of ripeness, accumulations
of meaningless minutes. The Brave Infant of the first two stanzas traces the
circle of "deepest lore" (10) in this poem of many circles. His virtue is the
courage not to live at all. Shorter even than that of the "Lillie of a Day," his
life represents the genuine desire of all mature men: "As, could they but lifes
miseries fore-see, / No doubt all Infants would returne like thee" (19–20).
The lesson of his "deepest lore" is that the life of Morison stands as a model
because of, and not in spite of, its brevity. Even the Stirrer, who spent sixty
years "sunke in that dead sea of life" (40), lived "by vertuous parts" for his
first twenty years: "How well at twentie had he falne, or stood!" (31). The
vexations of age itself seem to dissipate moral energy. It is one thing to say
that good men die young—this poem goes some way toward suggesting that
those who die young are good.

Years earlier, consoling himself for the death of his son, Jonson won-
dered if young Benjamin had not lived a happier life than his aging father:

> To haue so soone scap'd worlds, and fleshes rage,
>   And, if no other miserie, yet age?
>   ("On My First Sonne," 7–8)

Like the passage defining "my state" in "To Heaven," the phrase "worlds, and fleshes rage" is deliberately close to pulpit cliché. The tone of the next line intimates that, while the conventional rages of world and flesh may not be, after all, so miserable, "age" certainly is. This misery, if no other, the boy had escaped. I think our conclusion unavoidable: Jonson lived long with the depressions of *taedium vitae* and precisely to this extent he envied early death. An old stirrer, he knew that age inflicts more than one kind of deformity.

What Jonson knew of the weariness of age could not, in all patience, be acted upon. He loved his God and he dared not pray with Paul. Unlike Donne, he did not permit himself to consider the possibility of righteous suicide: he recognized his motives to be unworthy. As a poet commits himself to a predetermined pattern of meter and rhyme, fulfilling that pattern no matter what the cost in tedium, so Jonson committed himself to the design of a natural life. The words "social" and "public," so often used to epitomize his tone and thus his temperament, diminish him by trivializing his assumptions about this life, the sources of his knowing and his feeling. He stood tough in his patience. He was a melancholy man, full of shame and scorn—magnificently so. He deserves to exist in literary history as the man he was, not as a convenient figure to balance against the "private" and "meditative" John Donne in order that we may write our tidy but inaccurate history of seventeenth-century literature. There is indeed much conviviality in his lyric poetry, much wine and good food and noble friendship. There is wine at the climax of the Cary-Morison ode, as Jonson announces the successful reconciliation of Lucius Cary to the death of his friend: "Call, noble *Lucius,* then for Wine (75). One of the most complex in all of Jonson, the line is difficult in the responding—difficult morally—in the same way that a philosophical argument may be difficult conceptually. Of course the wine will be drunk in a mood of Christian consolation, for Morison has returned to God, having "leap'd the present age" (79). But the wine is also a sacrament of Stoicism for those who endure and, with the death of an "early" man, mourn their own inevitable disfigurement. It is hard consolation which makes peace with early death on the basis that long life is miserable, repetitious, and unavoidably wearisome. But Jonson and Cary drink together, mature men lifting their cups in the knowledge that all infants would, if they understood life, repudiate their birth. Only a profound festivity could survive this knowledge. The wine of the Cary-Morison ode partially celebrates this knowledge: eat, drink, and be merry, for yesterday you should have died. The public conviviality of Ben Jonson was, like his private love of God, hard won. If we examine even his most exuberant performances with minds attuned to the nuances of mood, we may well discover "a little winter-love in a darke corner."

A. RICHARD DUTTON

The Significance of Jonson's Revision of
Every Man in His Humour

A number of major changes marked the development of Jonson's career as a dramatist, but none is more striking than the difference of tone and approach between *Volpone* (1605) and *Epicoene* (1609). Professor Harry Levin [in "Jonson's Metempsychosis"] neatly summed up what has come to be the general attitude to this change in saying: "As [Jonson's] powers of realistic depiction came into full play, he gradually relinquished his loudly proclaimed moral purposes." This interesting assertion—based upon a fanciful analogy between the supposed "metempsychology" of Pythagoras's soul, described in *Volpone* (1.2.1–62), and the equally supposed mellowing of Jonson's satiric temper after that play—sees the conflation of two popular lines of thought on Jonson's career: Jonson the realist, the journalist-depictor of the foibles of his age, and Jonson the satirist who grew to be more tolerant and indulgent with age. Both are in their various ways myths, and to some extent they feed on each other, as may be evident in the words of one of their most enthusiastic, but least critical proponents, John Palmer [in *Ben Jonson*]. Regarding *Epicoene,* for instance, he states that "there are no intensities, and the moralist is silent . . . There is none of the satire which in *Volpone* bites into the substance of human nature, but a merry confounding of impostures and eccentricity." Merry confounding, indeed. "Volpone," he continues, "playing upon his dupes for the love of the game, is a moral portent. The rogues whom we meet in *The Alchemist* have no such signifi-

---

From *Modern Language Review* 69, no. 2 (April 1974). © 1974 by the Modern Humanities Research Association.

cance. Livelihood is the beginning and end of their endeavour, and the play ends merrily with the ablest villain of the pack successfully outwitting the rest and making his peace with authority." Ends merrily, indeed. "Jonson is nowhere more tolerant, open of mind and sense than in this play [*Bartholomew Fair*]. It is a fit expression of the merry England which was passing." Merry England? This picture of open-minded, avuncular amiability in the plays of the middle period leaves much to be desired—almost as much as Edmund Wilson's antithetical, pseudo-Freudian picture of a morose Ben Jonson [in *The Triple Thinkers*]. Nevertheless, the suggestion that the plays after *Volpone* are somehow more indulgent, less satirically wounding, remains widely held, so that even Jonas Barish [in "Ovid, Juvenal, and *The Silent Woman*] thinks in terms of "the geniality and relaxed moral temper of the later plays, as typified by *Bartholomew Fair*."

Of course, *something* does happen to the tone and character of the plays. We have lost the in-jokes and the backbiting of the plays belonging to the so-called War of the Theatres; there is none of the virulence of a Macilente, or the complacent smugness of a Crites—or, if they do appear, it is only to be parodied in a Surly or a Justice Overdo. No later play creates the same sense of insistent moral corruption as *Volpone*. But impressionistic accounts of a change of heart in Jonson himself are hardly adequate to explain the complex alteration of aims and techniques which produce the great plays of the middle period. The apparent strength of Professor Levin's statement hinges upon a genuinely acute observation—that the supposed change of "tone" or "attitude" in the plays after 1605 coincides with Jonson's adoption of fully-realized, contemporary London settings for his comedies. But the process of cause and effect is surely more involved than he suggests. Traditionally, of course, Jonson is, with Dickens, the quintessential London writer, but it is important to bear in mind that his earlier plays are not on the whole located in London. The obvious exception to that statement is *Every Man out of His Humour*, which is incidentally set in London; one scene is marked "The Middle Aisle of St. Paul's," and another "A Room in the Mitre," but Jonson can scarcely be said to capitalize on these settings, and the prevailing tone of the play is set by the stylization of the characters, which is quasi-Italian. With this exception, none of Jonson's plays to which we can fix a definite date was located in London until 1609, when *Epicoene* appeared. After that date, all the plays (excepting only *Catiline*) were unmistakably set in contemporary London, though this does become more nominal in the very late plays. The fact remains that Jonson had already written one masterpiece, *Volpone*, before making what appears to have been a deliberate and calculated switch to recognizably Jacobean London settings. The notion that Jonson gradually developed a talent for realism hardly seems to fit the facts. It was Swinburne who complained that: "There is nothing accidental in the work of Ben Jonson"; and it is as if Jonson deliberately appointed himself as playwright to the city, just as he had effectively become masque-maker to the Court at this period. No one appears to have commented much on this fact; Brian Gibbons, for instance, rather glosses over it when he includes Jonson's plays in the "genre" of "city comedy." It seems to me important, and it lends particular significance to the revision of *Every Man in His Humour*—the revised version of which was deliberately placed at the beginning of the 1616 Folio.

The date of the revision of the play is one of the more vexed problems of Jonsonian scholarship. Percy Simpson argues a strong case for 1612/13 in his edition of the play; more recent editors, like G. B. Jackson and J. W. Lever outline the difficulties more fully. The evidence is confusing and circumstantial, and conclusions can only be tentative, but there would seem to be good reason for supposing that the revision might occupy some of the time that Jonson was off the public stage, after *Volpone* (1605) and before *Epicoene* (1609). This does not preclude the possibility of further revision for the 1616 Folio, for which the prologue was obviously written. But the timing of the revision, though intriguing, is not crucial; what matters here is that we have an unparalleled opportunity to study the writer in his maturity (the period 1606–13—the accepted terminal dates of the argument— is certainly within the time of Jonson's best and most original dramatic writing) reassessing material he had already used much earlier in his career. Whatever date we choose, there can be no doubt that the revision is linked with the impulse which led Jonson to set his other plays in London. Certainly, no one who has deliberately compared the two texts of *Every Man in His Humour* could doubt but that the change of locale was a thoroughly calculated move. The London "colouring" is neither casual nor incidental, but comes as it were in strategic bursts, where it is most telling, most notably in the opening scenes; for instance, the idiotic Stephen grows pompous: "Because I dwell at Hogsden, I shall keepe companie with none but the archers of Finsburie? or the citizens, that come a-ducking to Islington ponds?" (1.1.47; Folio); "mine uncle here is a man of a thousand a yeare, Middlesex land" (1.2.3; Folio). The former passage is a completely original insertion; in the latter, the word "Middlesex" is interpolated in a bald line of the Quarto (1.1.82–3). One effect is precisely to define Stephen's milieu and the nature of his pretensions to the audience that Jonson was writing for; familiarity makes for ease of communication. On a very basic level, the local insertions act as clearer strokes of the pen in a rather blurred original picture: "over the fields to Moregate" was obviously much easier for Jonson's audience to conceptualize than a bare "to Florence." On this level, they are no more significant than Jonson's obvious efforts to clarify the sister / sister-in-law / brother / half-brother relationships complex, which is needlessly vague and confusing in the Quarto, or than the tightening-up of the denouement in the last act. We expect this kind of care from a professional.

Swinburne and others have seen more to it than that:

> Translated from the imaginary or fantastic Italy in which at first they lived and moved and had their being to the actual and immediate atmosphere of contemporary London, the characters gain even more in lifelike and interesting veracity or verisimilitude than in familiar attraction and homely association. Not only do we feel that we know them better, but we perceive that they are actually more real and cognisable creatures than they were under their former conditions of dramatic existence.
>
> (*A Study of Ben Jonson*)

Herford and Simpson are similarly enthusiastic about the Balzacian depiction of contemporary London manners:

> Ben Jonson knew too little of Italy for effective realism, even had this been his aim. The transfer to London liberated his vast fund of local knowledge. The London of the Folio is crowded with precise localities which have only vague equivalents in the Florence of the Quarto. It acquires a distinct physiognomy and atmosphere, as Florence never does.

The emphasis in both these accounts seems questionable: the former sees the revision in terms of a move towards a rather naive, nineteenth-century form of verisimilar realism, while the latter gives a faintly condescending impression of Jonson as a frustrated urban folklorist. Either of these accounts is surely misleading if taken in isolation, and not related to Jonson's art as a whole. And does the London of the Folio really acquire a "distinct physiognomy"? Although the play is recognizably located in London, the setting is essentially passive and incidental to the story. By comparison with Lovewit's house and Bartholomew Fair it is a feeble outline, in spite of the care that has been lavished on it. The revision points the way in which Jonson's technique improved and intensified, but it is not up to the standard of the best plays (even though Swinburne exalted it as virtually *the* best play). This is not simply a question of quantity—of how much realistic material is included—but of function; the setting of the revised play is adequate and a distinct improvement on the original, but it is not so integral to the drama as to form the basis of a completely new dimension to the satire, as I shall shortly suggest is the case in the best plays.

There would be little point in compiling a painstaking list of all the alterations; the general principles are agreed upon, even though interpretations of them differ. Jonson did not simply alter the locale of his play; we find ourselves short of differentiated terms to describe the kind of improvements in the characterization, the style of prose and verse, even, ultimately, the shape of the play—all of which contribute to what is generally recognized as the greater "realism" of the Folio version. A number of key passages reveal a thorough revision, affecting even basic word-style; Well-bred's intercepted letter, for instance, the main-spring of the action, is almost completely rewritten. There is less in the grandiose manner about Apollo and the Muses, which is part of a general toning-down of references to poets and poetry throughout the play, including the excision of the much-praised and often-quoted speech by Lorenzo Junior (5.3.312–43; Quarto). The early play smells very much of Jonson the young Renaissance poet, flexing his new-found muscles and glorying in his traditional powers, perhaps at the risk of identifying too readily with Lorenzo Junior. Although the function of the poet is implicitly a key issue in all Jonson's plays, it has little direct bearing on the action of this play and is properly deleted. It is perhaps the surest sign of Jonson's maturity in the revision that he had the heart to cut it out, in spite of its intrinsic merit. In place of the sententiousness of the original, the Folio-letter captures much better the bantering wit of the young man-about-town, revealing a closer attention to the type-veracity of the characters: "Doe not conceive that antipathy between us, and Hogs-den; as was be-tweene Jewes, and hogs-flesh" (1.2.74; Folio). The style is still affected and "clever" (this is part of Well-bred) but the idiom is snappier and more convincingly spontaneous (less "literary") in its flow of ideas than the original, and this makes Kno'well Senior's suspicious misunderstanding all the more credible. "Leave thy vigilant father, alone, to number over his greene apricots, evening, and morning, o'the north-west wall" (1.2.75; Folio). This is taken up by the slow-witted and literal-minded Kno'well Senior: "Why should he thinke, I tell my Apri-cotes?" (1.2.103; Folio). The result of such a tiny detail is a very neat and credible demonstration of old and young minds working on different wavelengths—which is perhaps the central theme of the play. It sets old Kno'well off on the chase.

It is notable how integrated the improvements are; the local and verbal realism—familiar settings, topical allusions, and a wider use of colloquial idioms (for example the pun on Hogsden)—all contribute to what we might

call an increased psychological realism. This is basically a technical improvement, rather than a fundamental change in Jonson's style; he is not attempting to achieve, for instance, a Shakespearian "roundness." On the contrary,
what takes place is a closer and more precise definition of Jonson's personal
idiom—a development of something already there in the Quarto. The changes
in old Kno'well's lines reveal his increasing grasp of character decorum, and
his ability to capture the quality of an eccentric, even deranged, personality.
There is a greater terseness to imply his suspicious and impatient mind. His
lines are recast to seem less studied and "balanced": for example, "Go to,
you are a prodigal, and self-wilde foole" (1.1.46; Quarto), becomes "You
are a prodigall absurd cocks-combe: Goe to" (1.1.54; Folio). The sense of
the line is scarcely altered, but the Quarto has no life in it at all, while the
Folio builds with indignation, giving a genuine stab to the "Goe to" at the
end. Stilted and artificial formulae, like the following advice to Stephano,
are simply omitted from the Folio:

> Chosen, lay by such superficiall formes,
> And entertaine a perfect reall substance.
>   (1.1.74; Quarto)

The net result of such changes is to achieve a harsh, realistic style of verse,
analogous to the baroque, anti-Ciceronian prose, so well analysed by Jonas
Barish. Kno'well Senior's reaction to the letter, which in the Quarto is pathetically tame: "Well, it is the strangest letter that ever I read" (1.1.176)
explodes in the Folio at the signature, "from the Windmill":

> From the Burdello, it might come as well;
> The Spittle: or Pict-hatch.
>   (1.2.92)

Once again, the psychological actualization and the London setting merge
perfectly and reinforce one another. Old Kno'well is not simply an abstract
"humour"—he is a manifestation of the London in the play, where suspicious, rather cynical old age is out of tune with regenerative nature and
society, represented here by the playful vitality of the young men.

There is a parallel example of more concrete and particularized dialogue
in the case of Kitely. A comparison with Thorello quickly reveals Jonson's
improved command of one of the fundamentals of his art: the precise definition and speech-depiction of an obsessively closed and fixed state of mind.
Kitely's jealousy is embodied in the nervous, erratic qualities of his speech;
his own description of the way his mind works, for instance, is adapted in

such a way that it expresses, rather than merely announces, the inner tension. The mellifluous, Shakespearian metaphor:

> my imaginations like the sands,
> Runne dribling foorth to fill the mouth of time.
>
> (3.1.43; Quarto)

becomes a less "poetic," but more anxious:

> my imaginations runne, like sands,
> Filling up time.
>
> (3.3.50; Folio)

Kitely's anxiety is acted out at length in this ludicrous scene, when he debates with himself whether to confide in Thomas or not. The basic idea, in the Quarto, is conveyed with a wild logic, which is obviously to the point, but it has little definition or dramatic sense; in the Folio, the insight becomes clearer, shrewder, and more explicit. When, for instance, he imagines some prevarication on Thomas's part about taking an oath of secrecy, he reflects:

> He is no puritane, that I am certaine of.
> What should I thinke of it?
>
> (3.1.80; Quarto)

In the Folio, this sober, abstracted reflection takes on new definition and concrete dimensions; this is achieved jointly by an infusion of realistic detail and a disjointed word pattern, which is helped by the over-running of the lines:

> H'is no precisian, that I am certaine of.
> Nor rigid Roman-catholike. Hee'll play,
> At Fayles, and Tick-tack, I have heard him sweare.
> What should I thinke of it?
>
> (3.3.88; Folio)

The deranged running-together of ideas adds far more weight to the question, and creates a much more convincing evocation of the jealous man.

By almost every criterion, in fact, the revised *Every Man in His Humour* is an improvement on the original; the diffuse plot is made slightly clearer, the denouement is shortened, made more straightforward and intelligible, while the characterization and the setting are more fully realized. But do the composite improvements constitute an essentially different kind of play? It would be a mistake to see the new psychological realism as an end in itself, the whole point of the changes, just as it was misguided of Swinburne and others to see the "verisimilar" realism of time and place as an end in itself. The fact is that Jonson's personal style and growing competence have stamped themselves on the revised version of the play; and with these qualities comes a fuller realization of his mature preoccupations. The commitment behind his writing is more surely engaged, and while that may express itself through psychological and verisimilar realism, these are only means to an end.

The most significant improvements in the later version of the play remain improvements within Jonson's own terms, and there are those who find these terms inadequate, however competently they are executed. Interestingly, it is Swinburne, who had a love-hate relationship with Jonson's writing, who best sums up the most deeply felt objection: "it is difficult to believe that Ben Jonson can have believed, even with some half-sympathetic and half-sardonic belief, in all the leading figures of his invention." However true the characters are to their age, however laboriously accurate Jonson is in their delineation, they lack "the sympathetic faith of the creator in his creatures," "the vital impulse of the infallible imagination." In short, they are not alive in the sense of suggesting the full complexity of persons in real life. The unspoken figure of Shakespeare stands in the background, and Jonson has suffered much for neither being, nor pretending to be, Shakespeare. A study of the revision emphasizes that Jonson never pretended to depict the "full humanity" of his subjects; for all the increase in realism, his concern for human life and values manifests itself in other ways. The act of creation for Jonson is also an act of judgement. There is a paradox in all his plays, which must lie behind Swinburne's doubts, between the patient effort which goes towards the solid depiction of his characters, and the structural logic of the drama, which is invariably reductive, bent on questioning and often destroying what he has created. He reveals a fully-engaged concern for humanity, for a sane and rational society, in his determination to ridicule and destroy manifestations of folly, which he regards as socially divisive and morally degenerate. Kitely and Kno'well Senior are simple examples of typical Jonsonian characters; Justice Clement—an uncomplicated *deus ex machina* of right-thinking and social harmony—arraigns them and bids them put off: "you, master Kno'well, your cares; Master Kitely, and his wife, their jealousie" (5.5.71; Folio). At this point, in complete reversal of the care which we have seen Jonson taking to present them, they cease to have any significance; they cease to have any existence, dramatic or otherwise. This has nothing to do with Jonson's alleged lack of "the sympathetic faith of the creator in his creatures"; it is the working-out of the moral and humane principle that lies at the heart of Jonson's drama. The realism that matters to Jonson is neither verisimilar nor, ultimately, psychological—though these are pieces of the pattern, means to an end—but moral.

The "characters," Kitely and Kno'well Senior, are manifestations of folly, embodiments of a diseased condition which is more than merely psychological and attacks the fabric of natural social harmony. The common distinguishing feature of such folly is that the afflicted creatures have lost touch with "reality," creating private worlds of fantasy and illusion in its place. It is in the tension between the supposed and the actual "reality" that Jonsonian drama is generated. We can see it as a function of the realism of the London settings to act as one of the terms of reference for what is real and true, in sharp contrast to the illusions that flourish among them. Bobadill, for instance, lets the ease of his bragging façade get the better of him, and he inadvertently slips into the truth when he mentions: "Turne-bull, Whitechappell, Shore-ditch, which were then my quarters, and since upon the Exchange" (4.7.44; Folio). The sordid reality of brothels and doss-houses suddenly appears, incongruously, in his fanciful bravado. This is only a small example, and the London setting in *Every Man in His Humour* does not really work consistently or cohesively enough in this way to advance the tension. Old Kno'well, Kitely, Bobadill and the rest are splendidly executed cameos, but the London setting does not give sufficient focus to suggest that they are all manifestations of a common condition; this, coupled with the fact that the action is too episodic, prevents the drama from achieving the inclusive, portentous quality of the best plays. It remains an indictment of follies, rather than an insight into human nature. G. B. Jackson makes a similar point: "London is a neutral setting in which society means a collocation of varied types; it cannot offer a hard ethical center. The constant insistence upon the locale, by providing a conceptual centre, goes some way towards disguising the lack of an evaluative center, but it is no substitute." This judgement is made in implicit contrast with Volpone's Venice, Truewit's London, Lovewit's house, and Bartholomew Fair, each of which constitutes, in her terms, "an evaluative center"—they are the stable realities against which the private follies which pass through them are measured.

This is true, but it is only a partial solution to what sets *Volpone, Epicoene, The Alchemist,* and *Bartholomew Fair* above the early "humour" plays (including the revised *Every Man in His Humour,* for all its improvements) and also above the so-called dotages. In these plays, Jonson comes closest to resolving the tensions which are ever-present in his art—the divergent aims of creation and destruction being one—by compounding them with those of the dramatic medium itself; that is, he equates the moral reality, which is expressed in the tension between the supposed and the actual, with the ambiguous reality of the dramatic illusion itself. He self-consciously plays around with what is real on stage and what only seems to be real. The role of Peregrine in *Volpone,* and the English elements generally (together with the subsequent parodying of the satirist-figures—Surly, Overdo, etc. and their privileged relationship with the audience); the double illusion of the boy-actor in *Epicoene; the special resilience of Face in his "master's wor- ship's house, here in the friers," which depends on his ability to be all things to all men, including the audience—as his closing address to them slyly hints; and the whole business of the contract between the author and the audience, coupled with the puppet-show climax, in Bartholomew Fair:* each of these is a function of what is real and what is illusory in the dramatic art itself. These are not merely technical tricks or embellishments, but underlie a se- rious intensification and growing sophistication in Jonson's art. In the early plays—and, in this respect, *Every Man in His Humour* remains an early play, for all its mature touches—the audience remained essentially outside the dramatic illusion, passing judgement upon it; the relationship between the play and the audience was essentially static, and the moment of dissolution, where someone with the role, if perhaps not the manner, of a Justice Clement finally ostracized the follies, left a vacuum in which the satirist seemed, all too patly, to have cured the ills of the world. The self-conscious and largely explicit playing with the dramatic illusion, which is a crucial feature of the best plays, helps to break down the formal barriers; it introduces a flexibility which is analogous to the moving camera in cinematography. It seems plau- sible to suggest that the strong contemporary flavour and the London settings of the plays after 1609 further help to break down the barrier between the stage and the audience, implicating the latter far more strongly *within* the process of recognizing and exposing folly. There are perhaps two major results of this shift: one is to involve the audience in such a way that, from being passive judges, they become agents within the satiric process, if not themselves objects of the satire; the second is to remove the bland finality of the early plays—the solutions of the plays are far more ambiguous, leaving essential problems, unresolved, in the laps of the audience.

Perhaps the most significant feature of the revision of *Every Man in His Humour,* then, is how limited, for all the neatening, tightening, and contem- porary flavour, the revision actually is. There is nothing to suggest that Jonson's basic aims have altered, or that his moral conscience is any the less stringent. On the contrary, an investigation of what the revised play lacks in comparison with the "realistic" plays of its own period suggests that the superiority of those plays is a matter of organization and of manipulation of the medium, rather than a thinning of the satiric impulse. With its episodic structure and the simplistic dismissal of its foolish characters, the Folio *Every Man in His Humour* remains an early play, its "moral purposes" self-evident to the on-looking audience. But it is a sign of maturity, and not geniality, that these are less "loudly proclaimed" when Jonson's attention shifts from the characters within his plays to their mirror images in the audience. Jonson's "powers of realistic depiction" do not portend a decline of moral fervour, but an ironic recognition of the actual powers of the satirist, which are limited by the capacity of the audience to recognize their own shortcomings when they see them. If Jonson does undergo a "metempsychosis" after 1605, it is not an indulgent frame of mind that he acquires, but the skills and wiles of the old Fox that he "mortifies" at the end of *Volpone*.

JONATHAN HAYNES

Festivity and the Dramatic Economy of Jonson's Bartholomew Fair

This essay tries to historicize the meaning of festivity in *Bartholomew Fair*. In medieval and early modern Europe festivity was, in the first place, a mode of social expression and organization—a point Bakhtin insists on in his great book on Rabelais [*Rabelais and His World*], although the point is regularly lost as Bakhtin's notion of the festive is imported into Anglo-American criticism, where festivity tends to become a purely symbolic or moral structure. Because it was fundamentally a social phenomenon, the sort of festivity Bakhtin describes disintegrated as its social basis disintegrated, and was reformulated in conformity with the new social conditions. That reformulation involved, in fact, the limiting of its radical social aspects and emphasis on a more inward and detachable symbolic and moral meaning. Such a process is of course very complex and does not happen overnight; but it seems clear that in 1614 Jonson felt he was writing at the moment of disintegration and reformulation, and intervened with his characteristic energy. At times he is quite polemical about it.

I want, then, to call attention to this historical aspect of the play, its role as witness of, and agent in, the transformation of festivity—a transformation that focuses with peculiar sharpness and delicacy the fundamental economic, social, cultural, and moral transformations of the early modern period. I will be investigating three sectors of the "dramatic economy" of the play: the commercial economy of Bartholomew Fair as Jonson represents it in his play; the economy of dramatic relations within the play; and the

From *ELH* 51, no. 4 (Winter 1984). © 1984 by the Johns Hopkins University Press.

theatrical economy of relations with the audience. More than a pun holds the larger dramatic economy together: its parts are interrelated and interdependent, and were changing together as part of the same broad historical process.

I

In Bakhtin's "festive marketplace" there is a "temporary suspension, both ideal and real, of hierarchical rank," preserving utopian memories of a primitive communism; all exchanges are between equals, and are frank and free, as is language, often to the point of obscenity and abuse; the physical body is reviled and celebrated; the air is full of a universal laughter.

> The marketplace of the Middle Ages and the Renaissance was a world in itself, a world which was one: all "performances" in this area, from loud cursing to the organized show, had something in common and were imbued with the same atmosphere of freedom, frankness, and familiarity. . . . The marketplace was the center of all that was unofficial; it enjoyed a certain extraterritoriality in a world of official order and official ideology, it always remained "with the people."

The utopian features of the festive marketplace are not to be understood apart from a good deal of squalor and violence and trickery; and detailed historical study of carnival behavior may qualify the absoluteness of Bakhtin's utopian claims. Still the main lines of Bakhtin's account of carnivalesque social behavior seem sound, and the historical problem that concerns us here is the erosion of the carnival tradition. This ancient pattern was still flourishing in Rabelais's France, but as Susan Wells has pointed out, it was breaking down in Jonson's London:

> just as the literal marketplace was, during the Jacobean period, becoming marginal, slowly being replaced by the private shop . . . so also the metaphorical arena of the marketplace, the arena of openness and play, outside the scrutiny of the church and the direct concern of the crown, was becoming compromised . . . first, by becoming simply the location of exchange and profit rather than a gathering place, a common space; second, by being circumscribed more tightly by the "official order," by losing its "extraterritorial status" and becoming integrated with the central apparatus of the government. . . .

Thus, while Bakhtin's *Rabelais* can present the marketplace as the place where the rights of the "lower bodily stratum" are legitimated, and where the popular subversive tradition of laughter, parody, skepticism, and utopian hope could be preserved, so straightforward a relationship to the marketplace was impossible for Marston, Middleton, and Jonson. Their marketplace, their city, and their space of celebration, were different.

["The Jacobean City Comedy and the Ideology of the City"]

City comedy, Wells goes on to say, explores the contradiction between the old communal marketplace, with its corporate ideology, and the new economy which rendered it obsolete; and it is city comedy

in which the popular festive traditions were most tellingly brought to bear on the problem of forming a new self-understanding for the commercial city. And indeed, the city comedy is rooted in forms that were connected, either organically or by analogy, with those traditions, and was performed before audiences who would have been both aware of the traditional forms of celebration, and unable to accept those forms uncritically.

Wells provides a very apt description of the problematic of *Bartholomew Fair*. The play is of course built directly on the representation of the festive marketplace, and nowhere does Renaissance literature bring us closer to the sights and sounds and smells of a popular celebration. All the central motifs of Bakhtin's festivity are here: the material bodily principle is magnificently embodied in the enormous flesh of the pig-woman Ursula and in her booth, which caters to all the body's needs (eating, drinking, defecating, fornicating); the fair people speak a pungent billingsgate; a mood of holiday license is evoked amid the noise and confusion and crowds; the plots follow the uncrowning, mocking, and humiliation of the bourgeois characters' pretensions to honor (Win Littlewit and Mistress Overdo), righteousness (Rabbi Busy) and authority (Justice Overdo and Humphrey Wasp). The play ends with a symbolic leveling, in which Justice Overdo is forcibly reminded that he is also Adam, merely flesh and blood, and is made to invite everyone home for dinner.

But there is at the same time a current setting the other way, which is finally decisive, drawing us away from participation in the festive marketplace and toward a criticism of it. We will look at how this works in the plot and in the relationship Jonson sets up with the theater audience, but the character of the Fair itself needs to be discussed first.

II

This most durable of fairs was changing—changing its face (Stow had noticed that the fairgrounds in Smithfield, just northwest of the walls, were being surrounded and encroached on by the expansion of the city; and in the year of the play the fairground was paved for the first time and improved in various other ways), and changing its function, or rather the relations among its functions. Very broadly, the Fair's history is the history of the specialization and fragmentation of the religious, commercial, and recreational aspects of what was originally one indivisible event. Its religious associations had been destroyed at the Reformation, when the monastery of St. Bartholomew was dissolved (heretics, however, continued to be burned there, and that ceased also after 1611). Commercially, according to the Fair's historian, Henry Morley, Bartholomew Fair was for centuries the most important cloth fair in England, and was important for trade in horses, cattle, and leather goods as well. During the Middle Ages all the shops in London were forced to close during fairtime and set up booths in the Fair if they wanted to continue to do business. (Such legislation was a standard accompaniment of the legal privilege of holding a fair.) But by 1614 the Fair no longer swallowed up the whole city, no longer *was* the city in a holiday mode; it now seemed an appendage of its commercial life, and its national and international role as a hub of trade had perhaps begun to decline, though this decay did not become serious until the Restoration. The commercial fair maintained its festive character, and as late as the Commonwealth could invent new customs that perfectly expressed the festive mode.

But Jonson's attention is devoted more or less exclusively to the pleasure fair that had grown up beside the commercial one. Northern, the clothier "who does change cloth for ale at the Fair here," is the sole representative of the cloth fair, and he is plainly off work when we see him. Jordan Knockem is a horse-courser, and may have some connection—apparently not an active one—with the livestock market, but he is also called a "Ranger of Turnbull" in the *dramatis personae,* and it is in this capacity of whoremaster and gamester (as well as acting proprietor of Ursula's booth) that we see him— that is where the fun and the money were, and that is where the future of the Fair was, too. From 1661 to the middle of the eighteenth century the Fair ran for a fortnight or even longer, rather than the statutory three days at the end of August, in spite of frequent attempts to prune it back. Critics complained that three days were enough for business, and that everyone knew the prolonged Fair "to be a mere Carnival, a season of the utmost Disorder and Debauchery, by reason of the Booths for Drinking, Music,

Dancing, Stage-plays, Drolls, Lotteries, Gaming, Raffling, and what not." The ever increasing crush of people from the burgeoning metropolis finally made it impossible to conduct business: "the element of sober trade was choked by its excessive development as a great pleasure fair. . . . [The] cloth trade in Bartholomew Fair died naturally; but the other trades that perished from it, died by suffocation."

The consequence of this separation of business and pleasure was that pleasure became a business. In Jonson's play the marketplace is sharply divided into buyers and sellers—two distinct classes. This economy of the pleasure fair is special because real money is traded for more or less worthless goods and services: hobby-horses and gingerbread men; pig sold at inflated prices for the privilege of eating it in the Fair; in short, all the staples of the vices of mind and body. Jonson wrote other plays about greed; the theme of this one is folly. So the buyers and sellers are also hucksters and fools; and, since the conditions of the Fair encourage the free play of the natural law that decrees that fools and their possessions should be separated by fair means or foul, the hucksters become sharpers and criminals, and the fools their gulls.

Appropriately Ursula's booth, where the pigs roast and the ale flows and the tobacco smokes in festive plenty, is also the front for the main criminal activities: it receives the purses that Ezekiel Edgworth and Nightingale steal, it houses Whit's prostitution ring, and it hosts the fights that Knockem arranges so cloaks can be stolen in the confusion. And the pig is overpriced, the ale and beer sold in false measures, the tobacco adulterated.

Nor are Urs and company the only criminals in the Fair, though they are its biggest operators. All of the fair people are ready to commit crimes when the occasion arises. The theme of adulteration—the first "enormity" Justice Overdo encounters, and a timely one—opens with Lantern Leatherhead's threat to reveal that Joan Trash's gingerbread-progeny are made of stale bread, rotten eggs, musty ginger, and dead honey (2.2.8–9). Lantern Leatherhead and Joan Trash will strike their booths and steal away without delivering the goods that Cokes has paid for. The costermonger will dump his basket of pears in front of Cokes, by arrangement with Edgworth, so Cokes can be robbed as he scrambles for the fruit. This is a minor moment, but typical, and nicely symbolic of what has happened to the festive: the heap of fruit which should accompany a communal feast is wasted as a ploy in a criminal operation. The world of the carnival is being restructured into the world of the coney-catching pamphlets.

The fairground has become a place where the representatives of the folly of a huge city fall into the clutches of an underworld. Within this underworld some of the communal solidarity of the festive marketplace is preserved. In spite of the abusive language the fair people use among themselves (which is itself a mark of the festive marketplace) they pull together: when Ursula is scalded everyone leaps to her aid; Joan Trash and Lantern Leatherhead call one another "brother" and "sister" when they are not quarreling; all the crimes are committed by a *team*. Ezekiel Edgworth, the Fair's golden boy, stands at the center of the economy of the underworld as virtuoso cut-purse, jovial principal customer of Ursula's whorehouse, and patron of a tarnished golden world of liberality and festive plenty. He always has money in his purse, we are told again and again, and always pays for everything (2.3.54–56, 4.24–26, 4.68). He offers to give Knockem half of what he has, though Knockem does not seem to be in on his game.

The underworld preserves the memories of a primitive communism and the freedom of exchange among equals, but being contained within an underworld changes their nature. The liberty of the fair people is limited—an evasion rather than a true (even if temporary) release. The law may in many ways be made over in the image of the Fair (the watch is corrupt, in league with the informer/bawd Whit, more interested in extorting five-shilling fines than in keeping the peace; Justice Overdo is a fool, and his court of Pie Powders a unique and perhaps faintly ridiculous legal institution adapted to the Fair) but it hangs heavy over them. Their talk is full of references to the cart, the whip, and the gallows. The disguised Overdo overhears Lantern Leatherhead and Joan Trash threatening each other with his name, and is satisfied: "I am glad to hear my name is their terror, yet; this is doing of justice" (2.2.25–26). The authority of his bench will continue to structure relations in the Fair, if only in a negative way; he is looked for on the bench even while he himself is in the stocks.

III

More important than the criminalization of the Fair is the creation of class barriers within it. Bakhtin insists on the "temporary suspension, both ideal and real, of hierarchical rank"—that *everyone* participates, and on equal terms. The underworld has an obvious vested interest in preserving the distinction between itself and its victims. Punk Alice complains when Mistress Overdo begins to compete in her market—"The poor common whores can ha' no traffic for the privy rich ones"—and beats her (4.5.64–65). The class lines are asserted from above as well.

It is true that the main plot (or plots—our descriptive vocabulary breaks down in the face of the profusion of this play) involves the disintegration of the two parties of bourgeois fair-goers we meet in act 1. Each individual is separated from his party and stripped of the emblem of his social position: Cokes loses his money and most of his clothes, as well as his fiancée; Busy loses his hypocritical superiority, and so on. By act 5 the leveling is completed, and the fair people and fair-goers go off to feast together.

This pattern is certainly saturnalian, yet I would argue that the bourgeois characters and their destinies are conceived in the terms of satiric comedy. Jonson's play mixes the two kinds of comic structure, and mixes the two kinds of social concern C. L. Barber associates with them:

> Satirical comedy tends to deal with relations between social classes and aberrations in movements between them. Saturnalian comedy is satiric only incidentally; its clarification comes with movement between poles of restraint and release in everybody's experience.

The bourgeois characters are all immediately recognizable types from other city comedies: Cokes the gullible heir, unable to hold onto his property; Wasp the irascible but impotent guardian; Mistress Overdo, whose trivial social pretensions do not disguise the heart of a whore; John Littlewit, infatuated with his own negligible wit and his connections in the sub-literary world of petty taverns and puppet theaters; his pretty and mindless wife, fair game for everyone since her husband is too foolish to hold onto her; her canting mother and her mother's hypocritical Puritan suitor. They are all ready for a fall; the conventions of city comedy demand their humiliation. Jonson despised the particular milieus from which they spring, and as individuals they represent the disjunction between social and moral status that particularly scandalized him, and which provides much of the tension in city comedy. They are propelled out of their class positions and into the Fair by their own folly and vice, and there poetic justice is done to them. (When Cokes is robbed Wasp asks him, "Are you not justly served i' your conscience now?" [2.6.101].) Quarlous, Winwife, Edgworth, and Nightingale are all concerned, in what is presented as a principled and quite disinterested way, that people get what they deserve. When all the strands of plot are taken together it may appear that everyone is losing his class character in one universal rhythm and experience; but it is also possible to see the play as a collection of destinies being met by (and *as*) individuals, expressed through conventions with an exact and limited social meaning. Jonson had as much scorn for those who, like Littlewit and Cokes, could not recognize class distinctions, who could not recognize when they were degrading and making fools of themselves, as he had for inept and unworthy social climbers like

Mistress Overdo; and as much contempt for those who couldn't hold onto their own as he did for those motivated by raw acquisitiveness. But this study of social and moral status and the sorts of social mobility attendant on it is inherently quite different from the suspension of rank during a period of festivity.

There are three characters who are neither fools nor knaves: Quarlous, Winwife, and Grace Wellborn. Grace represents female virtue in a rather schematic way, and is a victim of the corruption of the social order: specifically, she has been sold to Justice Overdo in the notorious Court of Wards. Quarlous and Winwife are also characters we recognize from city comedy: young gentlemen with wit and education (Quarlous says he has been to Oxford and the Inns of Court) but no money, on the make in the more fluid sectors of Jacobean society; usually to be found, as here, preying on the fortunes and women of foolish citizens. All three are from the gentry, but their class membership is threatened by legal or pecuniary problems. More or less from the moment we meet them we assume that the business of the comedy will be to confirm and secure them in their social position. This solidification of the hierarchy of rank runs counter to the festive in more than an abstract thematic way.

Grace and Winwife's marriage and Quarlous's fortune are made possible by the Fair, yet they never really participate in it. This point is made over and over very distinctly. Almost the first thing we hear Grace say is "Truly, I have no such fancy to the Fair, nor ambition to see it; there's none goes thither of any quality or fashion" (1.5.121–22). She is carried along anyway, but her icy reserve is never broken. Winwife and Quarlous follow, but they make it clear that they are trailing Wasp and Cokes, rather than visiting the Fair itself. They always enter their scenes looking for Wasp and Cokes, and speaking of them as a show: "We had wonderful ill luck to miss this prologue o' the purse, but the best is we shall have five acts of him ere night. He'll be spectacle enough!" (3.2.1–3) The Fair is an affront and a nuisance for Winwife, and for Quarlous at best a way to pass the time until Cokes reappears.

> WINWIFE: That these people should be so ignorant to think us
>   chapmen for 'em! Do we look as if we would buy ginger-
>   bread? or hobby horses?
> QUARLOUS: Why, they know no better ware than they have, nor
>   better customers than come. And our very being here makes
>   us fit to be demanded, as well as others. Would that Cokes
>   would come!
>   (2.5.12–17)

When Jordan Knockem recognizes them and extends the hospitality of the Fair, Winwife wants to refuse, and Quarlous accepts only in order to quarrel. Both insist on the distinctions Knockem assumes the Fair has suspended.

> KNOCKEM: Will you take any froth and smoke with us?
> QUARLOUS: Yes, sir, but you'll pardon us if we knew not of so much familiarity between us afore.
>
> . . . .
>
> KNOCKEM: Master Winwife, you are proud, methinks; you do not talk or drink; are you proud?
> WINWIFE: Not of the company I am in, sir, nor the place, I assure you.
>
> (2.5.33–35, 48–51)

Later, when Edgworth has stolen the marriage license for Quarlous, he offers to share his whores with his customary liberality—"I can spare any gentleman a moiety"—but Quarlous rebukes him violently:

> Keep it for your companions in beastliness; I am none of 'em, sir. If I had not already forgiven you a greater trespass, or thought you yet worth my beating, I would instruct your manners, to whom you make your offers. . . . I am sorry I employed this fellow; for he thinks me such: *facinus quos inquinat, aequat.*
>
> (4.6.20–27)

As the bourgeois parties of fools and coxcombs disintegrate, Winwife, Quarlous and Grace find each other and establish in the midst of the Fair their own little society based on the contrary values of self-possession and the manners that reflect a gentlemanly bearing:

> WINWIFE: . . . will you please to withdraw with us a little, and make them think they have lost you? I hope our manners ha' been such hitherto, and our language, as will give you no cause to doubt yourself in our company.
> GRACE: Sir, I will give myself no cause; I am so secure in my own manners as I suspect not yours.
>
> (3.5.269–74)

When Quarlous and Winwife turn on one another in their competition for Grace, she chooses her husband by lottery, as Valentines were chosen—a carnivalesque enough motif, but again her attitude is absolutely antithetical to everything the Fair stands for.

GRACE: Sure you think me a woman of an extreme levity, gentlemen, or a strange fancy, that (meeting you by chance in such
a place as this . . .) I should so forsake my modesty . . . as
to say "this is he," and name him.
QUARLOUS: Why, wherefore should you not? What should hinder
you?
GRACE: If you would not give it to my modesty, allow it yet to
my wit; give me so much of woman and cunning as not to
betray myself impertinently.

(4.3.19–29)

Barber quotes a relevant speech of Rosalind's as an example of the mood of
revelry in courtship: "Come, woo me, woo me! for now I am in a holiday
humour, and like enough to consent." Grace's stratagem of the lottery is
designed to keep Quarlous and Winwife both in expectation and working
for her until she is safely out of the Fair. Quarlous circumvents this strategy,
but it is a clever one.

Grace is an altogether unlikely heroine for the play, given that the dy-
namic of festivity forces everyone to join in its spirit and derides and punishes
those who do not, but she is the heroine of the play, not of the Fair; and, as
we are seeing, these are two distinctly different things. The "super-plot" that
centers on her is as formal as her character is: a pure comic plot of a girl
dispossessed by a ridiculous but powerful blocking figure, representing an
unjust and foolish society, who escapes from his authority with the help of
the young man she will marry. This plot floats on top of the plots involving
the bourgeois characters, plots which in turn are perched on top of the Fair
itself. It is there to represent a potential society of sense, which Justice Overdo
will not be able to provide even after his chastening. We would like to believe
in Grace, and in Winwife for her sake, but like Celia and Bonario in *Volpone*
their virtue is too cut off from the central energies of the play.

The plot reflects this problem by having its natural economy disrupted
by Quarlous, a character with the more ambivalent virtues of the city-comedy
gallants. Winwife may have got Grace, but Quarlous has managed to acquire
a legal document transferring Grace's wardship from Justice Overdo to himself—and he will make her compound for the privilege of marrying Winwife
just as Justice Overdo would have done. This twist by which boy gets girl
but his friend gets her money is highly unusual, if not unique. Quarlous has
also contracted a marriage for himself with Dame Purecraft, who has £6,000
and a roaring business defrauding her Puritan brethren. To make this match
he sacrifices our sentimental interest and his own sexual gratification—it was

Quarlous who in act 1 lectured Winwife on the foulness and unnaturalness of chasing this particular widow—but it is a nicely symbolic union, uniting the two sharpest operators in the play.

How are we to understand this deflection of the most fundamental comic plot type, in which the gentle characters never recoup their positions entirely—Winwife and Grace because they are left without their fortune, Quarlous because he is saddled with an unpresentable wife? It is not hard to see why Quarlous ends up holding all the cards. We have seen that he is as hostile to the Fair as Winwife or Grace, but he is much more willing to plunge in than the squeamish Winwife. He is quarlous, and it gives him opportunities to quarrel; but more importantly, he plunges into the marketplace because he needs money and there is a lot of property to be had by those aggressive enough to seize it from its imbecilic owners. He understands the marketplace as a place for accumulation, not festivity. His disguise as a madman shows he understands how to manipulate the symbol system of the Fair without believing in it himself. Like the cutpurses of the coney-catching pamphlets and the underworld figures of this play, he understands the uses of disruption. They turn every fight, every spilled basket, every commotion caused by another crime, into an opportunity for the man with a quick wit and a quick hand; the Fair for them is such a disruption on a giant scale, its festive trappings bait for their traps. Quarlous is playing a larger game: for someone in a socially marginal position a general disruption will create openings. Grace and Winwife stand to profit from the same situation, but it is Quarlous who has the virtues—alertness, aggressiveness, the ability to improvise, a detached but practical intelligence, and a willingness to get his hands dirty—that make him the master in this world. It is not especially reassuring to leave things in Quarlous's hands, but it makes sense.

The social function of festivity, we are told by everyone who has thought about it, is revitalization of the social order—but what constitutes revitalization depends on specific historical circumstances. So the festive moment is essentially conservative in a strong and stable society, potentially revolutionary in an unstable or sclerotic one. Jonson's play provides a complex diagnosis of his society. The bourgeois victims of the saturnalian pattern stand to profit (somewhat paradoxically) from the spirit of festivity in orthodox ways; they receive a moral regeneration consequent on their humiliation, and a truer relation to society to compensate for the loss of the dominance (social or economic) they should never have had. Before the social order is restored (and the bourgeois characters are restored to their positions as well as limited to them by the universal forgiveness of the denouement) the satirist works his will on them. Jonson's particular social concerns and his individual moral focus cut across the older social patterns of festivity, but they displace rather than erase them.

Quarlous and Grace and Winwife are never touched by anything like the spirit of festivity; the benefits they derive from the Fair are all practical. For the disenchanted lovers the Fair has only this in common with the world of romance: that it is full of accidents and happy chances through which they gain their freedom. The temporary unravelling of the social fabric allows them to reestablish who they rightfully *are,* by nature and birth. This is the sort of plot that makes people say that comedy is a conservative form. Their plot draws them through the Fair, but their relationship with it is always accidental. Quarlous on the other hand does his own plotting in the Fair; in it he establishes not what he *is,* but what he can *do.* His attitude is also post-festive, but he sees how to get ahead in the rough scramble the Fair permits. The suspension of normal social relations leads not to a primitive equality, nor to a pristine and ideal social order, but to an acceleration of the processes of social Darwinism. In the long run it was the realism of the English upper classes toward the changes in the economy, their participation in and mastery of those changes, which insured the stability of their rule and the relatively smooth and rapid development of English capitalism. It is not too much to see in Jonson's distortion of the normal comic economy a registering of this historical perception.

In a sense, then, Jonson's implied historical analysis of the disintegration of the festive marketplace requires and guarantees Quarlous's role. And socially Quarlous, Winwife and Grace are, I believe, the necessary objects of identification for the audience, or at least that part of the audience Jonson was most concerned to reach, the part which Wells says could no longer accept uncritically the traditional forms of festivity. This function is implied by their formal roles in the plot, and if it is not earned by the depth or warmth of their characters, it is made inevitable by the lack of any possible alternative. Like the gentlemen of Jonson's audience, we certainly do not want to see ourselves in the Overdos, or Busy, in any but the most universal and metaphorical way; and while we may be attracted to the underworld figures (Edgworth and Nightingale in particular), our admiration must be romantic and voyeuristic; in real life we know we would be their victims, not their friends. Similarly the coney-catching pamphlets may betray a fascination with the glamour and freedom and wit of the criminals, but they are always addressed specifically to gentlemen, lawyers, country yeomen, and so on, the very people likely to be robbed; and the pamphlets were sold, in the first place, as instructions in how not to be taken, what to watch for. The way the Fair is presented is calculated to put us on our guard, to suggest that if we cannot, like Quarlous, master its noise and confusion, its tricks and deceptions, we had better stay aloof, like Winwife and Grace. Their detachment and condescension and even scorn are there as models for our own reactions, or at least for a crucial part of them—the part that has most to do with our own social identity, the cool judgment which only fools fail to consult before they give themselves over to the confusion of the Fair; the part that warns us not to let go, that sets us apart.

IV

Jonson wrote an Induction to explore the issue of the audience's relation to the play, and the play's relation to the Fair, which is of the greatest interest for our examination of the social meaning of festivity. The central fact is clear enough: the Fair, still very much alive in Smithfield, is being represented in a commercial theater, before a paying audience, at a different time of the year. It is torn out of its social context, then, and made the object of art; and Jonson wants to be sure his audience sees the difference, that they reconstitute themselves as the proper sort of audience, not as a crowd in the festive mode.

The Induction begins with the appearance of the Stage-keeper, an exponent of the popular tradition, who complains about Jonson's appropriation of the Fair. He begins by accusing Jonson of failure to represent, or we might say reproduce, the Fair itself accurately.

> When it comes to the Fair once, you were e'en as good go to Virginia, for anything there is of Smithfield. He has not hit the humors, he does not know 'em; he has not conversed with Barthol'mew-birds, as they say; he has ne'er a sword-and-buckler man in his Fair, nor a little Davy to take toll o' the bawds there, as in my time, nor a Kindheart, if anybody's teeth should chance to ache in his play. . . . But these master-poets, they will ha' their own absurd courses; they will be informed of nothing! . . . Would not a fine pump upon the stage ha' done well for a property now? And a punk set under upon her head, with her stern upward, and ha' been soused by my witty young masters o' the Inns o' Court? . . . He will not hear o' this! I am an ass, I? And yet I kept the stage in Master Tarleton's time, I thank my stars. Ho! an' that man had lived to have played in *Barthol'mew Fair,* you should

ha' seen him ha' come in, and ha' been cozened i' the cloth-
quarter, so finely! . . . And then a substantial watch to ha' stol'n
upon 'em, and taken 'em away with mistaking words, as the
fashion is in the stage-practice.

(9–40)

His demands modulate from having actual characters transferred from
the Fair to the stage, to the reenactment of social rituals characteristic of fair
time (ducking whores), to fidelity to the popular tradition in the theater. The
naturalness of the transitions may remind us of the very strong popular
dramatic tradition that was always associated with the Fair, and of Bakhtin's
comment that the marketplace was "a world which was one: all 'performances' in this area, from loud cursing to the organized show, had something
in common and were imbued with the same atmosphere."

Jonson meets this attempt by the popular tradition to reclaim its own
directly: "He has, sir reverence, kicked me three or four times about the
tiring-house, I thank him, for but offering to put in, with my experience!"
(24–26) The Book-holder is sent out to drive the Stage-keeper off the stage,
and to establish the proper relation with the audience, even while recognizing
the stake of the Stage-keeper and the popular audience in the play:

the author hath writ it just to his meridian, and the scale of the
grounded judgments here, his play-fellows in wit. Gentlemen . . .
I am sent out to you here with a scrivener and certain articles
drawn out in haste between our author and you.

(49–54)

The opposition between the popular and coterie theaters is perfectly expressed in this moment: groundlings vs. gentlemen; the Stage-keeper with
his memories of an improvisational popular theater vs. the Book-holder and
Scrivener, men of the master-poet's written text; the communal possession
of, and participation in, a tradition that was always extra-official, "with the
people," vs. legal relations expressed in the formal articles the Scrivener reads
out: "Articles of Agreement indented between the spectators or hearers at
the Hope on the Bankside, in the county of Surrey, on the one party, and
the author of *Barthol'mew Fair* in the said place and county, on the other
party."

The Articles, to which the audience must agree before the play will
begin, are of course half in jest, but they also impose serious conditions
which could hardly be calculated more exactly to oppose festivity as a social
form. The first (and most fundamental) requires the audience to remain in

the places their money or friends have put them in for two and a half hours, while the other party presents them with a play—the audience is legally separated from the stage, made physically (if not mentally) passive, turned into consumers of a commodity rather than participants in a ritual. This is what Bakhtin says carnival cannot allow:

> In fact, carnival does not know footlights, in the sense that it does not acknowledge any distinction between actors and spectators. Footlights would destroy a carnival, as the absence of footlights would destroy a theatrical performance. Carnival is not a spectacle seen by the people; they live in it, and everyone participates because its very idea embraces all the people. While carnival lasts, there is no other life outside it.

The second article grants that "every person here have his or their freewill of censure, to like or dislike at their own charge, the author having now departed with his right: it shall be lawful for any man to judge his six pen'orth, his twelve pen'orth, so to his eighteen pence, two shillings, half a crown, to the value of his place; provided always his place get not above his wit." The play can be sold as a commodity, but judgment of course cannot (though it is being conceived of as private property); but the project of differentiating his audience into more or less fit and unfit, after bringing them all under contract, is one that Jonson pursued through his whole theatrical career. It is always possible that a man's place will get above his wit, but the organization of society into classes provides the metaphor for the hierarchy of wit, and the correlation between the two is assumed to be roughly accurate. (Jonson's own search for patronage at higher and higher social levels is based on this assumption.) Jonson does not value the opinions of his audience equally; he does not address them as a community of equals, but as a society differentiated by classes, and the experience of the play and their reactions to it will validate and reinforce that differentiation, not break it down.

The third article deepens the isolation of the spectator, stipulating that "every man here exercise his own judgment, and not censure by contagion, or upon trust, from another's voice or face that sits by him . . . as also, that he be fixed and settled in his censure, that what he approves or not approves today, he will do the same tomorrow." The audience is not to respond together, as a crowd, in one rhythm; they are to restrict their experience to what is provided from the stage, not what their fellows contribute; judgment is an affair of the isolated individual, free of time and space. The effect Jonson was aiming at would later be achieved by lowering the house lights—

although Eugene Waith has shown that Jonson returned to medieval techniques in staging *Bartholomew Fair,* the conditions he tries to establish an-
ticipate those of a later theater. Again we may contrast these conditions with
what Bakhtin has to say about festive laughter:

> it is not an individual reaction to some isolated "comic" event.
> Carnival laughter is the laughter of all the people. Second, it is
> universal in scope; it is directed at all and everyone, including
> the carnival's participants.

The fourth article stipulates that "no person here is to expect more than
he knows, or better ware than a Fair will afford; neither to look back to the
sword-and-buckler age of Smithfield, but content himself with the present."
This is a direct reply to the Stage-keeper, limiting his rights of expectation;
but, confident now of having established the conditions of his theater, Jonson
can accommodate the popular tradition. He meets the Stage-keeper's demands, one by one: "Instead of a little Davy to take toll o' the bawds, the
author doth promise a strutting horse-courser. . . . And then for Kindheart,
the tooth-drawer, a fine oily pig-woman with her tapster to bid you welcome." (The list can be extended further: Quarlous, a witty young master
of the Inns of Court, asks after a ducking-stool for Ursula, an ex-punk, now
bawd; Cokes plays something like the part Tarleton once did; there is a
watch with mistaking words.) Although Jonson will not go as far as Shakespeare in his *Tales* and *Tempests* to please a popular audience, "yet if the
puppets will please anybody, they shall be entreated to come in." Jonson
reels off his menu with the relish and energy of language of which only he
was capable; he is transforming the popular materials, giving them back
animated with his own magnificent art, displaying the fruit of his imagination
with what we might be tempted to call festive abandon.

But it is festive in a sense quite different from that of the popular
tradition. Michael McCanles has described Jonson's notion of festivity quite
accurately as a much more refined comic spirit, expressed not in a social
convulsion but in an individual moral posture. Ideally the festive does not
oppose quotidian values: both are contained and reconciled within a single
awareness, laughing but sane. The model for this typically humanist moral
stance is Jonson's imitation of Martial, "Inviting a Friend to Supper."
McCanles enumerates elements that *Bartholomew Fair* shares with Bakhtin's
festive, but finds that the play does not really fit Bakhtin's definition. Neil
Rhodes takes the same position in an argument about Jonson's style—his
comic prose has its roots in the Rabelaisian tradition Bakhtin describes, but
"his moral earnestness pulls him in an opposite direction," toward the eigh-

teenth-century desire for "'correctness,' for purity and firmness of language" [*Elizabethan Grotesque*]. The point I am concerned to make here is that the disjunction in the meaning of festivity is thematized and insisted on by Jonson, and can be historicized much more fully than is generally done. It is not enough to locate it in the literary history of prose style, or to account for it as a function of a purely personal moral sensibility, or a purely moral distinction between a "true" and a "perverted" festivity.

The transvaluation of festivity depends ultimately on the transformation of the social base that had supported it. As surely as enclosures and rack-renting undermined the festive life of the countryside, the changing functions of Bartholomew Fair changed the nature of the festive marketplace. In both country and city the more visible ideological and legal attacks on the traditional extraterritoriality of the festive were led by the Puritans and the legal apparatus of the government. In that battle Jonson was a conservative: the Fair defends itself gloriously against the Puritan and the Justice of the Peace in his play; the aristocratic values of poems like "To Penshurst" are well known; his "sons" would get sentimental about hock-carts and May-days.

Still, humanism had transformations of its own to work on the patterns of the disintegrating traditional society. If Jonson's conflicts with the popular tradition are concealed by the content *Bartholomew Fair* shares with it, they are revealed by the pointedness and violence of his appropriation of that content. On every level he is willing to absorb the popular tradition, but is unwilling to be absorbed by it.

This is clearest when the popular tradition in the theater gets in the way of the career Jonson was inventing for himself, and the master-poet kicks the Stage-keeper. In spite of the affection Jonson obviously felt for certain aspects of the popular tradition in the theater, he was also alive to everything in it that was moldy, stale, crude, and outmoded, and no one believed more vehemently that as a method of producing plays it was worn out. He built his career more clearly than anyone ever had on the assumption that the future lay with a new kind of artist, a figure he himself was busy constituting. This figure was articulated (and propagandized for) in the language of humanism, and perhaps its central feature was the personal autonomy that the traditional society could not support, but the emerging capitalist society did. The Jonsonian man of letters had a high profile as an individual, was a citizen of austere independence of judgment; his productions were thoroughly his own because they were thoroughly coherent and original, the product of an individual genius (this was true even when he was imitating someone else); his proprietorship of his own productions was expressed by editing his own *Workes;* and when he wrote for the theater he expected—against all odds—

that complex institution to be bent entirely to serving his will, embodied in a written text, at least for the duration of the performance. Jonson's self-definition as an artist, then, depended on his making it clear to his audience that they were spectators of his art rather than participants in what was going on onstage, either as Fair-goers or as coproprietors of the popular theater. So he always stresses that he has created an object for contemplation, pointing to its aesthetic and moral coherence. Jonson's art envelops the Fair, but the Fair must not envelop his art.

The corollary of this definition of the author is of course an audience as defined in the Induction to this most Brechtian of Renaissance plays: a watchful, wakeful audience, with enough personal autonomy to make independent judgments, and enough aesthetic experience and training to make the right ones. Such an audience is also a historical product, and Jonson could not, and did not, assume that it already existed in adequate form. The prefaces, epistles, inductions and epilogues to all of his plays are largely taken up with cajoling or coercing it into being. The members of Jonson's ideal audience were antithetical to the crowd of fair-goers in their psycho-social organization, and in the functions art played in their lives. The experience of festivity in its original social form had less and less to offer them, and it contradicted more and more clearly the polished manners and inward depth that characterized the seventeenth-century gentleman. There was a social need to redefine festivity, toward the sensibility McCanles finds embodied in "Inviting a Friend to Supper," and away from the grossness of fat Ursula. This new perspective is a consequence and a cause of the disintegration of the older pattern, and it guarantees the roles of Grace and Winwife and Quarlous in this incarnation of the Fair.

V

The more polished classes did not stop going to the Fair; if Grace was right in saying that no one of quality or fashion went in 1614, things had certainly changed by 1667 when Pepys, on one of his many excursions (usually at the head of a pleasure party), saw the King's mistress Lady Castlemayne emerging from a puppet booth. Pepys went to see *Bartholomew Fair* too, which was often revived just before or after fairtime. (During the Fair itself the theaters would sometimes close, and their companies would move into booths in the Fair for extremely lucrative runs.) It is odd but appropriate that the dynamics of the commercial theater drew *Bartholomew Fair* back towards Bartholomew Fair—the companies could capitalize on the play's realistic aspects, offering it as a fore- or after-taste of the real thing.

But the nature of fair-going had changed again—there is nothing in *Bartholomew Fair* like Pepys's slumming—and there is at least one piece of documentary evidence to show that Jonson's play was attached to the Fair by the culture of the Restoration and eighteenth century because the theatrical relation developed in it did in fact serve as an exemplary model for fairgoers: a model of the proper structure of perception, moral relation to experience, and social relation to community—a model called for by the Fair in particular but of course relevant to life in general. This document is a letter written by one Sir Robert Southwell to his son, who was in London with his tutor at fairtime in 1685:

> Dear Neddy,
>
> I think it not now so proper to quote you verses out of Persius, or to talk of Caesar and Euclide, as to consider the great theater of Bartholomew Fair, where, I doubt not, but you often resort, and 'twere not amiss if you cou'd convert that tumult into a profitable book. You wou'd certainly see the garboil there to more advantage if Mr. Webster and you wou'd read, or cou'd see acted, the play of Ben Jonson, call'd Bartholomew Fair: for then afterwards going to the spot you wou'd note, if things and humours were the same to-day, as they were fifty years ago, and take pattern of the observations which a man of sense may raise out of matters that seem even ridiculous. Take then with you the impressions of that play, and in addition thereunto, I should think it not amiss if you then got up into some high window, in order to survey the whole pit at once. I fancy then you will say—*Totus mundus agit histrionem,* and you wou'd note into how many various shapes humane nature throws itself, in order to buy cheap, and sell dear, for all is but traffick and commerce, some to give, some to take, and all is by exchange, to make the entertainment compleat.
>
> The main importance of this fair is not so much for merchandize, and supplying what people really want; but as a sort of Bacchanalia, to gratify the multitude in their wandering and irregular thoughts.

It is the whole broad humanist moral tradition that turns the Fair into a theater or a book, but it is Jonson's play that gives point to the metaphor. Neddy is to see the Fair through Jonson's play, and his experiences in the Fair should simply double the experience in the theater: "Take then with you the impressions of that play, and in addition thereunto, I should think it not amiss if you then got up into some high window, in order to survey the whole pit at once." The high window serves as a box in the theater, a half-crown seat. . . . It removes Neddy from harm's way, and provides the necessary distance for reflection. Without this distance—the aesthetic distance of book or theater—the Fair means nothing at all, is simply a "tumult" or "garboil." (Book and theater are now effectively synonymous, and stand together against the Fair.) There is no question of a social relationship with the Fair, or even of direct experience or involvement of any kind. The "man of sense" observes everything, but is never touched.

No one in Jonson's play is allowed to take notes with this much detachment, and we may well regret the loss of Jonson's ferocious engagement. The spirit of festivity has really passed away. Still Southwell realizes the tendencies in Jonson I have been discussing: he is the ideal audience Jonson stipulates in his Induction. He also shares with Jonson a sense of the Fair as a great revelation of the social and moral fabric, and particularly of the false economies supported by human folly. He has faith that moral reflection can encompass the Fair, in all its uniqueness and particularity, and as his letter continues it becomes clear that the attempt to do so was intensely stimulating.

As London grew the Fair grew too, until the Jonsonian humanist moral tradition associated with it was crushed to death, as the commercial fair had been, by the huge press of fair-goers. The literary tradition of the Fair ends with book 7 of *The Prelude,* where it epitomizes everything that is unnatural and inhuman about London. It comes up in Wordsworth's discussion of the relations that the structures the mind builds for itself have with outward things: Bartholomew Fair is his example of

> A work completed to our hands, that lays,
> If any spectacle on earth can do,
> The whole creative powers of man asleep!—
> For once, the Muses' help we will implore,
> And she shall lodge us, wafted on her wings,
> Above the press and danger of the crowd,
> Upon some showman's platform.
>
> (679–85)

The movement out of the crowd—tenser now—onto the showman's platform continues the structure of detached observation; and the point will be, as it is in Jonson and Southwell, the Fair as testing-ground for a special kind of seeing and comprehension—again an elite accomplishment, though now the "man of sense" has been replaced by the man with the Spirit of

Nature upon him. But the structural similarities are less impressive than the changed scene. It is hard to think of Wordsworth as an audience: the isolation of the spectator has deepened past the point where we can place him in any social relationship. Having escaped from the press and danger of the crowd, he becomes a seer, a lonely prophet.

What he sees is not a play but a phantasmagoria:

> What a shock
> For eyes and ears! what anarchy and din,
> Barbarian and infernal—a phantasma,
> Monstrous in colour, motion, shape, sight, sound!
> (685–88)

There are prodigies of all kinds to gaze at, and the masses who have come to gaze; the first are too unreal and the second too anonymous to fashion drama out of. No faces or character types emerge; the theme of a moral economy is obviated by the epistemological problem and an industrial image:

> Tents and Booths
> Meanwhile, as if the whole were one vast mill,
> Are vomiting, receiving, on all sides,
> Men, Women, Three-year's Children, Babes in arms.
> (718–21)

Jonson may have participated in the breakdown of the cohesion of his society, and of the popular theater audience in particular, but that cohesion is still very much with him. He was playing to an audience of the widest possible social range, from the groundlings at the Hope theater (a place "as dirty as Smithfield, and as stinking every whit," as Jonson ungraciously says at the end of the Induction), to the King, before whom the second performance of the play was given; and in the world Jonson represents a surprising number of people already know each other when the play begins. Connectedness was a fact in the social fabric, not just a possibility for the individual mind, as in Wordsworth.

That connectedness is denied and violated in several ways, as we have seen, but it is also reasserted at the end of the play, symbolically and ideologically, by the dinner at Justice Overdo's house to which everyone is invited. The communal feast is of course a central festive symbol and event. The New Comedy convention that ends the play with an offstage feast is highly convenient for Jonson, because it follows naturally from his comic plot, and because it postpones the feast until after the play is over. The feast would be the genuine festive experience, but it is hard to imagine it in the light of the still unresolved (and perhaps unresolvable) divisions the play has opened up. Can Grace really sit down with Ursula? How will Winwife get along with Quarlous, who has just defrauded his fiancée of her inheritance? The postponement confirms what the whole play has indicated, that real social festivity has become a utopian idea—not the utopian reality which is remembered and temporarily realized in Bakhtin's festive marketplace, but a purely symbolic event.

JONATHAN DOLLIMORE

Sejanus: *History and* Realpolitik

S*ejanus,* like *Mustapha,* seeks to represent the mechanisms of state power
and in so doing confronts without resolving the disjunctions between idealist
and realist mimesis, religion and policy, providentialism and *realpolitik.*

HISTORY, FATE, PROVIDENCE

The concluding paragraph of "The Argument" gives to history, politics
and ethics an explicitly providential perspective; essentially, political opposition is represented as "unnatural" to the extent that it deviates from a
divine prescription which happens to ratify the status quo. Even evil princes
are part of the design and therefore not to be challenged.

> This [i.e. the fall of Sejanus] do we advance as a mark of terror
> to all traitors, and treasons; to show how just the heavens are in
> pouring and thundering down a weighty vengeance on their un-
> natural intents, even to the worst princes: much more to those,
> for guard of whose piety and virtue, the angels are in continual
> watch, and God himself miraculously working.

The fact that *Sejanus* was thought seditious when first acted and Jonson
summoned to the Privy Council (and possibly imprisoned) might explain
why this passage was included in the first (1605) Quarto edition of the play,

From *Radical Tragedy: Religion, Ideology and Power in the Drama of Shakespeare
and His Contemporaries.* © 1984 by Jonathan Dollimore. University of Chicago Press
and Harvester Press, 1984.

two years after it was first acted, although left out of the 1616 folio, when presumably it was thought safe to do so. Whether or not "The Argument's" providentialist gloss was dictated by expediency the fact remains that most of act 5 involves a crude attempt to interpret history according to this same providentialist justice.

For plays like *Sejanus* shifts in contemporary historiography are of paramount importance. Machiavelli, Guicciardini, and Raleigh (among others) present history in terms which qualify, problematise and even contradict providentialist explanations. It is their conception of history which realist mimesis draws upon.

Jonson insisted on the importance for art of historical truth and, more specifically, of experience: "Experience, Observation, Sense, Induction, are the fower Tryers of Arts. It is ridiculous to teach any thing for undoubted Truth that Sense, and Experience, can confute" (Preface to *The English Grammar*). So detailed are the historical sources which Jonson provided for *Sejanus* that it has been described as a work of "historical realism," one disclosing as much about Jonson's present as about the past and thereby remaining "one of the most devastating accounts the drama has given us of dictatorship in action."

Historical writing of this kind came specially under the ban of the authorities and its writers ran serious risks; as we saw, Greville felt obliged to destroy one of his plays for fear of reprisals from the state, Shakespeare's *Richard II* was almost certainly exploited for seditious purposes, and, sure enough, *Sejanus* got Jonson in trouble with the Privy Council. Raleigh in the Preface to his *History of the World* expressed the danger in no uncertain terms: "who-so-euer, in writing a moderne Historie, shall follow truth too neare the heeles, it may happily strike out his teeth."

In the earlier acts of *Sejanus* history is presented as radically contingent; political power, not providence is the fundamental determinant:

> TIBERIUS: When the master-prince
>   Of all the world, Sejanus, saith, he fears;
>   Is it not fatal?
> SEJANUS: Yes, to those are feared.
> TIBERIUS: And not to him?
> SEJANUS: Not, if he wisely turn
>   That part of fate he holdeth, first on them.
> TIBERIUS: That nature, blood, and laws of kind forbid.
> SEJANUS: Do policy, and state forbid it?

TIBERIUS: No.

SEJANUS: The rest of poor respects, then, let go by:
            State is enough to make th'act just, them guilty.
                                              (2.165–73)

Thus speak the two most powerful men in Rome. Especially interesting is
the way that Sejanus conceives of "fate" as almost synonymous with
"power"; more generally, both Sejanus's amoral self-assertiveness and the
extent of its deviation from the moral norm—"the rest of poor respects"—
are sharply focussed in the semantic changes which "fate" undergoes. Tiberius's use of "fatal" suggests awareness of an extra-human agency to whose
influence even the prince is potentially subject; for Sejanus the prince subjects
fate. Fate is similarly conceived as personal power when at the end of act 1
Sejanus, after having refused to fight with Drusus (who has just struck him)
remarks in soliloquy:

> He that, with such wrong moved, can bear it through
> With patience, and an even mind, knows how
> To turn it back. Wrath, covered, carries fate.
>   (1.576–78)

Two things are happening here: first, stoic "patience" is being appropriated
for *realpolitik,* second—and relatedly—"fate" is made almost synonymous
with purpose (cf. Tiberius's remark to Sejanus: "Dearest head, / To thy most
fortunate design I yield" [3.502]). Sejanus's attitude to fate contrasts strik-
ingly with the fatalism of the virtuous and powerless people in this play; for
them "fate" either signifies the way events transpire (always beyond their
control) or the more or less vaguely conceived extra-human agency responsible for that outcome.

These semantic shifts are a primary manifestation of the underlying
tension in *Sejanus* between a pagan-secularist discourse and a Christian one,
each interrogating the other. In the earlier scenes it is the former which
dominates; even Silius and Arruntius offer a kind of choric commentary
which tacitly acknowledges the primacy of state power:

ARRUNTIUS: O desperate state
            Of grovelling honour! Seest thou this, O sun,
            And do we see thee after? Me thinks, day
            Should lose his light, when men do lose their shames,
            And, for the empty circumstance of life,
            Betray their cause of living.

SILIUS: Nothing so.
Sejanus can repair, if Jove should ruin.
He is now the court-god . . .
He will do more than all the house of heav'n
Can, for a thousand hecatombs. 'Tis he
Makes us our day, or night.
                                    (1.196–207)

Stressed too is the fact that ethical determinants have no external or objective existence; once again power is the sole criterion:

SEJANUS: Sir, you can lose no honour,
By trusting ought to me. The coarsest act
Done to my service, I can so requite,
As all the world shall style it honourable.
                                    (1.326–29)

Similarly, according to Macro, "A prince's power makes all his actions virtue" (3.717). The same relativist challenge lies behind the most subversive statement of Sejanus's *realpolitik:* "'tis place, / Not blood, discerns the noble, and the base" (5.11–12). Nobility, on this estimation, derives not from innate *virtus* but one's place within the power structure. This is the last of Sejanus's several repudiations of hierarchy, and it is made just before providentialist retribution sets in: we see, or are meant to see, Sejanus's *realpolitik* as nothing more than hubristic strutting. In a kind of supernatural melodrama Sejanus's statue belches black smoke and there leaps from it a "monstrous serpent" (5.37); his servants slip over and break their necks while ravens croak.

Sejanus remains sceptical:

What excellent fools
Religion makes of men! Believes Terentius
(If these were dangers, as I shame to think them)
The gods could change the certain course of fate?
                                    (5.69–72)

If the answer is "yes"—and at one level it is clearly meant to be—then fate is firmly relocated within a providential scheme and no longer the open-ended concept undergoing shifting definition in a power struggle which, dramatically disclosed, threatens to subvert that scheme.

Sejanus thus foregrounds a contradiction between the providentialist ratification of power and the demystifying strategies of survival and gain resorted to by those actually holding power; further, it substantiates Felix Raab's identification of such a conflict in Jacobean England: at the beginning of the seventeenth century the same men involved in ruthless struggles for power would also be those who, "in a different context, would defend the power of kings and/or popes in terms of Scripture, the patristic texts and scholastic philosophy. . . . That there was a basic contradiction between this conceptual framework and the world of affairs in which many of its exponents were involved is obvious" (*The English Face of Machiavelli*). In *Sejanus* this is nowhere more apparent than in the disparity between the paragraph from "The Argument" with which I began, and the sentence which immediately precedes it: "at last, when Sejanus least looketh, and is most secure (with pretext of doing him an unwonted honour in the Senate) he [Tiberius] trains him from his guards, and with a long and doubtful letter, in one day, hath him suspected, accused, condemned, and torn in pieces, by the rage of the people."

Of course there were those in the period who openly advocated both policy and a belief in providential design. Thus as early as 1548 we find William, Lord Paget of Beaudesert arguing that only "arte, pollycie and practise must helpe (for these be the meanes in myne opynion) that God will nowe vse for our helpe" (*Camden Miscellany*). This illustrates the way ideology may suppress contradictions but only by incorporating them within itself; if the element of suppression enables the process of ideological legitimation, that of incorporation offers the possibility of it being challenged: it renders the ideology potentially unstable—vulnerable, for instance, to the sceptical interrogation to which it was being subjected in the Jacobean theatre.

JOSEPH LOEWENSTEIN

Echoic Presence and the Theatrical Court: Cynthia's Revels

It remains outside the scope of this essay to perform an exhaustive analysis of *Cynthia's Revels*. But attention to Jonson's use of Ovid's fable of Echo and Narcissus can direct us beyond the play's attack on vanity, its most obvious and amusing, but perhaps least interesting, feature, to what I have called [elsewhere] the formalist tendencies of his mythographic habits. Ovid's fable authorizes a strain of antitheatricality in the play, an antitheatricality that is finally crucial to the theory of masque-making worked out in the play at large. The embodiment of Echo and her partial detachment from the tradition of the moralized Ovid will be seen as a revival of significances of echo found in those antique texts discussed . . . [elsewhere]. Specifically, Jonson's Echo raises the problem of imitation for the first time in his career, a problem that remains central to Jonsonian poetics; here, the treatment of imitation includes its dark twin—plagiarism—making this a matter of more than private concern. The War of the Theaters (only a skirmish, really—the combatants were friends again within about three years) was, for Jonson, the occasion for a public examination of the idea of originality, of poetic and moral authority in the theater; *Cynthia's Revels* is Jonson's defensive strike.

From *Responsive Readings: Versions of Echo in Pastoral, Epic, and the Jonsonian Masque.* © 1984 by Yale University. Yale University Press, 1984.

169

PLOT AND CURSUS IN *CYNTHIA'S REVELS*

. . . this studiously and laboriously erratic design.
                        —SWINBURNE, *A Study of Ben Jonson*

The play was written for the Children of the Chapel, a boys' company
which had been disbanded for sixteen years but which was reconstituted in
1600. *Cynthia's Revels* may have been the first play performed by this new
company, and it is almost certainly the play that the Chapel Children performed as their contribution to the extraordinary season of court revels
arranged for that winter. Elizabeth saw eight plays between Christmas and
Twelfth Night; on Twelfth Night alone, when the Chapel Children made
their court debut, the three major adult companies of London also gave
performances. It was Elizabeth's most lavish revels, a display of flamboyant
magnificence designed to demonstrate her inviolable power in the face of the
slight but persistent popular allegiance to Essex, who was then under house
arrest. In those words of Jonson's Cupid cited in the introduction to these
essays:

> The Huntresse, and Queene of these groves, DIANA (in regard of
> some black and envious slanders hourely breath'd against her, for
> her divine justice on ACTEON, as shee pretends) hath here in the
> vale of *Gargaphy,* proclaim'd a solemne revells . . . in which time,
> it shall bee lawfull for all sorts of ingenuous persons, to visit her
> palace, to court her NYMPHES, to exercise all varietie of generous
> and noble pastimes, as well to intimate how farre shee treads such
> malicious imputations beneath her, as also to shew how cleere
> her beauties are from the least wrinckle of austerity, they may be
> charg'd with.
>
> (1.1.91–95, 97–103)

Jonson, of course, colludes in Elizabeth's own theatricality. The Essex rebellion was being represented as mere willful aristocratic irregularity, not a
more profound and widespread dissatisfaction with price inflation, with the
proliferation of monopolies, with the decay of agriculture, and with all the
consequent social dislocations—a dissatisfaction that was beginning to receive perfectly lawful articulation in the House of Commons. Jonson's contribution was thus quite expedient, for its fundamental aim was merely the
critique and reform of aristocratic revelry.

In many ways, this program of reform was quite conservative, as was
the fashion of Elizabethan reform. Writing for the Chapel Children, Jonson

chose to reproduce many of the qualities of those plays that had won the
original Chapel Children such favor, the court plays of John Lyly. The reliance
on a mythological frame for the plot, the paring down of plot to leave a
purely paratactic dramaturgy (what Peter Saccio has called "situational dramaturgy") in which multiple exposure of characters and situations replaces
development, the final transformation of mundane situation by theophany—
all these point to particular Lylyan influence. Yet to speak of influence may
distort the matter, since the evocation of Lylyan dramaturgy is polemical. It
declares the return of the Chapel Children to the glories of their old manner
and advertises Jonson's abilities in this most acceptable mode. For political
reasons, Lyly himself was out of favor and, by 1597, had lost hopes of
reversion of the Mastership of the Revels to Sir George Buck, whose claim
on the office had also languished somewhat. Some lines in Dekker's *Satiromastix* suggest that Jonson aspired (or was suspected of aspiring) to this
post; much that was new to the Jonsonian manner in *Cynthia's Revels* be-
speaks just this sort of pretension. And yet there was much in Lyly that was
easy for Jonson to adapt, for Jonson's earliest plots (as indeed many of his
later plots) depend on a similar parataxis, on the juxtaposition of loosely
connected scenes, on discrete character groupings in which individual behavior intensifies without any sign of trasformation. In *Cynthia's Revels*,
Echo's cursing of the Fountain of Self-Love is followed by the moment when
Amorphus drinks the waters; Amorphus purveys these waters to the court—
but this line of plot is utterly fractured. Echo's curse comes in 1.2.; Amorphus drinks in 1.3.; in 2.5., the various court pages (another Lylyan touch)
go off as "yeomen of the bottles" in an antic procession to the fountain; in
4.1., the foolish ladies of the court are seen awaiting the return of the pages;
the water arrives in 4.4. And this description of the fractured line suggests
an even greater focus on the waters than the play actually maintains: the
references to this plot in 4.1., for example, occupy only the very first lines
of the scene, providing only a pretext for the ladies' assembly on the stage.
Finally, this unsophisticated sequence of actions has virtually no effect on
the social behavior and organization of the theatrical court. Rather, it provides a frame for an elementary education in courtiership (Amorphus in-
structing Asotus), advanced classes in courtiership (Hedon and Anaides
engaged in mutual instruction), and the frolics of Moria and her train. Jonson
provides very little teleological promise for the play; instead of plot we have
a concatenation of shows, filling but not shaping an interim. This is the first
of Jonson's plays to abjure the intermingling of prose and verse within the
same scene, and this technical choice emphasizes the dislocations of each

discrete shows requires a magical breach of the play's own conventions, depending upon a theophany.

One of the chief features of Lylyan drama, of course, is the use of mythological plots, usually from Ovid. Again Jonson follows the master: his Echo is explicitly that of the Ovidian story—Jonson would seem to be the first European playwright to employ just this Echo—and the Echo thus evoked is specifically a pathetic one. I have shown [elsewhere] how the antique etiologies of echo inscribe pathos upon the inhuman voice of nature, and although Jonson's scene feints toward a release of Echo from pathos into autonomy, "enricht with vocall, and articulate power" (1.2.11), it concludes by reenacting her loss of self-possession. In Ovid's tale, Echo interests herself in the scene of Narcissus's demise, interests herself even to the point of self-abnegation; here in *Cynthia's Revels* her recovery of independence is almost complete (though her speech remains bound to antecedent discourse by anadiplosis). But the recovery is brief and she soon flees to her traditional theatrical place offstage. So the scene reenacts that aspect of the Ovidian tale which works as an etiology of pathetically passive and marginal expression.

Perhaps this reenacted etiology of the marginal is what prompted G. K. Hunter's observation that "Echo is seen as the type of the clear-eyed and eloquent scholar-satirist, condemned to be only a voice, and for most of the time a voice disregarded by those who hear her"—in effect a suggestion that Echo, as well as Crites, speaks for Jonson [*John Lyly*]. Hunter suggests, that is, that the scene provides a poignant opening of a theme of critical marginality that is the play's most pervasive autobiographical element. But by granting Echo new freedom of speech, Jonson does more than fulfill his own wish to be heard; he also enables her to generate that thready plot which is the play's only sign of narrative coherence. She gains this power at some cost in dignity, for Mercury recognizes that her curse on the fountain is partly motivated by anger at the Cynthian vengeance wrought there:

> Fond ECCHO, thou prophan'st the grace is done thee:
> So idle worldings (meerely made of voice)
> Censure the powers above them.
>
> (1.2.93–95)

Having turned her opportunity for plaint against vengeance into her own reactive vengeance, Echo charts the potential pitfalls of transporting the techniques of comical satire into the practice of court dramaturgy.

Both the Echo-scene and the disguise of Cupid and Mercury strip the normal pattern of Lylyan theophany of its ethical power and purity. Cupid and Mercury seem to revel in the "privileges" of their subordination: as Mercury puts it, "O, what a masse of benefit shall we possess, in being the invisible spectators of this strange shew, now to be acted." They continue spectators throughout; even after Cupid's fullest moment of dramatic participation (in 5.7., when he takes a part in the first of Crites' masques for Cynthia), he quickly returns to join Mercury as viewer:

> *The Maskes joyne, and they dance.*
> CUP. IS not that AMORPHUS, the travailer?
> MER. As though it were not! doe you not see how his legs are in
> travaile with a measure?
> CUP. HEDON, thy master, is next.
> MER. What, will CUPID turne *nomenclator*, and cry them?
> (5.10.1–6)

This has indeed been their function throughout the play, to observe and describe, pronouncing expanded versions of the character writing with which Jonson had augmented the list of dramatis personae of *Every Man Out*, published during the preceding year. This function is most obtrusive in the second act, where their interventions provide a steady counterpoint through each of its four scenes, displacing action into empirical object. Their distance on the scene is reemphasized at the opening of 2.1., when Mercury advises Cupid, "since wee are turn'd cracks, let's studie to be like cracks" (ll. 4–5). The word becomes their favorite term for their new status, a slightly unusual bit of slang and one that the child actors of the induction are also fond of applying to each other; the term ties the speech of these gods to the extra-fabulous discourse of the Induction.

But Cupid and Mercury share the "benefit" of spectatorship and commentary with others. The scholar, Crites, is similarly marginal and, though less enthusiastic a spectator, similarly satiric. He passes an entire scene (3.4.) describing the multitude of theatrical fools who make up the "outer" court of Cynthia: "I have seene (most honour'd ARETE,) / The strangest pageant, fashion'd like a court, / (At least I dream't I saw it)" (3–5). This is, of course, part of an extended critique of the significance or value of appearance, a critique worked out in the character grouping of Anaides and Hedon as a satire on ostentatious costume (whether of body or of phrase), in the Amorphus-Asotus group as a satire on gesture, and in the Morian group as a somewhat diffuse attack on the arts of feminine appearance (as when Philautia recapitulates Narcissan crime by swearing by her own image in a glass). The critique occasionally strikes off subtler hits, as when Amorphus makes Asotus the horribly paltry gift of his own hat—"it is a relique I could not so easily have departed with, but as the *hieroglyphicke* of my affection; you shall alter it to what forme you please, it will take any blocke" (1.4.183–86)—and in so doing submits not only his own mutability to ridicule but also the contemporary idealization of "natural" or "necessary" signification, that ultimate overestimation of appearance manifest in the vogue of hieroglyphics. Yet Jonson is clearly interested in more than a mere attack on vanity, for he has read Ovid closely. The form of vice in Jonson's Gargaphie is held close to the form of transgression in Ovid's—the overestimation of the visual.

Crites takes his station as observer far less lightly than do Cupid and Mercury:

> I suffer for their guilt now, and my soule
> (Like one that lookes on ill-affected eyes)
> Is hurt with meere intention on their follies.
> Why will I view them then? my sense might aske me

The question opens a full range of questions about the ethics of gaze; perhaps Jonson's most Shakespearean verse, Crites' speech now takes on much of Hamlet's style:

> Or ist a raritie, or some new object,
> That straines my strict observance to this point?
> My spirit should draw a little neere to theirs,
> To gaze on novelties: so vice were one.

His reasoning then swerves wildly; ceasing to accuse his hungry eyes, he makes blindness first the sign and then the instrument of complete habituation to vice:

> Tut, she is stale, ranke, foule, and were it not
> That those (that woo her) greet her with lockt eyes,
> (In spight of all the impostures, paintings, drugs,
> Which her bawd costome dawbes her cheekes withall)
> Shee would betray, her loth'd and leprous face,
> And fright th'enamor'd dotards from themselves:
> But such is the perversenesse of our nature,
> That if we once but fancie levitie,
> (How antike and ridiculous so ere
> It sute with us) yet will our muffled thought
> Choose rather not to see it, then avoide it

The blindness of the vicious finally shifts to vice's self-delusion of invisibility—it is the child's oddly theatrical magic trick of covering the eyes and crying, "You can't see me":

> And if we can but banish our owne sense,
> We act our mimicke trickes with that free licence,
> That lust, that pleasure, that securitie,
> As if we practiz'd in a paste-boord case,
> And no one saw the motion, but the motion.
>
> (1.5.40–64)

Crites receives no correction in this play, is indeed one of the play's three moral authorities, yet the fascinating and subtle hysteria that laces through the imperious accusations of this speech seriously threaten that authority. To see is to be culpable; to be blind and then to believe oneself unseen is to be culpable: the vagaries of the argument are largely resistant to generalization, save that the argument manifests a pervasive ambivalence to the spectacular that endows vision and visibility with confused, but extreme, ethical import. When Dekker comes to Marston's aid in "the untrussing of the humorous poet," he reacts to more than the presumption to moral authority which Jonson makes in the person(s) of "Asper, Criticus, Quintus Horatius Flaccus"; Dekker's assault challenges the *conjunction* of Jonson's critical presumption with his manifest ambivalence to using spectacle as an instrument of criticism.

What distinguishes Jonson from his own critics is his eagerness to encounter methodological problems in the new practice of satiric comedy; in *Cynthia's Revels* Jonson tests the practice by subjecting spectatorship itself to spectacular treatment. The final device of the play, the Lylyan theophany of Cynthia, in some way abrogates this test, for it presents itself as an ideal spectacle for a fully redeemed spectatorship. Yet when Crites introduces the famous Hesperian hymn to Cynthia, "*Queene,* and *Huntresse,* chaste, and faire," with the words,

> Now thrive invention in this glorious court,
> That not of bountie only, but of right,
> CYNTHIA may grace, and give it life by sight.
>
> (5.5.70–72)

it is clear that the complex effects of gaze have not been simplified, for whether life is granted by the appearance or by the gaze of Cynthia remains unresolved here. Perhaps not ethically unresolved, of course, for as Cynthia herself observes,

> To men, this argument should stand for firme,
> "A Goddesse did it, therefore it was good:
> "We are not cruell, nor delight in bloud."

Yet this redemption of the spectacular from ethical ambiguity leaves a nagging question—

> But what have serious repetitions
> [theophany, masque; properly imitative creations]
> To doe with revels, and the sports of court?

This hardly resolves the ethical problematics of satiric comedy, proposing, as it does, an alternative form of purer type. The question may or may not be a "rhetorical" one, may be a statement of absolute disjunction between comedy and masque, or may be a legitimate inquiry into whether their continuity be possible. Intended for performance in the "private" theater and at court, *Cynthia's Revels* surely means the question in both ways, registering Jonson's discomfort with the lower spectacularity of comedy and questioning his own ability to extend himself successfully into a realm of higher spectacularity. And Jonson worries here about more than mere success, for into this play he imports the anthropologist's great problem of what constitutes the critical authority of the observer. Nearly all of Jonson's observers are somehow compromised—Mercury and Cupid because of their simultaneous participation in the scene of vice and their program to further corrupt Cynthia's court by afflicting it with amorous heat, Crites because of his visual taint neuroses, Echo because her rise to power over the scene of Gargaphie grows impassioned and augments the prevailing narcissism of the court. And as we shall see, even Cynthia's power is somewhat circumscribed by the follies of her train. Thus we can say that Jonson here not only anticipates a career of masque-making (perhaps even making a bid for the position of Master of the Revels) but also gives subtle inflection to those tragic studies in the observer's marginality which can be found in *Hamlet* and in the malcontent plays that follow from it.

Jonson shares an arresting foresight with his more honored peers, Spenser and Milton: the early work of all three poets gazes steadily toward the later products. Milton and Spenser rely, of course, on the traditional cursus of the Virgilian career, so that the *Shepheardes Calender* and "Lycidas" employ a traditional paradigm to render articulate and prophetic the youthful voices of their poets. Jonson, on the other hand, was doomed to exclusion from that traditional career, forced by social and economic pressure to make a living in the theater or remain a bricklayer—and there is no *cursus Terentii* to give inevitability to a playwright's progress. If we find in an early play, like *Cynthia's Revels,* the projection of later poetic activity, we cannot properly invoke the mysterious and implicitly typological vocabulary of foreshadowing. Almost nothing in *Cynthia's Revels* has the twilight charm of "Tomorrow to fresh fields and pastures new" (a charm at odds with the tripping fiction of the line's surface), precisely because Jonsonian anticipation is analytic and deliberate, an effortful construction.

CUPID'S COMEDY

> ATTICUS: *Come, let passe, let passe, let's see what stuffe must*
> *cloath our eares: what's the plaies name?*
> PHYLOMUSE: What You Will.
> DORICUS: Ist Commedy, Tragedy, Pastorall, Morall, Nocturnal, *or*
> Historie?
>
> —JOHN MARSTON, *What You Will*

The later, folio version of *Cynthia's Revels* (1616) offers special evidence that the pattern of the play is intended both as a plan for the masques and as a cursus. Jonson expanded the fifth act to include what Amorphus repeatedly calls a public "Act" or "Action," a competition at courtiership. Both Mercury and Crites participate as actors in these "sports of court," beating their opponents at their own games. This extended fifth act fits perfectly the clearer pattern, not of Lylyan court drama, but of Jonsonian masque—by the time the folio copy text went to the printer, Jonson had devised about a dozen masques and entertainments, and the form had achieved considerable stability—the interpolated courtly "duello" functioning as antimasque, the descent of Cynthia working as transformation scene, Crites' device taking the place of the masque proper. As deviser, Crites is redeemed from the actor's trade to which he had descended early in the act. His recovered status as spectator carries hitherto unavailable power: he is granted executive powers to match his critical ones, becoming master of Cynthia's Revels, not commentator on Moria's.

Thus the folio text traces a generic career. The diffuse comedy of the first four acts modulates to the patterned but vicious antimasque that opens the fifth act of the published version, finally unfolding into the masque of the concluding scenes. The original version of the play traces this same shift in genre (though without the antic composure of the antimasque, an aspect of the Jonsonian masque that developed only slowly and that *Cynthia's Revels* did not, in its original form, preconceive), but it traces the shift less as a simple progress from comedy *to* masque than as a disabling of comedy *by* masque. In the penultimate scene, Cupid sets about his business proper, brandishing his arrows "upon—it makes no matter which of the couples. PHANTASTE, and AMORPHUS, at you" (24–26; he does not actually shoot, fearing lest "CYNTHIA heare the twang of my bow," (22–23). This action has been long deferred, purposed in the play's first scene but suspended by the dissolution of plot into "strange shows." Cynthia's descent restores the possibility of teleological structure: it begins the action anew. Cupid now takes up arms, but nothing happens:

> CUPID. What prodigie is this? no word of love? no mention? no
>   motion?
> MERCURY. Not a word, my little *Ignis fatue,* not a word.
> CUPID. Are my darts inchaunted! Is their vigour gone? is their
>   vertue—
> MERCURY. What? CUPID turn'd jealous of himselfe? ha, ha, ha.
> CUPID. Laughs MERCURY?
> MERCURY. Is CUPID angrie?
> CUPID. Hath he not cause, when his purpose is so deluded?
> MERCURY. A rare *comoedie,* it shall be intitled, CUPIDS.
>
> (5.10.55–65)

The means by which Cupid's arrows have been enchanted are manifold. Crites cannot be wounded as he is already enamored of virtue, Arete, "whose favour makes any one shot-proofe" (110); those courtiers who have drunk of the Fountain of Self-Love are equally impervious.

There is another overarching cause for the impotence of Cupid's arrows: this larger cause is a transcendental version of the play's prevailing delusion, that clothes make the man. Mercury admonishes Cupid:

> Faith, it was ominous to take the name of ANTEROS upon you, you know not what charme or inchantment lies in the word: you saw, I durst not venter upon any device, in our presentment, but was content to be no other than a simple page. Your arrowes properties (to keepe *decorum*) CUPID, are suted (it should seeme) to the nature of him you personate.
>
> (ll. 84–90)

This radical principle of decorum provides that the theatrical signifier (name, costume) have absolute power over agency—the name has a certain preeminence here, as we should expect from Jonson—as the masque-self disables or sublimates the self of "the sports of court."

The double cause of Cupid's comedy—the masque's principle of decorum and the homeopathic protection of the fountain—is part of a larger pattern in the play, a pattern of generic rivalry between masque (*Cynthia's Revels*) and satire (*The Fountayne of Selfe-Love*). But the double cause is also sign of another pattern: throughout the play, moral restraint is conceived of as *multiple*. When, for example, Crites expresses doubts in his own capacity to make such a cast "dance truely in a measure" (5.5.8), Arete reassures him that

> What could never in it selfe agree,
> Forgetteth the *eccentrike* propertie,
> And at her sight, turnes forth-with regular,
> Whose scepter guides the flowing *Ocean*.

(a transcendental, extrinsic moral authority)

> And though it did not, yet the most of them
> (Being either courtiers, or not wholly rude)
> Respect of majestie, the place, and presence,
> Will keepe them within ring; especially
> When they are not presented as themselves,
> But masqu'd like others. For (in troth) not so
> T'incorporate them, could be nothing else,
> Then like a state ungovern'd, without lawes.
>
>   (19–30)

(A principle or principles of decorum again; a moral authority intrinsic to courtiership and, finally, to masquing.) The courtiers will be restrained by Cynthian magic, by courtly habit, and by the fidelity of substance to semblance: the second is an ethical power vested in the state, the last an ethical power devolving, by tradition, upon the artist; that power is analogous to, but independent of, the mystique of the state.

All this suggests grounds for rethinking the conventional appraisal of Jonsonian ethics, for though *Cynthia's Revels* shows the ethical vehemence that we are told to expect of Jonson (albeit shading off toward a critically problematic hysteria in the character of Crites), it seldom shows any *single-mindedness* about the sources of ideological authority. And because the sources of ideological authority for play and masque are manifold, the effects of such representations are necessarily manifold. It is thus not mere playfulness that motivates the sly oscillations in Jonson's dedication to *Cynthia's Revels*; rather, this dedication "to the speciall fountaine of manners: The Court" celebrates the variety of those forms of efficacy to which a representation can lay claim:

Thou art a bountifull, and brave spring: and waterest all the noble plants of this *Iland*. In thee, the whole Kingdome dresseth it selfe, and is ambitious to use thee as her glasse. Beware, then, thou render mens figures truly, and teach them no lesse to hate their deformities, then to love their formes. ... It is not pould'ring, perfuming, and every day smelling of the taylor, that converteth to a beautiful object: but a mind, shining through any sute, which needes no false light either of riches, or honors to helpe it. Such shalt thou find some here, even in the raigne of CYNTHIA (a CRITES, and an ARETE.) Now, under thy PHOEBUS, it will be thy province to make more: Except thou desirest to have thy source mixe with the *Spring* of *selfe-Love,* and so wilt draw upon thee as welcome a discovery of thy dayes, as was then made of her nights.

(1–10, 12–23)

This is a rather complex mimetic theory. The court is first conceived of as an originator or model of behavior, but it rapidly loses this ideal, icastic function and takes on the responsibility for what Frye would call a "low mimesis" of the ethical state of the commonwealth, with Jonson's Lords described as a representation of the Commons. And the conclusion of the dedication makes it clear that Jonson's play operates under the same representational theory, providing both model and mirror.

With the subliming of satiric comedy into masque, we are encouraged to think that principles of low mimesis might disappear from the play. Thus, when Cupid completes his "characters" of Moria and her train, Mercury asks, "Are these (CUPID) the starres of CYNTHIAS court? doe these *Nymphs* attend upon DIANA?" The eccentric critic responds:

They are in her court (MERCURIE) but not as starres, these never come in the presence of CYNTHIA. The *Nymphs* that make her traine, are the divine ARETE, TIMÈ, PHRONESIS, THAUMA, and others of that high sort. These are privately brought in by MORIA in this licentious time, against her knowledge: and (like so many meteors) will vanish, when shee appeares.

(2.4.105–11)

The plots of Jonson's masques, shadowed in this passage, are primarily plots of replacement, not of struggle, preserving the tendency toward parataxis in *Cynthia's Revels*. But in this early play, the struggle with the vice of spectacle is permitted to contaminate the concluding masque, and the power of Cynthia over love is shared out with the comic power of self-love. The play perpetually hedges its claims to what Saccio calls "anagogic form," the sudden supersession of the mundane by the transcendental. Thus we should interpret Cupid's prophetic history of the Morian regime carefully. When he speaks of her troop as brought in "against" Cynthia's knowledge, Jonson is, I think, being deliberately ambiguous. They are brought in secretly in order to evade a Cynthian notice that would automatically deprive them of their power; they are also brought in to oppose her, licentious folly battling against chaste knowledge. The play sustains itself both on a plot of replacement and on a plot of conflict.

The restraint of full anagogy marks even the play's most radiant moment with deft melancholy. In what may be Jonson's most famous lyric, Hesperus heralds that moment, calling for the descent of Cynthia:

> *Queene,* and *Huntresse,* chaste, and faire,
> Now the *Sunne* is laid to sleepe,
> Seated, in thy silver chaire,
> State in wonted manner keepe:
>   HESPERUS intreats thy light,
>   Goddesse, excellently bright.
>
> (5.6.1–6)

This is the play's most grave transition—though it is never quite complete—enacting the passage from day to night, the transfer of dramatic centrality from vice to virtue, and a shift into the lyrical mode even more extreme, perhaps, than that which begins the final act of *The Merchant of Venice.* The song finally insists on the sudden entry of the powers of nature into what has been a riot of culture at its most debased and enervated.

Yet the potent natural order here invoked is immediately entreated to slightly unnatural manifestation. In the next stanza Hesperus calls for what must occasionally involve a suspension of Cynthia's wonted manner:

> Earth, let not thy envious shade
> Dare it selfe to interpose;
> CYNTHIAS shining orb was made
> Heaven to cleere, when day did close:
>   Blesse us then with wished sight,
>   Goddesse, excellently bright.
>
> (7–12)

Part of the charm here lies in the uncertainty that must hover around the stanza. Is the cessation of the earth's envy to be taken as apocalyptic or as a merely natural occurrence, one stage in the cycle that is the "wonted manner" of the earth? The careful emphasis placed on the earth's penumbra in changing the moon's *appearance* preserves a sense of Cynthia's essentially inviolate nature, her transcendence, but that very particular emphasis on natural causality rescinds some of the unqualified epiphanic force of the first stanza. Permanent luminousness cannot finally be manifest; envisioned, it is only momentary:

> Lay thy bow of pearle apart,
> And thy cristall-shining quiver;
> Give unto the flying hart
> Space to breathe, how short soever
>   (13–16)

The shining is conceived as a brief arrest in a wonted hunt; the promise of pure arrest is finally excluded.

Echo's appearance anticipates this restraint of Cynthian power, for like Cynthia's her appearance and power are temporary. The echo-scene bears on later scenes in other ways as well. I have already discussed the marginal pathos of Echo, a pathos that contributes to Jonson's continuing analysis of spectacle and objectifies the uncertainties of his career; I have also mentioned her emblematic control over a thready satiric plot, a plot only partly suspended by Hesperus's song and Cynthia's descent. Yet the most unsettling aspect of the echo-scene remains to be confronted: despite the thematic and narrative bonds that join it to the rest of the play, the scene possesses a remarkable detachment. As Salomon Pavy describes it in the induction, the scene threatens to slip all ties to the succeeding shows:

> MERCURY, he (in the nature of a conjurer) raises up ECCHO, who
> weepes over her love, or Daffodill, NARCISSUS, a little; sings;
> curses the spring wherein the prettie foolish gentleman melted
> himself away: and ther's an end of her.
>
>   (49–54)

This separation of the scene heightens as it isolates. Though Echo's pettish blasphemy against Cynthia joins the scene to what follows, the tonal quality of the scene, its soft pathos, particularly distinguishes it. Her song, "Slow, slow, fresh fount," with its melancholy moralizing ("our beauties are not ours"; 1.2.71) and its motif of melting and dissolution, emphasizes her own tenuous substantiality; her plea to Mercury, "Suffer my thirstie eye to gaze a while, / But e'ene to taste the place, and I am vanisht," and his counteroffer, "Foregoe thy use, and libertie of tongue, / And thou maist dwell on earth, and sport thee there" (78–81), suggest that without special and mercurial intervention, voice and even the most furtive presence must remain mutually exclusive for her. To a very great extent, these, and Amorphus's boorish pursuit of the nymph as she flies the scene, efface her own verbal crime against Cynthia, helping to detach her from blame for complicity in the satiric plot; they loosen her bondage to moral allegory, preserving her as an isolate object of pity.

The complexity here may derive from a Jonsonian effort to juggle the two fables of Echo, the story of her love for Narcissus and the story of Pan's love for her. The first story was heavily moralized in the handbooks Jonson consulted; the second story, having been recovered to the literate community only lately, had received fresher, less tropological interpretations at the hands of Renaissance exegetes. In the *Dictionarium Historicum* of Charles Estienne (Paris, 1553), one of Jonson's favorite postclassical authorities on antiquities and the chief source for the mythography of *Cynthia's Revels,* the two tales may be found in adjacent entries. In the one, Echo signifies "iactantiam, haec spreta mutatur in sonum, hoc est, in rem inanem" (boasting which, once scorned, is transformed into sound, that is, into a nullity; sig. Bb_1r); in the other, "[Echo] physice coeli harmoniam significare dicitur, Solis amicam, tanquam domini [these are two referents of the fictive Pan], & moderatoris omnium corporum coelestium, ex quibus ipsa componitur atque temperatur" (the physical significance of Echo is said to be the harmony of the heavens. She is the mistress of the Sun, as Lord and Master of all the celestial bodies, of which this harmony is composed and tempered). The two interpretations—entering the play as stated blasphemy and demonstrated harmony—are not fully reconciled, which may help to explain both the uncertain import of the scene and the tonal privilege conferred upon it.

YET NOT PERPLEX MEN, UNTO GAZE: COURT MARGINALIA II

Despite his many debts—to Lyly, Peele, and Gascoigne; to the early English character writers; to Erasmus; to Ovid, Lucian, Martial, and Seneca—Jonson claimed real novelty for the play and hoped to found a new stage in his own career on its inventiveness:

> In this alone, his MUSE her sweetnesse hath,
> Shee shunnes the print of any beaten path;
> And proves new wayes to come to learned eares.
> (Prologue, 9–11)

It does not surprise us to find hearing designated as the discriminating sense here in the prologue; in the preceding induction, the children perform for "auditors" or for an "auditorie"—Jonson indulges in his own quirky flattery by reserving the term *spectator* for those who engage in a potentially culpable form of attention. He promises "words, above action," which would make the play's intended mode of existence extraspectacular, and oddly, this promise includes so full a reification of speech that (unlike the Kenilworth entertainments) to some extent it also shuns print. The virtue that Jonson claims for the play does not reside solely in this acoustic moment—he further promises "matter, above words" (Prologue, 20)—but the acoustic moment is secured as both median and mediator between scene and sense.

The privilege here conferred on sound, which records so much of Jonson's suspicion of the stage, continued through much of his career. In the *Discoveries* (first published in the 1640 folio), he generalizes from his own uneasy disposition when he remarks that "wee *praise* the things wee heare, with much more willingnesse, then those wee see." When Mercury reinstitutes the Macrobian Echo, figure for *harmonia coeli,* by calling for airy concert with her song, the harmonies provide an alternative to the spectacular world that Amorphus carries with him and that can never properly transcend the ethical, as the acoustic can. Echo's music is her chief claim on our sympathy, and it lifts her out of the realm of judgment. Unlike Spenser or Lyly, Jonson endorses an acoustic sublime.

Yet we may still wonder why Echo is betrayed to the spectacular, why she is embodied. In part, the embodiment is proof of the novelty to which Jonson lays claim in his prologue; he braves the challenge of Ausonius's epigram and thus perhaps grows guilty of the play's signal vice—"Vane fictor." Jonson's echo-scene employs theatrical embodiment to figure such contemporary metaphors of cultural history as revival, recovery, and renaissance; as the next essay will show, it is a theatrical figure that Jonson might have learned from Guarini. But unlike Guarini, Jonson gives this master trope of the theater over to ethical critique, questioning whether the embodied past will necesarily lead toward virtue and showing that, granted theatrical presence, the revived Echo stoops to convert her tragically deferred mourning to petty hybris.

Moreover, for perhaps the first time in the Renaissance, Echo again engages that complex of issues accumulating around the Echoes and echoes of Aristophanes, Longus, and Ovid, the problem of literary imitation. And it is the complexity of this problem that finally authorizes the complexity of Jonson's echo-scene.

Her first "free speech" renews a voice constrained for three thousand years:

> His name revives, and lifts me up from earth.
> O, which way shall I first convert my selfe?
> Or in what moode shall I assay to speake?
>
> (1.2.18–20)

Her perplexity figures Jonson's, for Echo, having just recovered from a purely nominal existence, speculates on a problem both psychological and grammatical: the question of mood is the satirist's problem par excellence. Is Juvenal's *saeva indignatio* or Horace's gentler manner more in order? Or, to shift from psychological to grammatical mood, does the moralist in the theater speak indicatives (mirror), jussives (model), or, if this last were possible, imperatives? We can shift still again, from these broader rhetorical questions to more particular issues in practical poetics. What is the proper mode of reviving antique genre and antique tale? How may the modern writer usefully convert prevenient utterance? (And one must, after all, convert the prevenient: the tenor of Echo's complaint against hoarding of beauties extends to literary property, as we shall see shortly.) Flat repetition is seen as bondage in this scene, and Mercury's induction to Echo's appearance, with its allusion to the tragic pressure to achieve mourning, together with Echo's resistance to silencing once the scene is underway, foreground her appetite for this conversion or recreation of self. This conversion is strenuously performed in Echo's every speech; we see her work through repetition to a fully expressive independence of speech as she breaks the bonds of anadiplosis which tie each speech to Mercury's. With each speech she gains anew the power of self-representation.

The theoretical problems of artful imitation receive a particularly grubby reinforcement later in *Cynthia's Revels,* when Anaides tells Hedon how best to mount an attack on Crites. The cherished idea of imitatio intrudes, scornfully represented as plagiarism:

> Ile instruct thee what thou shalt doe . . . . : Approve any thing thou hearest of his, to the receiv'd opinion of it; but if it bee extraordinarie, give it from him to some other, whom thou more particularly affect'st. That's the way to plague him, and he shall never come to defend himselfe. S'lud, Ile give out, all he does is dictated from other men, and sweare it too (if thou'lt ha' mee) and that I know the time, and place where he stole it, though my soule bee guiltie of no such thing.
>
> (3.2.54–63)

Hedon's hostility to Crites is everywhere marked by hysteria; here he is outraged that Crites hasn't noticed him (Anaides will later devise further revenge by encouraging the court to deprive Crites of their gaze). Yet in fact Crites has at least overheard their plot, and he responds with wily aptness: his soliloquy in the next scene is indeed dictated from other men, and the place where he stole it is Seneca's *De Remediis Fortuitorum* (7.1.) when it is not the *De Constantia* (8). The Senecan moral bombast that Jonson so often and so freely drew on throughout his career is here imported not simply for its content but because the appropriation of Seneca can serve as an *example*. The speech demonstrates the difference between the composite surface of courtiership and the imitative integration carried on in wisdom's self-construction. The charges of plagiarism are shown to be irrelevant (or at least that is Jonson's aim), not because Crites has demonstrated his independence from influence, but because he has managed to perform that perfect imitation which is "to make choise of one excellent man above the rest, and so to follow him, till he grow very *Hee*" (*Discoveries*, 2469–70).

The strategem of accusing Crites of plagiarism is the device of courtly bad conscience, as Amorphus's advice on courtiership makes clear. He tells Asotus to acquaint himself with Crites in order to steal his phrases:

> AMORPHUS: A quick nimble memory will lift it away, and, at
> your next publique meale, it is your owne.
> ASOTUS: But I shall never utter it perfectly, sir.
> AMORPHUS: No matter, let it come lame. In ordinary talke you
> shall play it away, as you doe your light crownes at *primero*:
> It will passe.
> ASOTUS: I shall attempt sir.
> AMORPHUS: Doe. It is your shifting age for wit, and I assure you,
> men must bee prudent.
>
> (3.1.43–52)

Phrases become coin in a court economy. Asotus is encouraged, though, to test his own credit as well. "See what your proper GENIUS can performe alone, without adiection of any other MINERVA" (3.5.99–100), says Amorphus on another occasion, but he seems hardly to suggest the test in true earnest, for when a faltering Amorphus resorts to citation from Kyd's *Spanish Tragedy* (following the example of his master), he is applauded: "O, that peece was excellent! if you could picke out more of these *play-particles,* and (as occasion shall salute you) embroider, or damaske your discourse with them, perswade your soule, it would most judiciously commend you" (118–22).

The issue of plagiarism cuts considerably deeper than these slight examples of courtly pretense perhaps suggest. Similar concerns with verbal theft are manifest in the induction, outside the fictive scene of Gargaphie, in the "real" scene of the mere stage. Pavy, hurt that the Author has given the prologue to another actor, decides to "tell all the argument of his play aforehand, and so stale his invention to the auditorie before it come forth" (35–37). He suggests that the audience is oddly obsessed with novelty, a suggestion he soon makes more explicit in his impersonation of a gallant who comes to sit on stage, rails at the company, and then demands to see the playwright "in the general behalfe of this faire societie here" (173):

> They could wish, your *Poets* would leave to bee the promoters of other mens jests, and to way-lay all the stale *apothegmes*, or olde bookes, they can heare of (in print, or otherwise) to farce their *Scenes* withall. That they would not so penuriously gleane wit, from everie laundresse, or hackney-man. . . . They say, the *umbrae,* or ghosts of some three or four playes, departed a dozen yeeres since, have bin seene walking on your stage heere: take heed, boy, if your house bee haunted with such *hobgoblins.*
>
> (176–81, 194–98)

This is the tenor of much of Marston's attack on Jonson in *What You Will* and of Dekker's assaults in *Satiromastix*—that his plays are composites of phrase and of genre, particularly of classical phrase and genre. Marston and Dekker had not yet made such criticism a matter of public record by the time of the queen's Christmastide revels of 1600–01, but these men were Jonson's colleagues; the place of these flytings on originality in the ensuing War of the Theaters suggests that they were aware of Jonson's particular sensitivity to the matter and that they may well have twitted him about his cherished imitatio already, arguing that such matters did not pertain to the theater. But the war established their pertinence.

In any event, *Cynthia's Revels* already manifests some defensiveness about the attractions and dangers of renovation and innovation. Indeed, the play dismisses the spectacular pursuit of perpetual novelty as folly, even while maintaining its claims for its own novelty. Property and nervous pride, then, may explain the considerable detachment of this echo-scene from the atmosphere and action that follows it. This detachment, together with the suppression of the moralizations of Echo, frees the echo-scene to represent a very tenuous materialization of voice, the conversion of poetry into a commodity within a modern theatrical marketplace. More poignantly, the isolation of the scene registers the pathos attendant on the invention of a self constructed out of the words of others.

STANLEY FISH

The Brave Infant of Saguntum:
The Self in Jonson's Verse

In the course of her incisive and powerful study of the rise of professionalism, Magali Sarfatti Larson identifies as one of the chief cognitive supports
of the professional ethos something she calls the "ideology of merit" [*The
Rise of Professionalism*]. By this she means what is to us the very familiar
notion (not to say conviction) that in modern corporate and academic life
one rises by virtue of native ability and demonstrated competence rather
than by the accidents of birth and fortune. Larson labels this notion "ideological" first because it is elaborated in the service of certain well-defined
interests (largely those of the corporate bourgeoisie), and second because it
masks what actually happens when the professional sets out to climb the
ladder of advancement. What the professional tells himself (because he has
been told it by others) is that as an individual, he is "essentially the proprietor
of his own person and capacities, for which he owes nothing to society";
but in fact, as Larson points out, he owes everything to society, including
the self whose independence supposedly enables and underwrites his achievements. That is to say, it is only with reference to the articulation and hier-
archies of a professional bureaucracy that a sense of the self and its worth—
its merit—emerges and becomes measurable. The ladder of advancement is
not only a structural fact; it is a fact that tells the person who occupies a
place on it who he is and what he has accomplished. By providing goals and
aspirations and alternative courses of action, the ladder also provides the

---

From *Representations* no. 7 (Summer 1984). © 1984 by the Regents of the University
of California. University of California Press, 1984.

189

very "means of self-assertion." "Career," Larson declares, "is a pattern of organization of the self"; or to put it another (less aphoristic) way, the self of the professional is constituted and legitimized by the very structures— social and institutional—from which it is supposedly aloof.

In Larson's analysis, professionalism and its contradictions constitute a departure from an earlier aristocratic model in which preferment is a function of a "traditional social hierarchy," and rewards are distributed on the basis of "social privileges" that pre-exist "the entry into practice." She has in mind, of course, the system or network of patronage that has recently become the object of so much scholarly attention; and while she is surely right to contrast that network—where access and mobility are largely determined by class—to the vertical passage offered by the mechanisms of education and training, the two worlds of modern bureaucracy and ancient privilege are alike in at least one respect: they present their inhabitants with the problem of maintaining a sense of individual worth within the confines of a totalizing structure. In the Renaissance as well as in the twentieth century, that problem is known by the word "merit." As Robert Harding has recently observed, theorists of patronage were as concerned as their modern counterparts that preferment be based, insofar as it was possible, on considerations of merit and virtue ["Corruption and Moral Boundaries in the Renaissance"]. To be sure, considerations of birth were themselves part of the "merit calculus"—"it is to be presumed," says one treatise, "that the son of a good father will bear himself heir of his virtues"—and merit, as Harding points out, "was conceived more in terms of innate talents rather than talents acquired by training and education," but still in all, it is clear from the evidence that the distinction between "true desert" and merely political and social preferment was as much in force (albeit in a somewhat different form) as it is today.

The fact that it was in force has an obvious psychological consequence: everyone wants to believe that his rewards have been earned rather than bestowed, and conversely, everyone wants to believe that his ill fortune is a comment not on his abilities, but on the perversity of a corrupt and blinkered system. In a modern bureaucracy it is harder to believe the second, since the system advertises itself as one that responds only to competence and genuine achievement rather than to the accidents of birth, or national or geographic origin. In the world of Renaissance patronage it is harder to believe the first, since every recognition or reward comes tagged with the name of someone who could have very well withheld it and to whom one is obligated in ways that cannot be ignored.

This is especially true of the court poet whose productions almost always

bear on their face the signs of subservience—dedications, occasional celebrations, flatteries, petitions, expressions of gratitude, recordings of debt.
How can someone whose work seems indistinguishable from the network of
patronage maintain a belief in its independence and therefore in the independence of his own worth and virtue? I propose in this essay to ask that
question by taking up the case of Ben Jonson, a poet whose every title would
seem to mark him as a man dependent not only for his sustenance but for
his very identity on the favor and notice of his social superiors. In what
follows I will proceed somewhat indirectly, moving from a revisionary account of Jonson's poetic strategies to an analysis of the relationship between
those strategies and his effort to assert his freedom and dignity in the face
of everything that would seem to preclude them.

Although Ben Jonson's poetry has been characterized as urbane and
polished, much of it is marked by a deliberate and labored awkwardness.
This is especially true of the beginning of a Jonson poem where one often
finds a meditation on the difficulty of beginning, a meditation that will
typically take the form of a succession of false starts after which the poem
stumbles upon its subject, having in the meantime consumed up to a third
of its length in a search for its own direction. Thus, for example, the poem
in praise of Shakespeare spends its first sixteen lines exploring the kinds of
praise it will *not* offer before Jonson declares at line 17, "I therefore will
begin," and even then what follows is a list of the poets to whom Shakespeare
will *not* be compared. In the "Epistle to Katherine, Lady Aubigny" (*The
Forrest*, no. 13) Jonson goes on for twenty lines about the dangers one courts
by praising before he draws himself up to announce "I, madame, am become
your praiser" (21). The opening of the "Epistle to Master John Selden"
(*Underwood*, no. 14) is more abrupt: "I know to whom I write," but although he knows, it is another twenty-nine lines before he hazards a direct
address and says to Selden, "Stand forth my object." In the Cary-Morison
ode (*Underwood*, no. 70) the halt and start of the verse is imitated by a
character—the "brave infant of Saguntum"—who draws back from entering
the world and therefore never manages to enter the poem, although he seems
at first to be its addressee. And in what is perhaps the most complicated
instance of the pattern, "An Elegy on the Lady Jane Paulet" (*Underwood*,
no. 83), Jonson melodramatically portrays himself as unable to recognize the
ghost of the Lady, who then identifies herself and immediately vanishes from
the poem, leaving the poet with the task of writing an inscription for her
tomb, a task he attempts in several aborted ways before resolving to leave

off heraldry and "give her soul a name" (22), a resolution that is immediately
repudiated by a declaration of poetic inability—"I durst not aim at that"
(25)—so that as we reach line 30 of the poem we are being told that its
subject cannot possibly be described.

What I would like to suggest in this essay is that Jonson's habit of
beginning awkwardly is not simply a mannerism but is intimately related to
the project of his poetry, and indeed represents a questioning of that project,
since the issue always seems to be whether or not the poem can do what it
sets out to do. The issue is also whether or not the reader can do what he
is asked to, for quite often the interrupted or delayed beginning of a poem
is part of a double strategy of invitation and exclusion in which the reader
is first invited to enter the poem, and then met, even as he lifts his foot above
the threshold, with a rehearsal of the qualifications for entry, qualifications
which reverse the usual relationship between the poet and a judging audience. Here the salient example is "An Epistle Answering to One That Asked
to Be Sealed of the Tribe of Ben" (*Underwood*, no. 47), where the reader
must stand with his foot poised for seventy-eight lines. But a more manage-
able though equally instructive example is a small, hitherto unremarked-upon
poem in the *Ungathered Verse*.

In Authorem

Thou, that wouldst finde the habit of true passion,
    And see a minde attir'd in perfect straines;
Not wearing moodes, as gallants doe a fashion,
    In these pide times, only to shewe their braines,

Looke here on *Bretons* worke, the master print:
    Where, such perfections to the life doe rise.
If they seeme wry, to such as looke asquint,
    The fault's not in the object, but their eyes.

For, as one comming with a laterall viewe,
    Unto a cunning piece wrought perspective,
Wants facultie to make a censure true:
    So with this Authors Readers will it thrive:

Which being eyed directly, I divine,
His proofe their praise, will meete, as in this line.
                            Ben: Johnson.

The tension that finally structures this poem at every level surfaces in
the very first line in the word "habit" which means both "characteristic

form" and "outward apparel." The tension lies in the claims implicitly made by the two meanings. The claim of one is to be presenting the thing itself while the claim of the other is limited to the presentation of a surface, and since that surface is a covering there is a suggestion (borne out by the examples of use listed in the *OED*) that what covers also hides and conceals. The uneasy relationship between the two meanings is brought out by the phrase "true passion." Can we truly see true passion if what we see is its habit? The question is not answered but posed again in line 2. Can a mind perfectly seen also be "attir'd?" Is the perfection we are asked to admire the perfection of the mind or of the dress that adorns it and therefore stands between it and our line of vision? The ambiguity of "habit" reappears in "straines" which, in addition to being an obvious reference to Breton's verse, carries the secondary meaning of pedigree or lineage. Is the perfect strain a perfect verbal rendering, i.e., a representation, or is it a perfect progeny, the direct offspring of the truth and therefore a piece of the truth itself?

As one proceeds through the first stanza, these questions are not insistent, in part because the poem's syntax has not yet stabilized. This syntactical hesitation is, as we shall see, typical of Jonson's poetry and allows him to keep alive options that will later converge in a single but complex sense. Thus, for example, it is unclear whether lines 3 and 4 are in apposition to "minde," and therefore descriptive of what the reader can expect to find, or in apposition to "Thou" (1) and therefore descriptive of the reader, who is required to do the finding. What is clear is that the description is negative, characterizing something or someone that does not show itself in modes or colors or even wit ("braines"). It is therefore with a particular sense of challenge that the second stanza issues its imperative "Look here!" Look where, one might ask, or at what, since we know that it cannot be at variegated surfaces or eye-catching fashions. The only instruction we receive is to look at "such perfections," but these perfections, whatever they are, have not been given any palpable or visible form; and almost as if to forestall a complaint that we have been assigned an insufficiently explicit task, Jonson delivers a pronouncement on those who find themselves unable to perform it: "If they seeme wry, to such as look asquint, / The fault's not in the object, but their eyes."

It is at this point that the relationship between the object (so carefully unspecified) and the reader's eyes becomes the poem's focus and its real subject. In the third stanza the requirements for right vision are forthrightly presented in a simile that is as complicating as it is illuminating. Perspective is a device by which one produces in art the same visual effects that are produced without artifice in nature. It is the manipulation of surface in order to produce the illusion of depth; it is the practice of deception in order to disclose the real; and it therefore, as Ernest Gilman has observed, "bestows a double role" on the artist "as truth-teller and liar, and on the viewer as either ideal perceiver or dupe" [*The Curious Perspective*]. The paradox of perspective—its "cunning" is designed to neutralize the deficiencies of its own medium—is the paradox already hinted at in the doubleness of "habit," "straines," and "shewe." Is what is shown a revelation or is it an interposition—a *"mere shew"*—that puts true revelation at even a further remove? Does Breton's work give its reader a sight of "true passion" or does it stand between that sight and his deceived eye? Are the "perfections" that seemingly "rise to the life" (always the tainted claim of illusionistic art) the perfections of appearance only? Such questions are not answered but given a particularly pointed form by the simile's argument, which contrasts the distortion that attends a "laterall" or sideways view with the view of a spectator who is correctly positioned. But that position has itself been forced upon him by the laws of perspective and by the manipulative strategy of the artist who deploys them. From within those laws and that strategy, the observer's judgment may indeed be "true" (11), but is it true to what really is, or true only to the constructed reality imposed on him by artifice?

In imitation of Jonson, I have deliberately withheld the context (or perspective) in which these questions receive an answer, the context of the court masque, a perspectival form at whose center is the figure of the monarch, at once audience and subject. In the theater presided over by Jonson and Inigo Jones, the king's chair occupies the only point in the hall from which the perspective is true. He is therefore not only the chief observer; he is what is being observed both by the masquers who direct their actions at him, and by the other spectators who must strive to see the presentation from his position if they are to "make a censure true." Moreover, since the masque is itself a celebration of the king's virtue, what he watches is himself, and insofar as his courtiers, in their efforts to align their visions with his, reproduce the relationship courtiers always have to a monarch, they are also at once the observers of an action and the performers of what they observe. One can no longer say then that the spectators are taken in or deceived by a contrived illusion, for they are themselves the cause of what they see, and in order to make a "censure true" they need only recognize themselves. There is no distance between them and a spectacle or representation of which they are the informing idea. The relationship between viewer and presentation is not one of subjection and control, but of identity; they are, in essence, the same, and because they are the same the court saw in the masque "not an imitation of itself, but its true self."

It is here in the notion of an observer who is both indistinguishable from what he sees and its cause that the ethical and epistemological dilemmas of representation are resolved or at least bypassed, and it is that notion which informs the concluding lines of stanza 3: "So with this Authors Readers will it thrive." Of course this line bears a perfectly reasonable sense as the conclusion to the simile's argument: the readers of Breton's work will judge it correctly to the extent that their line of vision is direct rather than oblique. But in the context of the masque experience, to which the entire simile has reference, a truly direct vision is the consequence of having recognized oneself and therefore of having become the reader of one's own actions—having become, in short, an author-reader. The composite noun which appears exactly in the center of Jonson's line is an answer (plainly there for all who have the eyes to see) to all the questions the poem implicitly raises. Insofar as the problem of the poem has been to find a position from which a reader of Breton's work can correctly judge it ("make a censure true"), that problem is solved by the assumption of an author-reader; that is, of a reader whose mind is attired with the same perfections as the mind informing the book. Judgment for such a reader will not even be an issue, since the act of judging implies a distance or a gap that has already been bridged by the identity, the sameness, of the censuring mind and its object. In this felicitous epistemology, perception is not mediated or "asquint" because it is *self*-perception; there is no obstruction between the eye and its object because there is literally nothing (no thing) between them. The dilemma of representation—its inability to be transparent, to refrain from clothing or covering—is no longer felt because representation is bypassed in favor of the instantaneous recognition, in another and in the work of another, of what one already is.

To solve the poem's problem in this way, however, is only to make the poem itself a problem, along with Breton's work. What exactly is their status? If what the fit reader would see in Breton's work is already in his mind, while others simply "want facultie," what is there left for the work to do? What *could* it do? And insofar as these questions apply to Breton, so do they apply equally to Jonson, who is as much "this author" as anyone else, and is certainly *this* author in relation to *this* poem. Isn't its work as superfluous as the work it purports to praise? Isn't its reader, its author-reader, directed to look at something he already is? All of these questions are rendered urgent by the first word of the concluding couplet, "Which," a word that is itself a question: "Which"? To what does it refer? The only possible candidate in the third stanza is the "cunning piece wrought perspective" of line 10, but it can hardly be that which is to be "eyed directly," since the noun-phrase is part of a simile, of an indirect or lateral approach, and is therefore by definition at a remove from direct perception. No matter how far back one goes in the poem, a satisfactory referent for "which" will not be found; *which* is just the point. The pronoun that stands in for nothing present or available refers to the perfection the poem cannot name because any name or habit serves only to obscure it. "Which" is a sign within the poem of what it cannot do, and a sign also of what is required of its reader as well as of the reader of Breton's work, to eye directly, that is, without any intervening medium, to find in himself what no poem or habit can represent. A reader who can so "eye" will not take from the poem, but give to it the center that will always escape its representational grasp, and the true act of communication which then follows is described (but not captured) in the sonnet's amazing final line: "His proofe, their praise, will meete, as in this line."

"His proofe, their praise" completes the work of "Authors Readers" by bonding the two agents together in a reciprocal and mutually defining relationship. His proof, in the sense of "that which makes good" his effort, is their praise; i.e., by praising him they give evidence of his work's merit. But that praise is also *their* proof, that is, by providing his proof, they prove themselves capable of recognizing his merit and thereby attest to its residence within themselves: "His proofe, *their* praise." But of course this immediately turns around to become once again the matter of his praise. By fashioning a book that calls for a praise that reflects on the praisers, Breton "proves out" in the sense of producing good results, and therefore earns still another round of praise; their proof, *his* praise. This self-replenishing circuit of proof and praise, praise and proof is reflected in still another meaning of proof, "a coin or medal usually struck as the test of a die, one of a limited number" (*OED*). It is in this sense that Breton's work is a "master print," a die that strikes off coins in its own image, something that at once tests and is tested (attested) by the absolute sameness of its progeny; it is an object that confers value and has its value conferred on it by the activities of those it makes. Of course this is equally true of Jonson's poem, which is the progeny of Breton's work, a piece of praise that is both Jonson's and Breton's proof, and a die that potentially extends the circuit to those of its readers who can receive its stamp and so become pieces of producing (proving) currency in their turn.

All of these meanings are concentrated in the problematic assertion that the meeting of proof and praise occurs *in this line*. The problem is that on one level, the level on which the poem finally never performs, nothing meets in this line. To be sure, the words "praise" and "proofe" meet, but they are not filled in or elaborated in any way that would validate the claim of the line to contain the essences for which they stand. But on another level, the level on which the poem acts out an antirepresentational epistemology, the absence at the center of the line is what makes the assertion good, provides its proof; for the line in which "praise" and "proofe" meet is not the physical (external) line of print and paper but 1. the line of vision established by the instantaneous self-recognition of eyes similarly clear, eyes that communicate directly and without mediation, and 2. the genealogical line that is continually being extended whenever another author-reader is moved to write or praise (they are one and the same) and so give proof of his membership in the community of the clear-sighted. The members of that community eye directly because they have been "eyed" directly, that is, given eyes, by the inner vision that makes them one. They see the same perfection not because some external form compels them to recognize it, but because it *in*forms their perception so that it is impossible for them to see anything else. They see themselves; they see the same. In that sense they have "eyes divine" and they can even announce themselves, as Jonson does, with the indirection characteristic of this poem, as "I divine."

It is a remarkable little poem, but it is also I think, altogether typical and points us to a recharacterization of Jonson's poetry in which some of the more familiar terms of description will be called into question. First of all it will hardly do to label Jonson a poet of the plain style if his poems continually proclaim their inability to describe or "catch" their objects. That inability is not only proclaimed; it is discoursed upon at length in the very poems that announce it. The poet dares not aim at the soul of Lady Jane Paulet because "it is too near of kin to heaven . . . to be described" (29–30). The mind of Lady Venetia Digby cannot be captured by the usual metaphors "The sun, a sea, or soundless pit" (*Underwood*, no. 84, 4, 12). These, Jonson explains "are like a mind, not it" (13). "No," he continues, "to express a mind to sense / Would ask a heaven's intelligence; / Since nothing can report that flame / But what's of kin to whence it came" (13–16). In some poems Jonson seems to claim just that status for his art, as when he declares in the "Epistle to Katherine, Lady Aubigny," "My mirror is more subtle, clear, refined, / And takes and gives the beauties of the mind" (43–44). But as it turns out what he means is that his poem is a mirror in the sense of being blank, empty of positive assertions, filled with lists of what Lady Aubigny is not, of the companions she does not have, of the masks she does not wear, of the paths she does not take, of the spectacles and shows from which she turns. The poem does not so much occupy, but clears its ground, so that when Jonson says of it that it is a glass in which Lady Aubigny can look and see herself (29), his claim is true because there is nothing in it or on it—no account, no description, no representation—to prevent it from functioning as a reflecting surface. She will see nothing in it but her own "form" which she shall find "still the same" (23).

Jonson's poems of praise (and this means most of his poems) are all like that; they present the objects of praise to themselves; they say in effect, "Sir or Madame So and So, meet Sir or Madam So and So, whom, of course, you already know." Once this is said, the poem is to all intents and purposes over, although the result paradoxically is that it often has a great deal of difficulty getting started since it is, in effect, all dressed up with nowhere to go. Epigram 102 says as much in its first two lines: "I do but name thee Pembroke, and I find / It is an epigram on all mankind." Epigram 43, "To Robert, Earl of Salisbury," is even more explicit: "What need hast thou of me, or of my muse / Whose actions to themselves do celebrate." In Epigram 76, the process is reversed; the poet spends some sixteen lines imagining a proper object of this praise only to dismiss in line 17 what he has written as something merely "feigned" before declaring in line 18, "My Muse bad Bedford write, and that was she." Of course if he had hearkened to his muse in the beginning and had written the name Bedford, there would have been no need to write the poem, a crisis that is avoided by making that realization the poem's conclusion. Given an epistemology that renders it at once super-fluous and presumptuous (it is "like a mind, not it"), a Jonson poem always has the problem of finding something to say, a problem that is solved char-acteristically when it becomes itself the subject of the poem, which is then enabled at once to have a mode of being (to get written) and to remain empty of representation.

Representation is the line of work that Jonson's poems are almost never in, except when their intention is to discredit; and indeed it is a discreditable fact about any object that it is available for representation, for that availa-bility measures the degree to which it is not "kin to heaven" and therefore can be described. The clearest statement of this esthetic of negative availa-bility is Epigram 115, "On The Townes Honest Man," who is not named, because as Jonson explains, "But, this is one / Suffers no name but a de-scription" (3–4); that is, he is the exact opposite of those (like Pembroke and Lady Bedford) who can be named, but not described, because descrip-tion can only "catch" surfaces and coverings, and is itself a covering. The point, of course, is that the town's honest man is all surface; he has no stable moral identity and therefore there is nothing *in* him to which a name could be consistently attached. He is a creature of momentary desires, whims, interests, and movements, and therefore his non-essence is perfectly captured by the ever-changing surface and moment to moment adjustments of verse. The very incapacity of Jonson's poetry even to approach the objects of its praise makes it the perfect medium for the objects of its opprobrium. The chameleon-like actions of the town's honest man (usually thought to be Inigo Jones) are chronicled with a particularity and directness one never encounters in the poems addressed to Jonson's patrons and heroes. When he says at the end of the poem "Described, its thus," he has earned the claim, and when he asks "Defined would you it have" and answers, "The Townes Honest Man's her errant'st knave" (34–35), the pun on "errant'st," at once greatest and most erring, tells us why a definition of the usual kind will not be forthcoming. By definition a definition fixes an essence, but if an entity is always in motion, is always erring, it has no center to be identified and it cannot be defined; it cannot receive a name.

What we have then in Jonson's esthetic are two kinds of poetry: one that can take advantage of the full resources of language in all its representational power, although what it represents is evil; and another which must defeat and cancel out the power of representation, because the state it would celebrate is one of epistemological immediacy and ontological self-sufficiency. What one wants is not something "like," but "it," and therefore what one doesn't want is a poem. Depending on how it is read, the sixth stanza of *Underwood,* no. 84.4 ("The Mind") is descriptive of both kinds of poetry:

> I call you muse, now make it true:
>   Henceforth may every line be you;
> That all may say that see the frame,
>   This is no picture, but the same.
>   (21–24)

If this stanza were to appear in Epigram 115, its every line would be "you" in quite a literal sense, since the "you" in question would have not one identity, but the succession of "identities" that fill every line. Every line can also be a reference to the art of painting (the dismissal of which is the subject of *Underwood* no. 84.4), and in that sense too every stroke of the artist's brush in Epigram 115 fully captures whatever momentary form the town's honest man has taken. Anyone who looks at this picture—that is, at this portrait of movement and instability—will see the same, that is, will see perfectly represented the endless self-fashioning that makes up the life of the "errant'st knave." The same stanza reads quite differently, however, when we relate it to the "mind" of Lady Digby, the drawing of which Jonson claims to be able to "perform alone" (3), without the aid of the painter. That boast does not survive the third stanza and the realization (which I have already quoted) that "nothing can report that flame / But what's of kin to whence it came" (15–16). Of course that would be no report at all, since to report is to convey something to another, whereas in this transaction (if that is the word) what is of kin simply recognizes itself, recognizes, that is, the same. At this point the poem is running the familiar Jonsonian danger of asserting itself out of business, and, in what amounts to a rescue mission, the poet moves to save it by turning it over to its subject / object: "Sweet mind, then speak yourself" (17). This injunction or invitation or plea can be read in several ways: "Sweet mind, speak in place of me," a reading that preserves the poem's claim to communicate, although with a borrowed voice, or "Sweet mind, speak yourself," in the tautological sense of declaring yourself as opposed to the mediating sense of speaking *about* yourself, which shades into "Sweet mind, speak without mediation, without aid, without voice, without poem, but simply by being."

It is these latter two readings that finally rule as the mind that is bid to "say" remains just out of reach of the verse and of the reader's apprehension. Indeed, the poem anticipates its own repeated failure when it asks to know "by what brave way / Our sense you do with knowledge fill / And yet remain our wonder still" (18–20). How can something that is the cause of all knowledge be itself unknown, remain presentationally silent, be our wonder *still* (always, unmoving, quiet)? The question is not answered but given a succession of experiential lives, as every attempt to make the mind speak, to give it a habit as it were, collapses under the weight of its own inadequacy. Richard Peterson describes these lines as "an evocatively tactile and mobile representation of Lady Digby's mind" [*Imitation and Praise in the Poems of Ben Jonson*], but if anything is represented it is the failure and impiety of representation; and if the verse is mobile, it is because whenever it seeks to rest, it finds that its object has once again escaped. (Again compare "On The Townes Honest Man" where the escaping or dissolving of a nonobject is what the poem accurately and repeatedly mimes.)

Our possession of that object is at its firmest (although most abstract) at line 55 when it is described as "polisht, perfect, round, and even," but even that hermetic and closed form is presented as a thing of the past that "slid moulded off from heaven" (56). The sliding continues in the next stanza as the mind is embodied in a succession of forms that are always in the act of disintegrating, a cloud, oil (but as it pours forth), showers, drops of balm, in every case a substance that is passing into a state more rarified than the one in which it is being "presented." In line 63 the verse toys with us by promising a moment in which the mind "stays," but it stays to become a "nest of odorous spice"; that is, it doesn't stay at all. Neither does it rest, despite the teasing appearance of that word at the beginning of line 65, where it is immediately glossed by the phrase "like spirits," and, moreover, "like spirits left behind." Even this fleeting image is itself left behind as it is expanded to include the alternatives of "bank or field of flowers," flowers which are said to be begotten by a "wind" (67) that enters the poem as an image of the ever-receding mind: "In action, winged as the wind" (64). In the impossible but typically Jonsonian logic of the poem the mind as wind begets itself.

The mind finally comes to rest inside the person of Lady Digby, where it was before this self-extending and self-defeating search for representation began. "In thee . . . let it rest" (68) is the poem's final admission of defeat; "it" will remain enclosed; it will not come out; it will not be brought out; it will not be represented. Instead it will remain in communion with itself, with what it possesses and informs. When Jonson says, "yet know with what thou art possesst" (70), the circuit of knowledge has been narrowed to the space between Lady Digby and her mind, which is no space at all; there is literally no room for anything else because she entertains only ("but") such a mind. The exclusivity of this fellowship is not broached but made more apparent when it welcomes another member, "God thy Guest" ("But such a mind, mak'st God thy guest"), who is at once guest and host, possessor and possessed. The circle of this trinity closes out everything, and especially the poem of which one can now truly say, "This is no picture, but the same." If every line is Lady Digby it is only because every line has emptied itself out in the impossible effort to capture her, leaving her and her guest and those of kin to whence they came in a state of perfect self-recognition, with nothing and no one (including the would-be observer-reader) between them.

One could say then that the poem displays what George Herbert would call a "double motion." It enacts the defeat of representation by never quite being able to present its object, and it more or less "chases" that object to the portals of its proper home, where, as in the last scene of *The Pilgrim's Progress,* one catches the barest glimpse of a kind of community that is open only to those who are already members of it. That community can no more be described or "caught" than can the minds of those who populate it. Just as the mind of Lady Digby or of her unnamed counterpart in the poem "To the World" can only be characterized in terms of the actions it shuns and the obligations it does not recognize, so can the society in which such minds "really" live be characterized only in terms of what *cannot* hold it together or constitute its order, the structures of power, wealth, preferment, influence, everything in short that Jonson refers to as "Nets," "Toys," "baits," "trifles, traps and snares," "gyves," "chains," "engins," "Gins" ("To the World, A Farewell," 8, 12, 18, 24, 30, 34, and 36). These, he says in "An Epistle to Master Arthur Squib," "are poor ties, depend on those false ends. / Tis virtue alone, or nothing that knits friends" (11–12). The ends in question are both the purposes or motives of those who allow themselves to be defined by society's values and the ends or rhymes (poor ties) of poems that issue from and support those same false values. In either case the true knitting is accomplished by "nothing," that is by *no thing* that is visible or measurable, but by a virtue that escapes, because it is a substance apart from, either the lines of influence in the world or the lines of description in a poem. The true poem and the true community are alike in that neither can be equated with the outward forms (of rhymes, honors, rank) that apparently tie them together.

In effect, then, Jonson is continually asserting the unreality both of what fills his poems—titles, offices, estates—and of the society in which those surfaces are the false measures of worth. It would seem therefore that he is no more a social poet than he is (except in a very special sense) a plain-style poet, and for the same reason. The plain style, as Wesley Trimpi and others have taught us, is particularly suited to the accurate representation of what men actually do in response to the pressures of everyday life"; but Jonson's interest is in what some men and women, including himself, actually *are* in a realm of being wholly removed from the everyday, even though it happens to occupy the same temporal space. The very appropriateness of the plain style to one kind of society renders it entirely inappropriate to the society that Jonson so pointedly declines to represent even as he invites us to join it.

Of course, as we have seen, that invitation is not an invitation at all, but a test, for it functions less as a means of expanding the community than as a device for closing the door in the face of those who are not already "sealed." As such a device, the poetry performs an action precisely analogous to the granting of favor and preferment by the wealthy and the powerful to those who petition them. It names who is in and who is out and awards not knighthoods, or offices or commissions or pensions or lands, but membership in the tribe of Ben. In a way, then, it is a social poetry, but only in the sense that it sets up, by refusing to describe, a society that is in direct competition with the society whose details fill its lines; by appointing himself the gatekeeper of that society, Jonson manages (at least in his poetry) the considerable feat of asserting and demonstrating his independence of the "poor ties" that supposedly constrain and define him. In short, Jonson establishes in these poems an *alternate* world of patronage and declares it (by an act of poetic fiat) more real than the world in which he is apparently embedded. He invokes the distinctions that structure (or at least appear to structure) his material existence—distinctions of place, birth, wealth, power—but then he effaces them by drawing everyone he names into a community of virtue in which everyone is, by definition, the same as everyone else. He calls his heroes and heroines by their proper titles—Lady, Sir, Lord, Knight—but then he enrolls them in his list under the title they all indifferently share.

That is why, despite the signs of specificity that are everywhere in the poetry, everyone in it is finally interchangeable. The only true relationship between members of a Jonson community is one of identity, and no matter how many persons seem to crowd into a poem, the effect of the argument is always to reduce them to one, to the same. The first five lines of Epigram 91, "To Sir Horace Vere," is almost a parody of the technique:

> Which of thy names I take, not only bears
>   A Roman sound, but Roman virtue wears:
> Illustrious Vere, or Horace, fit to be
>   Sung by a Horace, or a muse as free;
> Which thou art to thyself.
>
> (1–5)

Here the community is formed by dividing its one member into two, and then declaring (in a declaration that would hardly have seemed necessary before the poem began) that the two are the same. When the newly reunited Horace Vere is declared fit to be sung by another Horace or even by a muse of different name but like spirit ("as free"), it would seem that the population of the community is expanding; but it immediately contracts when the "muse as free" is identified (a telling word) as "thou thyself," and the absolute closedness and self-sufficiency of the community is reconfirmed. One is hardly surprised to find that the rest of the poem is concerned with what Jonson, as now superfluous muse, will *not* do. "I leave thy acts," he says, explaining that if he were to "prosecute" in detail Vere's every accomplishment, he would seem guilty of flattery; and if he were to celebrate some and omit others he would seem guilty of envy. It is a nice rationale for furthering the project of this poem, which is to get written and yet say nothing at all. Jonson *does* announce that he will say something about Vere's "Humanitie" and "Pietie," but he says only that they are "rare" (16) and "lesse mark'd" (14), which they certainly are in this poem if by "mark'd" one means set down or described. The poem ends without having taken one step from the circle formed by the two names (really one) in its title, "To Sir Horace Vere."

In an influential essay, Thomas Greene has called our attention to the prominence in Jonson's poetry of the notion of the "gathered self" which is always to itself "the same" (Epigram 98.10), a self whose ends and beginnings "perfect in a circle always meet" (Epigram 138.8), a self which presents such a closed face to the world that it is invulnerable to invasion and remains always "untouch'd," a self which may appear to travel and undergo changes in location and situation, but in fact never moves at all ["Ben Jonson and the Centered Self"]. What I am suggesting is that as objects and as discourses Jonson's poems are themselves gathered and closed in exactly these ways: rather than embracing society they repel it; rather than presenting a positive ethos in a plain style, they labor to present nothing at all and to remain entirely opaque. Greene asserts that "the concept of an inner moral equilibrium . . . informs . . . Jonson's verse"; but it would be more accurate to say that the concept of an inner moral equilibrium *escapes* Jonson's verse which is always citing the concept as its cause, but never quite managing to display or define it. It remains "inner" in a stronger sense than Greene's argument suggests; it remains *locked* in, forever inaccessible to any public inspection or validation. In its determination never to reveal what moves it, Jonson's poetry repeatedly enacts the teasing career of the brave infant of Saguntum, always only "half got out" before it hastily returns and makes of itself its own urn, so that we are left to say of it, "How summed a circle didst thou leave mankind / Of deepest lore, could we the centre find" (*Underwood,* no. 70.9–10).

JOHN HOLLANDER

Ben Jonson and the Modality of Verse

Considering that they are the work of a literary genius, Ben Jonson's poems have had a curious critical fate. The epoch that most intimately responded to their virtues never singled them out for special praise, while our own age, so acutely conscious of history, acknowledges their importance and success and at the same time retains a fundamentally unsympathetic view toward them, seldom praising without apologizing. It is true that the importance of Jonson's non-dramatic works as a source for the whole current of poetic style during the course of the seventeenth century has only been adequately assessed during the past several decades. But even at the height of the Augustan style whose origins must be traced to Jonson's influence, the fame of his poems lagged behind that of his plays, and even further behind that of his personality.

There is perhaps some irony in this. In the audaciously entitled *Works* that the poet himself, in 1616, collected in the folio format until then reserved for editions of the great writers of antiquity, it was the lyric and epigrammatic portions that were popularly neglected in favor of the plays that at the time seemed to have even less right to publication under the presumptuous rubric of "dramatic literature." Jonson was, in every sense, a man of letters. He always devoted great attention and care to the cultivation of an organized *oeuvre* or corpus of literary creation. To be fair to him, one should include in a balanced selection of his "poems" examples of all the verse and prose, dramatic and non-dramatic, lyrical, satiric, critical, didactic,

From *Vision and Resonance*. © 1985 by Yale University. Yale University Press, 1985.

and occasional, that he left behind him. Poetry, Jonson knew, meant "making," and the senses of "things," "actions," or "deeds" are partially conveyed in his translation of "*opera.*" On the other hand, what we would today call "poems" he would consider a misleading category, lumping together and blurring distinctions between the sub-species populating his literary world. A lack of sympathy with Jonson's attachment to just these distinctions between literary genres has led to the peculiar judgment and appreciation of his poetry characterized by the critical attitudes of the present age. That peculiar judgment has crystallized about a rival for Jonson's laurels: for if his greatness as a dramatist has always had to contend with often inappropriate comparisons of his plays to Shakespeare's, it is only recently that his poems have seemed to lurk behind the obliquely cast shadow of those of John Donne.

It was the rediscovery of Jonson's contemporary, and Donne's critical canonization in the past forty years, that have helped to establish the very criteria by which, three hundred years after his death, a poem is considered to be a poem. In the narrowest view of these criteria, Jonson does seem a strange sort of poet, perhaps. He informs us (through the offices of the obliging William Drummond of Hawthornden in his *Conversations*) that he wrote his poems out in prose before versifying them. It is only the Romantic belief that poetry is somehow inspired and mysteriously spontaneous, or the post-symbolist insistence that a poem must *be* its own meaning, scheme, and purpose, rather than have separable skeleton, flesh, and organs, that can make us blush for Jonson at such a remark. Donne's poems, far from having been formalized out of prose statement, resist even our own efforts at prose paraphrase; and Donne is, or at any rate until very recently has been, a model English poet.

It must always be remembered that Jonson often writes in the metaphysical style, and that in one mode of writing, at least, the two poets are almost indistinguishable, as continued scholarly argument about the authorship of one of the elegies in *The Underwood* would suggest. But in general, we may oppose them to each other. Where Donne is grotesquely original, Jonson strikes us as being overly imitative. Jonson, moreover, seems at once to brandish his Classical learning like a weapon, and to depend upon it for guidance and support, as if he were momentarily both halt and blind. Donne, conversely, subtly inoculates his rhetorically violent arguments with doses of sacred and profane lore. Donne is an ironist with no stage for which to write, and his poems seem as a consequence to condense the complicated structures of dramatic irony into a dramaturgy of image and tone: in a sense, Donne's poems are all dramatic monologues. Jonson, on the other hand, is a moralist with no pulpit. He makes of his theater a kind of complicated moral machine for projecting human behavior onto a screen so constituted as to reveal the true nature of that behavior, a nature always kept hidden by the distorted perspectives of mundane interests and commitments. For Jonson all of literature has this same moral purpose, and the poet is a secular priest.

But there are even greater differences between the two. Jonson, a schematic and devoted prosodist, declared that "Donne, for not keeping of accent, deserved hanging"; it is in just this metrical roughness of Donne's, however, that so much modern interest lies. Jonson writes in what look to be many styles, but all of Donne's verses, sacred or secular, amatory or satirical, songs or letters, are very much the same sort of intellectual ceremony, synthesizing the occasional and the spontaneous. It is this spontaneity of the dramatic rather than the inspirational sort that we miss in Jonson. Donne's wit often constructs a public or even a universal occasion from the most intimate and private ones, and "makes one little roome, an every where." But Jonson's occasional poems are frankly public, and it is significant that he makes pioneer attempts to adapt to English the Pindaric ode, that most ceremonial of forms.

A rewarding contrast might be drawn between two typical "occasional" poems: Donne's pair of "Anniversary" poems, in which the death of a patron's little daughter becomes the occasion for a lament over the passing of an epoch in the West's intellectual history, and Jonson's uncompleted elegy on the wife of Sir Kenelm Digby. In "Eupheme," Jonson commits himself to eulogistic extravagances, but struggles against them:

> What's left a *Poet*, when his *Muse* is gone?
> Sure, I am dead, and know it not! I feele
> Nothing I doe; but like a heavie wheele,
> Am turned with an others powers. My Passion
> Whoorles me about and to blaspheme in fashion.!

Aside from a punning reference to the lady's heroic name in "blaspheme," it was just the charge of blasphemy that Jonson leveled at Donne's first "Anniversary," perhaps having taken much of it far too literally. But in "Eupheme," Jonson's own literalness often leaves him breathlessly hyperbolic.

Although Jonson indeed esteemed "John Donne the first poet in the world in some things," he added later on that Donne "for not being understood, would perish." The irony here is that our day, which understands Donne so well as to have resurrected and animated his remains, should still

misunderstand Jonson in some basic ways. The same influential judgment of
T. S. Eliot that praised Donne as one who "knew the anguish of the marrow /
The ague of the skeleton" could not approve of Jonson without insisting that
"His poetry is of the surface." This, I feel, lies close to the heart of the
question of Jonson's reputation as a poet today. Modern poetic taste distrusts
surfaces because they seem too detachable, and demands the extrusion of
the core of a poem, so to speak, onto its outside. For us, the meaning of a
poem consists in its imagery and elaboration as much as in its "subject,"
and the separation of "sense" from expressive content in poetry is the arch-
heresy of orthodox reading today. Yet Jonson insists on in theory, and demonstrates often enough in practice, a view of the nature of poetry depending
on the notion of a "core" of prose sense or even moral purpose, surrounded
by an exterior added by art, rather than secreted by the poem's soul within.
Similarly, his widespread use of Classical sources as models, texts, and
themes, as well as for direct translation, seems to modern sensibilities somehow *inauthentic*. Indeed, the Classic poetry upon which he most frequently
draws—Horace, Catullus, Juvenal, Martial, the corpus of Greek verse called
the Anacreontea—itself tends to buckle under the same analysis of structure
and texture that college students are today taught to apply to English poetry
as a test of its very essence.

Beyond all these things, however, modern poetic theory requires of a
poet a consistently recognizable language of his own, a characteristic voice
sounding through any masks he may choose to wear, and overriding the
accents of any style or manner he may elect to use. For a true poet, we feel
today, all occasions, subjects, forms, and conventions must come under the
absolute command of one governing style, and a major poet like W. H. Auden
was often treated suspiciously by many otherwise sympathetic readers precisely because of his *use* of so many voices and techniques. But here again,
Donne serves as textual authority, and here again, Jonson resists automatic
commendation. With Donne, lyric, epigram, longer satire, and prayer are
all, as I have already observed, the same kind of poem. With one or two
dubious exceptions, none of the *Songs and Sonnets* are primarily lyrical,
affecting us as being, first and foremost, song texts. Jonson's most celebrated
lyrics, however, such as the too-heavily anthologized "Drinke to me, onely,
with thine eyes," or the "Hymn to Diana" from *Cynthia's Revels,* have
accumulated about them modern critical clichés concerning their "purely"
lyrical character primarily because of their radical difference in manner from
his odes, and even greater difference from his satires and epigrams. Jonson's
lyrics seem "lighter" than his other poems; it is certainly true that, in contrast
with Donne's, they are more properly "songs."

If we look through the body of Jonson's non-dramatic poetry, we come across his own schematic arrangement of various types of poem, both in the 1616 folio edition and in the larger posthumous publication of 1640. The epigrams form a collection of their own. Then follows *The Forrest,* a short selection of pieces of many sorts that he considered at the time to be his very best accomplishments. In the 1640 folio, Jonson prefaced his volume called *The Underwood* with the explanation that

> With the same leave as the Ancients call'd that kind of body *Sylva* or *Hule,* in which there were workes of divers nature, and matter congested; as the multitude call Timber-trees, promiscuously growing, a Wood, or Forrest: so am I bold to entitle these lesser Poems, of later growth, by this of Under-Wood, out of the Analogie they hold to the *Forrest*

It is not surprising, incidentally, to find him carrying through this "analogie" in the naming of his prose miscellany, *Timber, or Discoveries Made upon Men and Matter. . . .* But with the exception of the separate compilation of epigrams, Jonson's categories are based upon the departments of a literary *oeuvre,* and arranged with respect to relative importance, rather than to distinctions between literary genres as such and as represented in the poems themselves.

The fact that Jonson took these modes or forms utterly for granted is quite significant for any clear understanding of what he meant by poetry, or for that matter, by literature in general. One of the most overpowering myths of Classical antiquity was that of the power of music at the hands of heroes like the poet-musician Orpheus. Of all the lore about ancient music that was transmitted through the Middle Ages down to Jonson's time, the notion of what I shall call modality most fascinated Renaissance thinkers and writers who sought to understand that fabled power. The modes or keys of ancient music, called Dorian, Lydian, Phrygian, etc., were all held to affect the hearer's feelings and actions, each in its prescribed way. (Thus the Dorian had a manly and martial character, the Lydian was held to be voluptuous and relaxing, the Phrygian, frenzied, and so forth. The modern musician may think in terms of a whole species of distinctions corresponding to that drawn by the Romantic imagination between a "happy" major key and a "sad" minor one.) Great importance was attached to these modes, to the kinds of poetic texts conventionally sung to their melodies, the occasions appropriate to the use of each, and their respective characters. Socrates, it will be remembered, carefully indicates which modes are to be permitted in Plato's Just City. In general, the idea of modality in the music of the ancient world becomes a kind of standard or model of the relation of musical or poetic form to content or purpose.

Now for a Neoclassicist like Jonson, the music-poetry of antiquity is the unfallen ancestor of all literature, and Orpheus's lyre a heraldic bearing. The idea of musical modality thus expands into a general literary principle, analogous to the Greeks' purely musical one, in an age whose literary program aimed at the achievements, if not at the actual forms, of Classical literature. And thus, for a writer like Jonson who believed in a vital tradition embracing the poetry of the ancient and modern worlds, never use styles, forms, and conventions to be thought of as spontaneous channels of expression, shaped by the unique identity of the poet, his experience, and his voice. Only a Romantic writer would insist on that triumph of feeling over form. Rather would the Neoclassicist employ forms and styles of modes of discourse having certain quasi-musical effects upon the reader, perhaps, but more clearly serving as a proper vehicle or designation of an occasion, a subject, or an attitude. Granted the notion that art is to be a mirror of life, the relationship between poetic form and poetic purpose, between the public or private occasion of a literary utterance and the mode or style proper to it, becomes a moral one.

In praising a sentence of Demosthenes, the Hellenistic Pseudo-Longinus accounts for its power not only by allusion to its *dianoia,* "thought," but because of its *harmonia,* "melody": "Its delivery depends wholly on the dactyls, which are the noblest of rhythms and make for grandeur—and that is why the most beautiful of all known meters, the heroic, is composed of dactyls. Here is a beautifully framed example of what would become a dogma of Classicism: a form or mode is seen to possess an ethos or attribute of its own by nature, rather than because of an association with certain kinds and occasions of utterance. A modern formalist critic would say just the opposite about the dactyls, namely, that they acquired an aura of grandeur because of their conventional use in heroic, epical poetry. Jonson, like many good Renaissance scholars, knew something of the arguments in antiquity about whether powers of language and music were to be ascribed to nature, or to convention. But like all Renaissance poets who drew on antiquity for anything more than stylistic models, he grasped the force of the idea of the naturalness of stylistic effects, and lived with that idea as with a most useful fiction.

He retained always a vigorous and healthy attitude toward the relation between the modern and the antique. He castigated Spenser who, he felt, "in affecting the Ancients, writ no language," although we may suspect that other aspects of *The Faerie Queene* may have troubled him as well, and that

by concentrating on the language, he was anticipating the strategy of twen-
tieth-century Moderns like Eliot and Pound in rejecting Milton, Spenser, and
much more poetry of the past that posed aesthetic and moral problems far
deeper than stylistic ones.

Jonson took no part in the attempt to employ Classical quantitative
meters in English. He seemed firmly committed to the English iambic pentameter line from the outset. Drummond of Hawthornden reminds us that
Jonson distrusted longer lines, denouncing the translations of Homer and
Virgil "in long alexandrines as but prose," and having no patience for the
twelve-syllabled line of Drayton's *Poly-Olbion*. With his knowledge of the
ancients, Jonson must have understood well that the accentual decasyllabic
that descended (although his generation did not yet know this) from Chaucer
would have to do a variety of jobs in English poetry. In Classical verse, the
modalities, or generic associations, of various meters are sharply differentiated. Thus, Classical iambics (usually an iambic trimeter of six feet because
iambs and anapests were always doubled up as two to a foot) was a con-
versational meter, used on the stage and hence for some of Catullus's invective, for example. The heroic hexameter was the line of epic and, in the
tradition that Theocritus inaugurated and Virgil confirmed, of pastoral ec-
logue. The couplet was the meter of inscription, epigram, and, later, satire
and epistle. A modulation from one to another could constitute a revision
of a genre. Thus Ovid's joke, in the first two lines of the *Amores,* about how
he had originally planned to write of high heroic doings, but Cupid, the
naughty thing, came along and filched a foot from his second line (thus, it
went without saying, transforming the hexameters into elegiac couplets of
alternating hexameter and pentameter lines). A modern analogue of this
might be an improvising pianist who muttered as he played about how he
had meant to play a rousing march in C major, but Sorrow came along and
sadly draped three blue flats on his melody.

Jonson realized early that the English-stressed decasyllabic would have
to serve as iambics when unrhymed on the stage, as hexameters and as
elegiacs both when indented; similarly, he would translate iambics of the
Catullan sort by a shorter English line, usually tetrameter. The iambic pentameter line, he knew, would have to do, on and off the stage, for high and
low matters. His brilliant translation of Petronius's epigram about sadness
after sex that begins "Doing a filthy pleasure is, and short" maintains that
wonderful balance between the schematic written grammar and the spoken
force that we associate with Milton (the Latin original goes "*Foeda est in
coitu et brevis voluptas*")—the sequential build from one of the paired mod-
ifiers of "pleasure" to the second, last, and most telling being the inner

"narrative" of the line and the moral it embodies. It is no wonder that Jonson had written a (now lost) "discourse of poesie both against Campion and Daniel, especially the last, where he [proved] couplets to be the bravest sort of verses, especially when they are broken like hexameters." Here was Dryden's, and Pope's, direct ancestor.

Jonson thus seems to follow directly upon Sidney in his understanding of the relation between form and genre, and of the necessity of building a new world of expression, wielding style in the purposes of truth and right, upon the ruins of the ancient one. "He cursed Petrarch," Drummond tells us, "for redacting verses to sonnets which he said were like the tyrant's bed," by which he meant that of Procrustes; but as we shall see a bit further on, his one sonnet is an anti-sonnet, not merely because of distaste for the format, but out of revulsion against the institutionalized Petrarchan convention. (This did not prevent him, in "Eupheme" or, brilliantly, in the masques, from wrenching the rituals out of their normal molds, and reapplying the rhetorical and mythological strategies of celebration.)

Jonson's interest in form, then, is by no means superficial. The brilliance and permanence of many of his achievements in a purely technical direction lie close to the foundations of what he considered to be the fundamental problems of the man of letters. For him, poetry was the same mirror of life that it was for his contemporaries. It exercised a moral function by *illuminating* on the stage the hiding place of folly and vice, by calling down in satire nasty self-interest for what it is, celebrating the knowledge and generosity of individuals in commendatory poems, etc. But for Jonson in particular, the glass of poetry presented in addition a view of what might be. He flourished in a spiritual climate too close to the miasmas of medieval despair over nature, and was of too fierce and loathing a temper himself, to partake of any optimism for the economic, social, and religious consequences of the sixteenth century. Neither is his Neoclassicism to be considered a historical nostalgia for golden days: the virtues he responded to in Augustan Rome concerned what he felt to be a model relationship of literature to life, while life was as petty and vile, he knew, as ever. But without necessarily apologizing for any old order, he made his task as a poet the representation of the ideals of what he felt to be the most important Establishments of his day: aristocracy, order, and a kind of humanist orthodoxy. Prior to all these, perhaps, lay a notion of courtesy, no hodgepodge of chivalric ideology and scraps from medieval writers, but a more universal idea of civilization involving knowledge and enlightenment allied with power and effectiveness. Literature was for Jonson the language of that courtesy. The understanders of that language were the various aristocracies of enlightened courts, literate theatrical audiences, university intellectuals in public service, and a learned reading public. When eventually the playgoers proved too fickle, the court unappreciative of his greatest efforts in the form of the masque, and readers in general too unsubstantial an entity, he must have turned, in his later years, for more than consolation to the group of surrogate sons calling itself the "Tribe of Ben," and including in its numbers most of the distinguished poets of the Caroline age. The coterie of such younger men of letters as Herrick, Carew, and James Howell, such public men as Sir Lucius Cary, Sir Kenelm Digby, the Earl of Newcastle, and others, turned exclusively about "St. Ben," its unwobbling pivot in a mad world. It is perhaps as much as anything else the doing of this "cult of personality" of Jonson's later years that Jonson's public figure seemed for so long to eclipse the light of his works.

But the idea of a civilized society as well as its microcosm in the literary cabala of the Tribe of Ben were both modern versions, for Jonson, of the idea of a literate community that emerges from even a cursory reading of Classical writers. The sense of Augustan Rome that we get from its poets, for example, suggests the paradoxical condition of a tight coterie upon which, nevertheless, no sun could ever set. Jonson knew that of all the aristocratic Establishments, the most carefully preserved, pruned, cultivated, and revered is The Past. His Neoclassicism was the one element in his poetic program that brought together questions of purpose, theory, and actual practice. It is no wonder that his basic notion of what poetic language is by nature, and of how and when it was to be used, was so strongly conditioned by his self-adopted kinship with Latin writers.

The many modes of Jonson's poetry, then, betoken no superficiality or inconsistency. Although there may be recognized everywhere in his range of accomplishment the combination of toughness of wit and vigorous delicacy of control that characterize Jonson's unique poetic elegance, to list his very best poems is to include an astonishing variety of successes. From the half-wry, post-pastoral lyric of the "Celebration of Charis" or "The Musicall Strife," for example, is a considerable stylistic distance to the dramatic climax of the magnificent "Elegie on the Lady Jane Pawlet":

> What Nature, Fortune, Institution, Fact
> Could summe to a perfection, was her Act!
> How did she leave the world? with what contempt?
> Just as she in it liv'd! and so exempt
> From all affection! when they urg'd the Cure
> Of her disease, how did her soule assure
> Her suffrings, as the body had beene away!

> And to the Torturers (her Doctors) say,
> Stick on your Cupping-glasses, feare not, put
> Your hottest Causticks to, burne, lance or cut:
> 'Tis but a body which you can torment,
> And I, into the world, all Soule, was sent!

Then there is the dual brilliance of the famous "Come my Celia, let us prove": in its original context in the superb seduction scene in *Volpone,* it is no mere Classically imitated *carpe diem* lyric, but rather an expression as well of the whole play's themes of acquisition and deceit. But as printed with a companion piece in *The Forrest,* it presents itself to us as a Catullan adaptation made with an almost gnomic concision. Different again is the extreme Mandarin elegance of "To Penshurst," whose authoritative couplets frame a poetry of statement rather than of gesture or indirection:

> The earely cherry, with the later plum,
> Fig, grape, and quince, each in his time doth come:
> The blushing apricot, and woolly peach
> Hang on thy walls, that every child may reach.
> And thou thy walls be of the countrey stone,
> They'are rear'd with no means ruine, no mans grone

Even the complimentary conceits woven into the splendid tribute not only to the ancestral home of the Sidney family, but to a whole way of life as well, look ahead to the near-Augustan tone of Andrew Marvell: the "ripe daughters," a few lines further on, have baskets that "beare / An embleme of themselves, in plum, or peare." The tone of the closing lines might be said to resound at the tonal center of Jonson's highest commendatory mode:

> Now, *Penshurst,* they that will proportion thee
> With other edifices, when they see
> Those proud, ambitious heaps, and nothing else,
> May say, their lords have built, but thy lord dwells.

Jonson is perfectly capable of using the resources of metaphysical poetry, however, as in the great Pindaric ode, "To the Immortall Memorie, and Friendship of that Noble Paire, Sir Lucius Cary, and Sir H. Morison." At the very opening image, based, it is true, upon an obscure incident mentioned in Pliny, the wretchedness of a world that cuts off virtuous lives is figured forth in a conceit that makes one think of the wilder excesses of an extreme poet like John Cleveland:

> Brave Infant of *Saguntum,* cleare
> Thy comming forth in that great yeare,
> When the Prodigious *Hannibal* did crowne
> His rage, with razing your immortall Towne.
> Thou, looking then about,
> E're thou wert halfe got out,
> Wise child, did'st hastily returne,
> And mad'st thy Mothers wombe thine urne.
> How summ'd a circle didst thou leave man-kind
> Of deepest lore, could we the Center find!

In the antistrophe immediately following, however, Jonson employs a more Classically expository language to clarify that "deepest lore":

> Did wiser Nature draw thee back,
> From out the horrour of that sack,
> Where shame, faith, honour, and regard of right
> Lay trampled on; the deeds of death, and night,
> Urg'd, hurried forth, and horld
> Upon th'affrighted world:
> Sword, fire and famine, with fell fury met;
> And all on utmost ruine set;
> As, could they but lifes miseries fore-see,
> No doubt all Infants would returne like thee?

And then, again, Jonson is capable in the same frequently underrated poem of violent grammatical tricks, such as when he expresses the shock of the breach of friendship occasioned by Morison's death through a likening of the two men to the constellation of the Gemini ("this bright *Asterisme*" he calls it), and then writing

> To separate these twi-
> Lights, the *Dioscuri*

whereby, as already mentioned [elsewhere], the "twin lights" are separated, by the enjambment of the line, from the unified word "twilights" in which they were joined. Here the meter imitates the action of death by cutting the word apart even as death divided the two men. In the previous stanza, Jonson has also employed a striking enjambment, where Morison leaps "the present age, / Possest with holy rage," into eternity. The strophe ends: "And there he lives with memorie: and *Ben*," and there one tends to come to a full stop. But the next strophe begins "*Jonson,* who sung this of him, e're he went /

Himselfe to rest." This is no arbitrary shock, but is again a kind of pun-by-discovery. Just "*Ben*" may appear over-familiar; with the addition of the enjambed line, the poet, as he would have been known by the living Cary, the late Morison, and the whole "Tribe of Ben" becomes the public figure, the author of the *Works*. Thus is the poem labeled with the poet's dual name, expressing his private and public roles and duties.

But Jonson has countless other modes of performance. Even in satire, he can be as personal as in the account of the burning of some of his writings in the "Execration upon Vulcan," or in his attacks upon Inigo Jones. He can adopt the traditional genre of mock-epic for the magnificently Rabelaisian "Voyage" (which was apparently too scatalogical for Swinburne, incidentally, whom he would have thought barely capable of shock). He can adopt the varying tones of "Ben" the critic, in epigrams addressed to his fellow writers like Donne, Selden, and Drayton, and of the public "Ben Jonson," in occasional pieces on broader subjects.

Aside from the public theater itself, the "loathed stage" which he could never quite leave, perhaps the one poetic mode which Jonson found most congenial was that of the court masque. This peculiar form, for Jonson almost a miniature world of humane letters, is lost to us as dramatic literature today for it is impossible to resurrect the theater in which it occurred. The most devoted archaeology and technology might reproduce some of the brilliant scenic and mechanical effects of Jonson's great collaborator and eventual rival, Inigo Jones, or allow us to hear the music of such composers as Alfonso Ferrabosco. But nothing could ever really duplicate the total milieu relating author, musician, performer, and audience. Masques were more than merely festival pageants full of singing and mythological figures and clever stage machinery. The Jacobean masque was an elaborate kind of dramatized court dance, in which some courtiers themselves participated, while others observed, with the monarch, from the vantage point known as "The State." The masque in Jonson's hands became, over a period of more than thirty years, a unique poetic instrument. With the sovereign, his court, and "The State" in a Hall on Twelfth Night, say, and the world enclosed, so to speak, in a more ideally compacted microcosm than the "wooden O" of the public theater, the poet could lead his nobility through a series of allegorical dances. The texts of the songs surrounding and accompanying them explained and moralized the very patterns, often, of the intricate series of dance figures, just as their melodies and rhythms provided the proper measures to govern them. In Jonson's masque *Pleasure Reconciled to Virtue,* for example, the masquers, costumed as pleasures and virtues, are led through a "laborinth

of love" by Daedalus, the fabulous artificer of antiquity. As they "put themselves in forme" for the various dances, he sings

> Come on, come on; and where you go,
>   So interweave the curious knot,
> As ev'n th'observer scarce may know
>   Which lines are Pleasures, and which not.
> First figure out the doubtfull way
>   At which, a while all youth should stay,
>   Where she and Vertue did contend
>   Which should have Hercules to frend.
> Then as all actions of mankind
>   Are but a Laborinth, or maze:
>   So let your Daunces be entwin'd,
> Yet not perplex men unto gaze.
> But measur'd, and so numerous too,
>   As men may read each act you doo.
> And when they see the Graces meet,
>   Admire the wisdom of your feet.
> For Dauncing is an exercise
>   Not onely shews the movers wit,
>   As he hath powre to rise to it.

Here is the perfect combination of "pleasure and profit," that Renaissance
cliché about the purpose of art to which Jonson did not hesitate to give
assent. But in this masque, moral subject, poetic figure and dramatic action
are all unified. (Is the first stanza actually *metaphorical*, by the way, or rather
a literal injunction to embodied abstractions about the structure and value
of their imminent dance?) The animated moral emblem of the masque, moreover, might be said itself to approach most closely to Jonson's ideal of the
proper role of poetry in the real world, involving the principals of The State
not as spectators only, but as amused, amusing, and profitable participants,
instructed both in and by allegorical roles by the poet himself. Such songs
as these (and, of course, the masques include almost every type of dramatic
and nondramatic lyric as well) are supreme cases of the lyric doing the work
of dramatic, speculative, and didactic poetry as well. But they can do so
only because of the perfect, artificial literary milieu in which they are conceived. As the work of such scholars as Stephen Orgel has shown us, the
masque remains in some senses the form of Jonson's most original poetic
achievement.

Yet the range of his technical accomplishments is quite broad. Among its high points must be mentioned the establishment of the couplet in form and purpose as it was to continue through the century, and the extremely original and personal tone, texture, and form of the odes. For lyrics Jonson employs a variety of forms extending from the tetrameter couplet (analogous to the meters of the Anacreontea?) to the complicated stanza forms taken by pastoral madrigals. Certain forms he eschews utterly. His sole sonnet is almost a joke; "To the Noble Lady, the Lady Mary Wroth" at once casts aspersions on the form as a kind of Sunday painting, and manages to celebrate most delicately the Lady's own accomplishments in just that form.

> I that have beene a lover, and could shew it,
> > Though not in these, in rithmes not wholly dumbe,
> > Since I exscribe your Sonnets, am become
> A bitter lover, and much better Poet.
> Nor is my Muse, or I asham'd to owe it,
> > To those true numerous Graces; whereof some
> > But charme the Senses, others over-come
> Both braines and hearts; and mine now best doe know it.

It is the same impulse operating here that accounts for the "Fit of Rime against Rime," in which he can choose no other instrument to launch his complaint about the necessary barbarisms incidental to the carving of literature out of the living, rather than the dead, language. Jonson uses all the attacks on the debased state of modern languages and their need for rhyming that were employed in the turn-of-the-century debates over prosody. At the end of the poem, he condemns the imaginary inventor of rhyming to a fate no worse than what must have been the endemic agony of a conscience-ridden Classicist who, unlike Thomas Campion, for example, refused to write quantitative poetry for polemical purposes alone, while hewing to the line of rhyme in all the rest of his work:

> May his joynts tormented bee,
> > Cramp'd forever;
> Still may Syllabes jarre with time,
> Still may reason warre with rime,
> > Resting never.

Jonson's mastery of the short poem led him to avoid, in all but satires, the kind of drawn-out, dialectical elaboration which Donne delighted in producing. Consider the perfection of the little poem on the hourglass, from *The Underwood:*

> Doe but consider this small dust,
>　　Here running in the Glasse,
>　　　　By Atomes mov'd;
>　　Could you beleeve, that this
>　　　The body ever was
>　　　　Of one that lov'd?
> And in his Mistris' flame, playing like a flye,
>　　Turn'd to cinders by her eye?
> Yes; and in death, as life, unblest,
>　　　To have exprest,
> Ev'n ashes of lovers find no rest.

This is like a collapsed version of a Donne song, starting with a formal reading of the emblem of the hourglass (what does it mean? here is the signification: etc.) and ending up where Donne might have after several stanzas and much brilliant digression. It is brilliantly, and tactfully, compressed, and calls to mind several lines from Herbert's "Church-Monuments"; a Latin original on which it is based is three elegiac couplets, but Jonson modulates with line length and half-rhyming (the opening "dust" never rhymes with "this" or "was," and comes to an uneasy rest of closure in the triple-rhymed, final "rest"). Similarly, "My Picture Left in Scotland," with its opening casual paradox "I now thinke, Love is rather deafe, then blind" closes in a bluster of material from the opening of Donne's "The Canonization":

> My hundred of gray haires,
>　　Told seven and fortie years,
> Read so much wast, as she cannot imbrace
>　My mountaine belly, and my rockie face,
> And all these through her eyes, have stopt her eares.

Between the intimately private and the didactically public, there are many modes, and Jonson played in them all.

But even Jonson's most personal triumphs of technical skill and concern cannot put off post-Romantic objections to his imitativeness. Originality and novelty are recent virtues, and the Renaissance did not demand of "making" or "feigning" as poetry was frequently called in English, that it work out of whole cloth. But even against such a background, Jonson seems often to be doing patchwork. Translations, adaptations, and borrowings appear almost everywhere in his poetry. A particular poem may echo several different sources, while the same classic text may show up in several poems. His "translations" proper never aim at preserving a particular poem, however, but at carrying over a method, a style, a way of writing, thought, and life.

But Jonson's adaptations betoken no failure of imagination; rather they reveal a particular kind of mind. Edmund Wilson, in an extremely provocative essay in literary psychology, likened Jonson to James Joyce, and the similarities he draws between the two writers apply to the question of their use of literary reference and allusion as well. Both Joyce's and Jonson's learning is like a kind of hoarding. Lines, phrases, patterns, shapes (as, with Joyce, sounds, fractions of syllables, rhymes, puns) become the objects amassed in the store of knowledge—in his feelings for language, Jonson seems much like one of his own stage misers. Learning is for him not so much a play of light upon, or elevation of, the self, or a metamorphosis in the inner life, but rather an accumulation of treasure which cannot help but overflow.

Moreover, Jonson, like Joyce, aims at the creation of language itself. The latter sought in his later writing to make the One Great Statement that, once made, would render all other assertions tautological or trivial, and he tried to cast that Statement in a Universal Language, assembled from all the tongues of men and of angels. But Jonson makes no attempt to go beyond English. Rather, he attempts to mark off a literary dialect within it, manipulating larger instead of smaller linguistic elements. He selects building blocks from Classic writers in much the same way that Modern poets will come to choose forms or styles in this eclectic age. Today, times past and places distant are raided for metrical and rhetorical schemes, or even for the very notions of what a poem *is*, in an attempt to find an authority broader and more compelling than that given by the uses of the previous generation. Jonson's tags, phrases, and comparisons become the counters in no universal language, but rather in a particular civilized one. It is the language of poetry whose ultimate constituents are not so much words, but rather combinations of and ways of using them.

And finally it must be said that Jonson's very way of being derivative was in itself original. F. R. Leavis has pointed out that if Jonson's followers in the seventeenth century seem to derive more from his own Classical sources than from Jonson himself, it is because "the indebtedness to Jonson's models is of a kind that it took Jonson's genius in the first place to incur; if the later poets learnt from these models, they had learnt from Jonson how to do so." This is undoubtedly true; but it should be added that Jonson's own pioneer concerns were for creating discourse in an ideal community, within which the literary dialect would be as speech. His Classical allusions and quotations are not covert tricks hiding cosmic jokes, as in Joyce, just as his poems, unlike those of Donne, Herbert, and Vaughan, for example, are not modeled on difficult texts for study, contemplation, and close reading, rather than upon songs, letters, dialogues. Their allusions aim at being recognizable accents, recognizable not only to a coterie of poets and gentlemen-scholars, but to a whole culture as well. If the notion of a civilization seems today to demand something larger, and the idea of humanistic literacy to be something smaller, perhaps, than it was for Jonson, his poetry nevertheless remains a monument of a literature that sought to engage life, but on its own terms. This is surely at once the oldest and the most urgently modern demand made upon the poetic virtue.

For the student of poetic form, Jonson's contribution to literary history is immense. In his grasp of the modality of verse, of the inevitable "choice of meter" which must be made, he advances the original contribution of Sidney. The latter's myriad attempts at all sorts of lyric forms were in the main, experimental: whether in the variety of meters in which he versified the Psalter, or the quantitative poems in the *Arcadia*, sheer compositional exuberance, and the exigencies of a particular moment seem to be at work. It is either a matter of trying on a form for its own sake, or casting about for a structural idea. But there is no sense of metrical genre about Sidney's shorter poems. With George Herbert, we have a radical extension of Sidney's practice in one direction, that of expressiveness. The overflowing variety of invention in *The Temple*, the scores and scores of unique through-composed and strophic patterns—all these seem directed not at a modal or generic variation, but at an internalized array of states. The form is frequently "read" tropically or figuratively by the language of the poem cast in it. Each form, as each poem for Wallace Stevens, is "the cry of its occasion."

Another Sidneyan experimentalist is Coleridge, using an array of meters but so enmeshed in the Romantic struggle to evolve new genres that although he is keenly aware of Classical and Neoclassical modality, he is torn between theorizing about it and practicing in a more expressive tradition as far as metrical "choice" is concerned. An extreme of non- or even anti-modal variation of style in the short poem is presented by Thomas Hardy, who makes us feel uncomfortable, often, at a decision about form which seems to have been taken in caprice, and then stuck to at all costs. Indeed, it is just out of such a sense of difficulty overcome that he is frequently able to generate formal, rhetorical, and structural force. But Hardy is almost the textbook case of want of modality; perhaps it is traceable to his having started a serious poetic career so late in life, and bursting into the blossom of verse so frenziedly because his poems, although written since his twenties, had been more a matter of the left hand until he gave up novels in the 1890s. It was not a matter for Hardy of finding a voice by searching for style and form, but of singing as many songs as possible.

Hardy's vast formal and structural repertoire exerted, as by his own frequent admission, a considerable formal influence on the young W. H. Auden, who was also absorbing Edward Thomas, Frost, Hopkins, early Germanic verse structures, and, later on, Rilke and Brecht. But after an early, self-consciously experimental approach to form, Auden developed a keen modal sense, and he became in the twentieth century the epitome of the master craftsman of verse. Modern poets can take one of two directions, it seems, in moving toward a characteristic use of form, in seeking to "learn a style from a despair" of belated arrival in a world where forms are not given, where style is not canonical. One of these is that of American Modernism, following the Emersonian injunction to "mount to Paradise / By the stairway of surprise"—in short, to seize early enough upon a poetic tessitura of one's own, to frame a mode of singing, as it were, that would make any other formal style impossible. The effect is to dissolve genre: it is not that the poet wishes to make distinguishable, say, "a short, ironic meditation on landscape by Poet X," but rather only "a Poet X poem." The other tradition is best exemplified by Auden, and in this he was Ben Jonson's heir in our age. His grasp of the competing necessities of the public and private realms were mirrored not only in his poetic morals but in his stylistic practice; using a vast array of forms, styles, systems, differentiating between private messages, songs, sermons, inscriptions, pronouncements, and so forth, he made of his technical brilliance more than merely a matter of his own delight. In craft began, for him as well as for his predecessor Jonson, responsibilities.

MARIJKE RIJSBERMAN

Forms of Ceremony in Ben Jonson's Masques

Ben Jonson's development as a writer of court masques is generally conceived as a linear process of progressive mastery over the art form, as the gradual realization of a single dramatic vision. The early masques are accordingly seen as apprentice-pieces, bearing the Jonsonian stamp, but falling short of the peculiar perfection of the later work. This conception of "the Jonsonian Masque" as a unified corpus of texts is informed by a tendency to regard it as a "literary" form, in contradistinction, presumably, to the masques written by Jonson's contemporaries. The term "literary" functions as a covert value judgment here, setting a standard by which the early work is barely visible at all. It seems to me that this unwittingly normative procedure is a reflection of the fact that the "mature" work is more readily assimilable to our usual notions of what constitutes (good) drama. It is relatively independent of the situation of its performance, and as a consequence the text acquires its customary self-sufficiency and something we might wish to describe as organic form. Stephen Orgel's objections to the early work in *The Jonsonian Masque,* which remains the most authoritative account to date, are made precisely in these terms. The "transformation scene," as he calls the transition from the anti-masque to the main masque, is not motivated by the text, but frequently resorts to a *deus ex machina* for its resolution. The different parts of the masque are thus improperly integrated, so that the work remains fragmentary, not to say formless. While I have no wish to argue that the early masques are superior to the later ones, although a good case can be made for *Hymenaei,* it seems to me that they are widely divergent in what they seek to accomplish. The current "literary" approach obscures such differences and does not do full justice even to the later work.

For all their traditionally literary qualities, Jonson's masques call for a different perspective, which takes into account the peculiar nature of the masque as royal ceremony, and can discern its radical difference from, say, a play staged at court for the king's diversion. The masque is determined by its nature as a gigantic, collective act of prostration before the monarch, sincere or otherwise, and is accordingly inseparable from the setting of its performance. As ceremony, it is—or should be—in seamless relation to its context, and the masque must integrate its fiction into the reality of the court environment if it is to achieve form and meaning at all. It is necessary, therefore, to pay attention to the way in which the masque negotiates this hurdle and attempts to break down the barrier between itself and the audience. The ceremonial nature of the masque is further determined by the relation of the fiction to the realm of the superhuman, both the royal and the divine, that is to say, by the way in which it ties the different levels together in the figure of the king. An understanding of the ceremony in turn crucially affects our understanding of the more purely literary aspects of the masques, such as the degree of metaphoricity of the allegory, or the motivation and mechanics of the transformation scene.

In the attempt to define the way in which the masque insinuates itself into the texture of ordinary reality, a clear break between "early" and "late" becomes visible in Jonson's career as a masque writer. It appears, in fact, that the earlier masques, up to *Oberon* (1611), are far more ambitious, in that they attempt to actively intervene in reality. They display a high seriousness in aesthetic vision which commands respect even where Jonson fails to realize it, at the same time that it must strike us as dangerously near the grandiose. Whereas the later masques are self-consciously textual allegories, which do not attempt to transcend their marginal nature but resign themselves to their linguistic impotence, the early masques, most clearly *The Masque of Blackness* and *Hymenaei,* are performative, in the sense that a "speech act" may be performative. They tend to rely on gestural, as opposed to verbal, signification to a far greater degree than the masques written after *Hymenaei,* and it is the gesture which is given the function of bridging the gap between the masque and its context. The early masques come close to being religious rites. They are almost sacramental in nature, and are actually parallel to the sacrament of the eucharist in intent. The early masque strives to open itself out and enforce upon reality its higher meanings, as delineated in the narrative by allegorical devices, through literalizing the metaphors it deploys, somewhat in the way the sacrament of the eucharist, in the doctrines of con- or transubstantiation, literalizes the symbolic meanings of the bread and wine. In so doing, the eucharist attempts to bring about an irruption of the divine into the texture of merely human reality and transform it permanently. A similar argument may be made for the early masques: they literalize the topos of the monarch as sun, and as (semi-) divine being, and thus attempt a form of homage which goes far beyond mere celebration or glorification. Jonson here arrogates to himself the office of establishing and confirming King James's legitimacy, attributing supernatural powers to him in the process and bestowing divine sanction on his reign. As if to prove the validity of his conception of the monarch—which, we may note, was met with considerable skepticism even then—he creates a situation in which James's supernatural power is to become operative not only within the fictional reality of the masque, but in actual political life. These situations in the early masques, which do not have full-fledged anti-masques, constitute the transformation scene. While we may argue with Orgel that the resolution is thus brought about by *deus ex machina,* it is hardly true that it is imperfectly motivated.

Obviously, there are great problems attached to this peculiar ceremonial strategy, which Jonson by no means in all cases knows how to deal with. In *The Masque of Blackness,* for instance, he sets up a situation to Queen Anne's specifications, to which he cannot provide the required solution. The plot, if it deserves that name, concerns a number of Ethiopian ladies, danced by the queen and eleven noblewomen of her entourage, whose skins are supposed to have been scorched black when Phaëton had his misadventure with the chariot of the sun. They have been told that another sun, which never sets and sheds its beams on a country the name of which ends in "tania," possesses the power of bleaching them back to their original hue. James, of course, is the referent of the riddle, the solution and explanation of which is phrased in the following way:

> With that great name Britannia, this blessed isle
> Hath won her ancient dignity and style,
> *A world divided from the world,* and tried
> The abstract of it in his general pride.
> For were the world with all his wealth a ring,
> Britannia, whose new name makes all tongues sing,
> Might be a diamond worthy to enchase it,
> Ruled by a sun that to this height doth grace it,

Whose beams shine day and night, and are of force
To blanch an Aethiop, and revive a corse.
His light sciential is, and, past mere nature,
Can salve the rude defects of every creature.

After the riddle has been solved, by recourse to the topos of the royal sun
and by the attribution of power "past mere nature" to James, the Ethiopian
ladies naturally present themselves to the monarch, with the petition that the
desired transformation be accomplished. The shift of the fictional place of
action from Britain's shore to the actual situation at court moves the masque
across its own boundaries into reality. A double movement takes place by
which the stage has come to include the audience, but by which at the same
time reality invades the fiction. Instead of enforcing the familiar idea that
"all the world's a stage," and showing James and his court to be an illusion,
the illusion tries to prove its reality by drawing the real person of the king
into its sphere. A further interpenetration of the two realms through the
transformation scene Jonson has clearly been working towards (that is to
say, an actual blanching of the Aethiops) would clinch the argument that
James is divine and permanently change life in Britain through his benign
influence. Such a literalization of what started out as a fairly hackneyed
metaphor would carry over the divine from the masque into reality.

Before turning to the greatest problem Jonson has thus set himself up
for, we may note another difficulty involved in this strategy. The idea of
James as ruler by divine sanction did not command universal assent. Indeed,
James disseminated it himself as a piece of official propaganda. Jonson shows
himself uncomfortable with the idea too, and is hesitant in elevating James
to divine stature. In his contribution to the king's entertainment at the royal
entry into London (1603), he only *compares* the royal family to gods in the
epithet "godlike race." He apparently felt compelled to justify the figure even
so, as he provides the following gloss in the printed text: "An attribute giuen
to great persons, fitly aboue other humanity, and in frequent use with all the
greeke Poets, especially *Homer.*" In *The Masque of Blackness,* James is provided with a divine lineage, being styled "Neptune's son" (181), about which
Jonson is again rather defensive. He explains the device in another gloss:
"Alluding to the rite of styling princes after the name of their princedoms;
so is he still Albion and Neptune's son that governs." Clearly Jonson was
not very happy with the conceit, but evidently his conception of the masque
at this stage required elevating the monarch to divinity. As classical mythology does not provide sufficient authority for the conceit, the blanching
of the daughters of Niger becomes indispensable, not only as the device by

which the fiction might be integrated into reality but also on the less ambitious homiletic level.

Unfortunately, the literalization is impossible: James obviously cannot be put to the test and asked to take the soot off the skins of the masquers by some magical gesture, the way Elizabeth, for instance, can be asked to settle the shepherds' dispute and restore the peace in Sidney's *Lady of May,* despite the risk that she make the wrong decision. If Jonson had gone through with the projected transformation scene the entire structure of the masque would have come tumbling down, exposing the fiction rather than enforcing it, and vitiating any degree of interpenetration and alignment with actual court life still possible. At the last moment the masque veers back into metaphor, giving the ladies a bleaching formula and telling them to come back in a year. The net result is that the masque, instead of realizing the divine in the person of the king and actualizing it for his court, stops short at delineating the commensurability of the royal with the divine, and keeps the two realms strictly apart. The daughters of Niger are personifications of such things as abundance, splendor and sweetness. The device of having them repair to James's court associates his reign with the good qualities they personify. Jonson suggests, then, that Britain under James is commensurable to a higher reality, but *The Masque of Blackness* remains an allegory, unable to transcend its fictionality. Anticipating a later argument, I may point out that this is essentially the strategy serving the later masques. But it is not because Jonson's goals in *The Masque of Blackness* proved unattainable that he reverts to the use of allegory later on, as his triumph in *Hymenaei* shows.

The occasion of *Hymenaei* (1606), the political marriage of the Earl of Essex to Lady Francis Howard, provided a considerably more auspicious narrative situation for Jonson's purposes than the queen's wishes for *The Masque of Blackness* had turned out to be. *Hymenaei*—which consists of two parts, the masque proper and a barriers, performed on two successive nights—is a celebration of the wedding at the same time that it is, in its overall structure, a celebration and consecration of the monarch in whose honor it was performed. The basic narrative situation is the reenactment of the marriage-rite, which is transposed to a higher level and becomes a rite by which James is wedded to his subjects, and a demonstration of his divine power. The fictional situation is merged with the actual situation of the performance in such a way that all differences are leveled out. The groundwork is thus laid for the coalescence of the divine and the human realms into a perfectly continuous unity. The opening song announces "mysteries" (59) and "rites" (63) to be performed in the masque, from which the profane are to be excluded (57, 66). The "mysteries," apart from having a simple intradiegetic reference to the wedding ceremony, also refers to the masque as a whole.

Whereas in *The Masque of Blackness* James is for the most part simply a passive on-looker and addressee, failing at the crucial moment to take an active role, he is given a number of parts to play in the action of *Hymenaei*. He retains his actual character when he enters the fictional realm, however, and does not impersonate any but his ordinary self. As a consequence, his presence bestows actuality upon the fictional situation. He is immediately drawn into the action by Hymen in his opening speech:

> What more than usual light,
> Throughout the place extended,
>   Makes Juno's fane so bright!
> Is there some greater deity descended?
>
>   Or reign on earth those powers
> So rich, as with their beams
>   Grace Union more than ours,
> And bound her influence in their happier streams?
>
>   'Tis so: this same is he,
> The king, and priest of peace!
>
> (72–81)

James is thus celebrated again for having united the kingdoms of England and Scotland and for his—not always appreciated—pacifism. He becomes a rival to Hymen, god of marriage and union, who immediately acknowledges James as a superior. The implication is that James is a deity of a higher order than Hymen, but the claim is not definitively made. Hymen's " 'Tis so" could be an answer to either of the questions asked in the first two stanzas of the poem, and does not actually decide whether James is to be regarded as a "greater deity" or a human being who holds the office of mediator between God and man. The epithet "priest of peace" strengthens the suggested possibility that James's divine power is not his own but held by proxy only. This solution is more felicitous than the one in *The Masque of Blackness,* as it asserts that James possesses divine power without going so far as to make the potentially blasphemous claim of divine stature for him. Jonson adheres to the same strategy throughout the masque, as for instance in the closing speech of the barriers spoken by Truth. Truth has just successfully defended the propriety of marriage and the blessedness of divinely ordained unions against Opinion's attacks. She has thus vindicated James as priest presiding over the rite. Truth closes her defense with a gesture of submission to James, resigning her attributes to him:

> This royal judge [i.e., James] of our contention
> Will prop, I know, what I have undergone;
> To whose right sacred highness I resign
> Low, at his feet, this starry crown of mine,
> To show his rule and judgment is divine.
> (845–49)

Again Jonson refrains from claiming divine stature for James, while granting him the possession of divine power, to which he here adds the royal incapacity to err.

James presides over the marriage-rite being performed in the masque, then, as the supreme priest of union and peace on earth. However, James is not in the first place associated with marriage, and in the course of the masque the focus is shifted to other forms of union under his influence. The rite burgeons out from a simple wedding ceremony to a ceremony confirming the peaceful union of Britain with neighboring nations, the union of England and Scotland, the union of the monarch with his subjects, and the union of subject with subject. Reason's remonstration with the unruly humors and affections, who descend upon the scene just before the rite is to be performed, indicates that it is also Union which "makes souls with bodies mix in love, / Contracts the world in one, and therein Jove, / Is spring and end of all things" (124–26). We are reminded here that James is the head of the Church of England, the supreme "priest" in the nation. The unions formed under his auspices are informed by a Platonic love, directing his people to God, "the spring and end of all things," rather than coming to rest in himself. James's powers are not only *asserted* in *Hymenaei*, however, but actually demonstrated throughout the masque. As priest of union, he binds the bride and groom in wedlock, and binds his subjects to himself and to each other in the first night's entertainment, the masque proper. The high point of the evening, its transformation scene, is the moment just before the bride and groom are led off to the nuptial bower. The masquers form a circle linking hands, and are urged by Reason to make obeisance to James and receive his blessing:

> Now move united and in gait,
> As you in pairs do front the state,
> With grateful honors thank his grace
> That hath so glorified the place,

> As in a circle you depart
> Linked hand in hand, so heart in heart
> May all those bodies still remain
> Whom he, with so much sacred pain,
> No less hath bound within his realms
> Than they are with the ocean's streams.
> Long may his union find increase
> As he to ours hath deigned his peace.
>
> (377–88)

Under James's auspices and influence the human circle has been formed, and, with his subjects paying him homage now, the union is consecrated. He is not just metaphorically the priest of union, then, but is actually made to perform the ceremonies. This time the attempted literalization is achieved: the divine is actualized in the figure of the king and made operative, so that it is also realized on the level of ordinary humanity.

We may also note that Jonson has improved on his device of shifting the place of action to the actual court setting, by which he negotiates the crossing of fictionality and reality in *The Masque of Blackness*. In *Hymenaei*, the place of action is a middle ground between the celestial and the sublunar—a hallowed spot where marriages are consecrated and where heaven and earth meet. It is also a middle ground of human nature, where the spiritual and carnal are harmonized and prepared for union, as symbolized by divine Reason and her handmaidens on the one hand, and the human affections on the other. After the initial disciplining of the humors and affections, they assist at the wedding in perfect harmony with Reason. In the revels the entire audience is drawn into this sacred spot, implying that they too have been sufficiently purified to tread its ground. Through the constant crossover from fictionality into actuality in the addresses to the king and in the role he is given to perform, the place of action is also intimately connected to the place of performance, Whitehall. As a consequence the hallowed spot may be identified with Britain. The masque thus also effects a hallowing of the country as sacred to union and peace.

On this reading of the masque, an interpretation of Jonson's introduction to the printed text becomes possible which diverges from the one current among critics of Jonson and the masque form. Jonson's introductory polemic with the tastes of his audience is usually read as an early version of "An Expostulation with Inigo Jones." The poem is an indictment of his former collaborator as a purveyor of light entertainment and a mere manipulator of spectacular stage effects, who caters to the frivolity and flabby tastes of his audience. The association of the introduction with a text written a quarter of a century later both assumes and confirms that the earlier text is an expression of Jonson's "mature" conception of the masque form, and precludes the recognition that Jonson is actually commenting on the ritual nature of *Hymenaei*. He identifies his own contribution with the real substance and significance of the masque, describing his work as its "soul" (6, 8), as opposed to the fleeting spectacle, "the outward celebration or show" (11–12) in which it is embodied, and which can be credited to Inigo Jones. The traditional interpretation cannot make much more of this terminology than that through it Jonson announces his own seriousness of purpose, and his endeavor to base the masque on classical mythology, in the face of the alleged frivolity of the court audience and of the king's architect. The phrase "more removed mysteries" (16–17) in particular cannot be given any specific content, unless it is read as a rephrasing of Jonson's statement that he devised "the most high and hearty inventions to furnish the inward parts, and those grounded upon antiquity and solid learnings" (14–15). This reading would suggest that Jonson proposes to write allegories that draw on his firsthand knowledge of classical literature and on the emblem books and compendia of iconographical lore so popular at the time. There is, however, no pressing reason for regarding the two phrases as identical in content. Moreover, the results still remain vague, as allegory may take a wide variety of forms. Only in dissociating the introduction from the "Expostulation" and connecting the "more removed mysteries" with the "mysterious rites" that have a "mystic sense" (137), as Reason describes the wedding in the masque, does a more precise reading become available. The soul/body opposition used in the introduction may also be connected with the same opposition as delineated in one of the glosses, where Jonson explains that the humors and affections are "brought in before marriage as disturbers of that mystical body and the rites which were soul unto it." It seems to me that the conclusion inevitably is that Jonson conceived of *Hymenaei* as a whole in ritual terms. What he complains about in his introduction is that no one bothered to understand the "mystic sense" of his work.

None of the masques conceived after *Hymenaei*, however, conform to the ritual pattern, so that we may consider the introduction as Jonson's statement of a poetics he was already in the process of abandoning. Indeed, there are elements in *Hymenaei* which foreshadow the strictly allegorical methods he was later to rely on exclusively. In the debate between Truth and Opinion concerning the propriety of marriage, for instance, Opinion advances the argument that the single state is preferable because it secures one's self-sufficiency and gives one a center in oneself:

Where virgins in their sweet and peaceful state
Have all things perfect, spin their own free fate,
Depend on no proud second, are their own
Center and circle, now and always one.
To whose example we do still hear named
One god, one nature, and but one world framed,
One sun, one moon, one element of fire,
So, of the rest; one king that doth inspire
Soul to all bodies in this royal sphere.

(717–25)

Truth makes an immediate rejoinder with the questions "And where is marriage more declared than there? / Is there a band more strict than that doth
tie / The soul and body in such unity? / Subjects to sovereigns?" (726–29).
James's union with his subjects is thus a figure of marriage and of the union
of body and soul, and vice versa. In this scheme James is the model rather
than the priest of peaceful union, and all the different kinds of union celebrated are only metaphorically related. Marriage, in Truth's defense, is an
allegory of all higher unions, such as the union of king and subjects. The
humors and affections also prompt allegorical exegesis, in a gloss provided
for those too "thick" to see with their own eyes. It is worth quoting at
length:

First, as natural bodies, so likewise in minds, there is no disease
or distemperature but is caused either by some abounding humor
or perverse affection; after the same manner, in politic bodies
(where order, ceremony, state, reverence, devotion are parts of
the mind) by the difference or predominant will of what we metaphorically call *humors* or *affections* all things are troubled and
confused. These, therefore, were tropically brought in before marriage as disturbers of that mystical body and the rites which were
soul unto it, that afterwards, in marriage, being dutifully tempered by her power, they might more fully celebrate the happiness
of such as live in that sweet union to the harmonious laws of
nature and reason.

The metaphorical relation between the humors and affections and the forces
that disrupt and distemper the body politic, to be subdued in a literal or
metaphorical marriage, again make explicit that marriage is a figure for the
tie between James and his people. Jonson has here reached a point where the
later masques stop short, but beyond which he takes *Hymenaei* by appointing

James priest of the rites, so paving the way for the literalization of the allegory. This literalization brings about the irruption of the divine into sublunar reality and the transcendence of the fictionality of the masque by which its meanings are enforced.

A number of reasons may be adduced for the change in Jonson's basic conception of the masque, from a ritual to a homiletic form. The most obvious reason one can point to is that Jonson became disappointed with James, as so many of his contemporaries were. Sad reality will have led him to the rejection of the idea that James possessed divine power. There is a hint of another reason in the text of *Hymenaei* itelf, where Jonson laments the transitoriness of "the first night's solemnity" (520). He remembers that the masque "was of power to surprise with delight, and steal away the spectators from themselves" (525–26). He recognizes at the same time that his power did not last beyond the duration of the performance, and that the spectators were lifted to a higher awareness only temporarily: "Only the envy was that it lasted not still, or, now it is past, cannot by imagination, much less description, be recovered to a part of that spirit it had in the gliding by" (529–32). The masque is too dependent on the pomp and splendor—on Jones's mere fleeting spectacle—for its effects. The transcendence Jonson achieves is severely limited and for the most part simply ignored, and he seems to have recognized the futility of his attempts to improve reality through the masque.

The Masque of Beauty (1608), conceived simultaneously with *The Masque of Blackness,* though performed three years later, still more or less adheres to the old pattern. *The Masque of Queens* (1609) on the other hand, is single-mindedly earthbound. The transformation scene, from the antimasque to the main masque presenting the House of Fame and history's most virtuous queens (among whom Queen Anne), is brought about, insofar as it is brought about by anything at all, by the appearance of Heroic Virtue. The virtuous queens are decidedly mortals, and having nothing of the divine about them. Their virtue is commensurable with a higher reality, from which, however, they are cut off, just as the masque remains cut off from it. Heroic Virtue describes the purpose of the masque in announcing that Fame "to this lesser world and greatest isle / Tonight sounds Honor" (371–72). Extolling Britain is indeed all the masque does or tries to do. It is instructive to pay more detailed attention to *Oberon* (1611), which is more inspired than *The Masque of Queens,* and in which the new structure has fully crystallized.

At the beginning of *Oberon*'s main masque, a sylvan describes the purpose of the night's entertainment in terms of the new homiletic approach:

"A night of homage to the British court, / And ceremony due to Arthur's chair" (240–41). All traces of mysteries and rites have vanished, though the word "rites" is still used to describe the action, as in the lines, "That all that shall behold the rites / Performed by princely Oberon and these knights, / May without stop point out the proper heir / Designed so long for Arthur's crowns and chair" (281–84). The rites performed by Oberon, danced by Crown Prince Henry, consist in the official coming out of the young prince— a social rather than a religious occasion. The most interesting aspect of the masque is the confrontation and implicit power struggle between Henry and James, which is resolved when Oberon and his companions "pay / Their annual vows" (245–46) to the king. The religious, ritual nature of the masque has evaporated, leaving as its only function a celebration of James's royal virtues and a demonstration of his subjects' continued loyalty. With the ritual pattern the claim to James's divine ordination has vanished. His legitimacy is now established from a very different, merely historical, per-spective, on the basis of the claim to descent from Arthur—a conventional piece of Tudor propaganda, as Orgel points out, which Jonson used quite often in the later period. He is consequently praised only for human attain-ments. The song by the two fays (286–97) gives a catalog of his virtues, comprising "majesty," "glory," "wisdom," "knowledge," "piety," in short "every virtue of a king," but nothing divine. Some of the old terminology is still in evidence—as in James's "sole power and magic" (249)—but it carries no conviction and is absorbed into the new rhetoric, which paints the mon-arch as "the matter of virtue, and placed high. / His meditations to his height are even, / And all their issue is akin to heaven" (258–60). There is some ambiguity about the word "akin" here, but the primary meaning is un-doubtedly that of similitude, commensurability, rather than "blood" rela-tion. The other topoi employed in the descriptions of James must also be read as similes. The judgment that James is "a god o'er kings" (261) merely means that he is better and greater than other kings, not that he is a god. The sun topos even proclaims its metaphorical nature in its outward form: "he holds his course as certain as the sun" (270). Because James possesses the human virtues to an extraordinarily high degree, his subjects do him homage and pledge themselves to him. They look to him for protection, and profess, through the sylvan, that he is the cause that they live "Sustained in form, fame and felicity, / From rage of fortune or the fear to die" (251–52). The masque gives no other reason for this state of affairs, however, than that James is wise and pious, and, above all, a pacifist. The principal homiletic speech, spoken by Silenus, even has a smack of the prescriptive, rather than the descriptive, about it: "He is a god o'er kings, yet stoops he then, / Nearest a man when he doth govern men, / To teach them by the sweetness of his sway, / And not by force" (261–64). The principle of *praecipere laudando* seems to have replaced the ritual pattern.

Oberon is one of the masques Orgel discusses at length, and one of those he deems imperfect, as the transformation scene moves the center of attention outside the fiction to James in his own person. But although it moves beyond its fictional boundaries, the masque does not really open out, as *Hymenaei* did. The entire fictional world of the masque confronts the king and pays its respects to him—upon which nothing really happens. James is not given a role at all, except as addressee of the homilies. He never enters the fictional realm, which, in turn, does not really cross over into actuality, except for that one tense moment of confrontation between the king and crown prince. The masquers withdraw again into the fiction—which, significantly, is situated in fairyland—and they take the audience with them during the revels. Order and harmony have been achieved within the fiction by the appearance of Oberon and Silenus at the beginning of the main masque, and the audience is taken up to its level. There is almost a note of defiance in the circumstance that James is left behind, while his son represents the principle of order and harmony in the ideal world of the main masque. Be this as it may, the ideal is transitory and is dispelled by Phosphorus, the herald of the day, as if to suggest that the harmony achieved in the masque is a mere dream rudely broken by morning.

The masque Jonson wrote almost simultaneously with *Oberon, Love Freed from Ignorance and Folly* (1611), is a comparatively slight piece, but interesting, as it may be taken as an almost programmatic statement of Jonson's new poetics. The basic design is very simple, turning on the solution of a riddle cast in almost the same terms as the one in *The Masque of Blackness*. Again, Albion, as an alternative name for James, is the answer. The situation is crucially different from that in Jonson's first masque, however. This time Love is asked to solve the riddle by the Sphinx, and if he succeeds he will have freed the "eleven daughters of the morn" held captive by the mythical monster. If he fails he will lose his life. Jonson explains the allegorical meanings of this scheme in a lengthy gloss worth quoting entire:

> The meaning of this is that these ladies, being the perfect issue of beauty and all worldly grace, were carried by love to celebrate the majesty and wisdom of the king, figured in the sun, and seated in these extreme parts of the world, where they were rudely received by ignorance on their first approach, to the hazard of their affection, it being her nature to hinder all noble actions; but that

the love which brought them thither was not willing to forsake
them, no more than they were to abandon it, yet was it enough
perplexed, in that the monster ignorance still covets to enwrap
itself in dark and obscure terms, and betray that way, whereas
true love affects to express itself with all clearness and simplicity.

This manages to be quite uncomplimentary to England and to James's court,
and takes back all the earlier masques said in praise of him. He is still
honored in the riddle and the gloss for his wisdom and majesty, but is at
the same time accused in no uncertain terms of malgoverning his country.
He cannot dispel ignorance, he is unable to protect the visiting ladies from
the monster that holds his kingdom and reign in its grip, and, lastly, he does
nothing for those who honor him. Significantly, it is not he who frees the
ladies from the clutches of the Sphinx and destroys the monster, but Love,
with the intervention of the priests of the muses. In another gloss, appended
to lines 211–14, Jonson explains that even Love is impotent, and does not
have the wisdom sufficient to conquer the Sphinx, until "divinely instructed."
The implication is that James, being unable (or worse, perhaps unwilling) to
do anything against the Sphinx, has not received divine instruction, and that
his wisdom is of a sort inferior to that finally attained to by Love, with the
aid of the muses' ministers, the poets. The overall structure of the masque
conforms to the estimate of James and his reign implicit in the allegory, that
is to say, it quite ignores him. Love makes a bow to the monarch in solving
the riddle, and the masque momentarily opens itself up to the court, but
immediately withdraws again. Love supplants the king as object of celebration, and is actually crowned by the Graces, because "Without his happy
wit / All form and beauty had been dead" (270–71). James is even deposed
from the sun topos by Aurora's daughters: it is their "beams" which make
it "ever day" in Britain. Moreover, their loss would have meant the undoing
of Nature too, which means that everything, including James, depends on
them and the love that protects them. Accordingly, the masquers pledge
themselves to Beauty rather than to James:

> We wish to see it [i.e., Beauty] still, and prove
> What ways we may deserve;
> We court, we praise, we more than love;
> We are not grieved to serve.
>
> (306–9)

These lines are spoken after the revels in which the entire audience dance,
which means that James's entire court—with the sole exception of himself—

are included in these "we's." The masque explicitly and deliberately turns away from the king and from court reality, and remains locked in its own allegory, the ideal world where only beauty is served, into which the audience is also admitted. In the very last line another perfunctory bow is made to James, who is styled "sun throned in the west," which acknowledges his continuing presence, but at the same time intimates that he is a setting sun. James remains an onlooker shut out from the ideal fiction for which his own court deserts him.

Another significant feature of *Love Freed* is that divine instruction is mediated through the priests of the muses, who thus rescue Love and Beauty. Jonson describes the priests in a gloss as "all that have the spirit of prophecy." In Jonson's time, the tradition which conceived of poetry as divinely inspired, visionary allegory was losing ground to the new humanist aesthetic, which regarded poetry mainly in terms of moral instruction, but it was still sufficiently alive to justify the identification of the priests with allegorical poets here. The conclusion follows that it is poetry which rescues Love and Beauty and dispels Ignorance, and that it is Jonson himself who does so in this particular instance. In other words, Jonson now takes the role he earlier allotted to James, and literature takes over from ritual and from royal influence in establishing the higher reality the masques strive to actualize, if only for the duration of the revels. Divine power is no longer made operative in reality but only within the fictional realm, and it is not James who wields it but the poet. The masques come to rest in their own literariness.

Love Freed definitively establishes the general pattern of the later masques: a pattern of more or less backhanded homiletic to the king, of self-conscious literary artifice, and of a flat refusal to try to transcend fictional limits. It does not, however, plumb the depths of Jonson's eventual estimate of James. In *News from the New World* (1620), the masquers are enjoined to look at James's face "Whence you as from a mirror take / The sun's reflected light" (308–9). The bottom line of James's gradual depreciation is reached in *The Gypsies Metamorphosed* (1621), where Jonson portrays James as presiding over a group of robbers and gypsies by way of a court. Jonson is also more explicit on occasion about the literary, textual nature of the late masques, which are self-enclosed to the point of seeming unaware of the audience. In *Pleasure Reconciled to Virtue* (1618), the audience is no longer simply drawn into the fictional realm and lifted up to its higher order of being, in which pleasure and virtue have been reconciled. In Daedalus's first song the dancers are told to dance in such a way that

men may read each act you do,
And when they see the graces meet,

> Admire the wisdom of your feet.
> For dancing is an exercise
>   Not only shows the mover's wit,
> But maketh the beholder wise,
>   As he hath power to rise to it.
>   (237–43)

The masque as a whole is given a literary status, then, and the audience will only be taken up into its ideal reality and be made wise as they have power to "read" the masque and lift themselves up to its level. Jonson has here inscribed the figure of reading into the visual effects and appropriated them, scoring a hit at Inigo Jones. History has proved him right in thinking the literary ingredient in the masque to be the most valuable and permanent.

Chronology

1572	Ben Jonson born, probably on June 11, in London, some time after his father's death.
(?)1574	His mother remarries a bricklayer.
1583–88	Attends Westminster School, studying under Master William Camden.
1588–96	Apprenticed to his stepfather; he also fights as a volunteer soldier in the wars in the Netherlands (exact dates unknown).
(?)1594	Marries.
1597	Acts in a strolling company, and collaborates on *The Isle of Dogs* (now lost), for which he is imprisoned on charges of sedition.
1598	*The Case Is Altered* and *Every Man in His Humour* performed; is imprisoned after killing an actor in a duel, but freed on pleading the right of clergy.
1599	*Every Man out of His Humour* performed.
1600	*Cynthia's Revels* performed.
1601	*Poetaster* performed.
1603	Son Benjamin dies. *Sejanus* performed, but hissed off the stage.
1605	Voluntarily goes to prison to join his collaborators Marston and Chapman (*Eastward Ho!*), who had been imprisoned on charges of mockery of the Scots.
1606	*Volpone* performed.

1609	*Epicoene* performed.
1610	*The Alchemist* performed.
1611	*Catiline* performed, unsuccessfully.
1612–13	Acts as tutor to the son of Sir Walter Raleigh on his French tour.
1614	*Bartholomew Fair* performed.
1616	Publishes a folio edition of his *Works; The Devil Is an Ass* performed; is granted a government pension (which he never receives).
1618–19	Goes on walking tour of Scotland, visiting Drummond of Hawthornden along the way.
1619	Receives an Honorary M.A. from Oxford University.
1623	House destroyed by fire; some work in progress is lost.
1626	*The Staple of News* performed.
1628	Partially paralyzed by a stroke; appointed Chronologer of the City of London.
1629	*The New Inne* performed and hissed off the stage.
1632	*The Magnetic Lady* performed.
1633	*A Tale of a Tub* performed (probably written much earlier).
1637	Dies on August 6, and is buried in Westminster Abbey.

Contributors

HAROLD BLOOM, Sterling Professor of the Humanities at Yale University, is the author of *The Anxiety of Influence, Poetry and Repression,* and many other volumes of literary criticism. His forthcoming study, *Freud: Transference and Authority,* attempts a full-scale reading of all of Freud's major writings. A MacArthur Prize Fellow, he is general editor of five series of literary criticism published by Chelsea House.

JONAS A. BARISH is Professor of English at the University of California at Berkeley. He is the author of *Ben Jonson and the Language of Prose Comedy* and *The Antitheatrical Prejudice.* He has edited *Ben Jonson: A Collection of Critical Essays* and a casebook on *Volpone* as well as the text of *Sejanus* for the Yale Ben Jonson.

EDWARD B. PARTRIDGE is Professor of English Emeritus at Tulane University. He has written the classic *The Broken Compass: A Study of the Major Comedies of Ben Jonson,* and edited *Bartholomew Fair.*

GEOFFREY HILL is generally acknowledged to be one of the finest poets currently writing in English. His volumes of verse include *For the Unfallen, King Log, Mercian Hymns* and, most recently, *The Mystery of Charles Peguy.* He is also the author of *The Lords of Limit: Essays on Literature and Ideas,* and of numerous articles on poetry.

STEPHEN ORGEL teaches in the Department of English at Johns Hopkins University. He is the author of *The Jonsonian Masque* and *The Illusion of Power.* He has also edited the complete poems of Christopher Marlowe and numerous anthologies of literary criticism.

WILLIAM BLISSETT, Professor of English at the University of Toronto, is the editor of *A Celebration of Ben Jonson.* His writings include, besides work on Elizabethan drama, *Long Conversation: A Memoir of David Jones.*

THOMAS M. GREENE is Professor of Renaissance Studies and Comparative Literature at Yale. His critical works include *The Descent from Heaven, Rabelais: A Study in Comic Courage, The Light in Troy: Imitation and Discovery in Renaissance Poetry,* and *The Vulnerable Text.*

WILLIAM KERRIGAN is Professor of English at the University of Virginia, and an authority on Milton. His work includes *The Prophetic Milton* and *The Sacred Complex: On the Psychogenesis of Paradise Lost.* He is also coeditor of *Interpreting Lacan* and *Taking Chances: Derrida, Psychoanalysis and Literature.*

A. RICHARD DUTTON is Lecturer in English at the University of Lancaster and has written widely on Jonson. His work includes *Ben Jonson: To the First Folio* and an edition of *The Epigrams* and *The Forest.*

JONATHAN HAYNES is Professor of English at Albion College. He has written on the work of George Sandys.

JONATHAN DOLLIMORE is the author of *Radical Tragedy: Religion, Ideology, & Power in the Drama of Shakespeare and His Contemporaries.* He also coedited with Alan Sinfield *The Selected Plays of John Webster.*

JOSEPH LOEWENSTEIN is Assistant Professor of English at Washington University. He is the author of *Responsive Readings.*

STANLEY FISH, Professor of English at Duke University, is the author of *Surprised by Sin: The Reader in Paradise Lost* and *Is There a Text in This Class?*

JOHN HOLLANDER is A. Bartlett Giamatti Professor of English at Yale University. His most recent books include *The Figure of Echo* and *Powers of Thirteen,* a poetic sequence.

MARIJKE RIJSBERMAN is in the Department of Comparative Literature at Yale University and is working on a study of seventeenth-century allegory.

Bibliography

Babb, Howard S. "The 'Epitaph on Elizabeth, L. H.' and Ben Jonson's Style." *JEGP* 62 (1963): 738–44.

Bamborough, J. B. *Ben Jonson*. London: Hutchinson, 1970.

Barish, Jonas. *Ben Jonson and the Language of Prose Comedy*. Cambridge: Harvard University Press, 1960.

———. "The Interpretation of Jonson's Courtly Spectacle." *PMLA* 61 (1946): 473.

———. "Jonson and the Loathéd Stage." In *The Anti-Theatrical Prejudice*, 132–54. Berkeley and Los Angeles: University of California Press, 1981.

———. "Ovid, Juvenal, and *The Silent Woman*." *PMLA* 71 (1956): 213–28.

Barton, Anne. *Ben Jonson, Dramatist*. Cambridge: Cambridge University Press, 1984.

———. "*The New Inn* and the Problem of Jonson's Late Style." *English Literary Renaissance* 9 (1979): 395–418.

Beaurline, L. A. *Jonson and Elizabethan Comedy: Essays in Dramatic Rhetoric*. San Marino, Calif.: Huntington Library Press, 1978.

Blissett, William Julian Patrik and R. W. Van Fossen. *A Celebration of Ben Jonson*. Toronto: University of Toronto Press, 1973.

Bryant, J. A. *The Compassionate Satirist: Ben Jonson and His Imperfect World*. Athens: University of Georgia Press, 1972.

Campbell, Oscar J. *Comicall Satyre and Shakespeare's Troilus and Cressida*. San Marino, Calif.: Huntington Library Press, 1965.

Cunningham, Dolora. "The Jonsonian Masque as a Literary Form." *ELH* 22 (1955): 93–124.

Dessen, Alan C. "*The Alchemist:* Jonson's 'Estates' Play." *Renaissance Drama* 7 (1964): 35–54.

Donaldson, Ian. *The World Upside Down*. Oxford: Oxford University Press, 1970.

Duncan, D. *Ben Jonson and the Lucianic Tradition*. Cambridge: Cambridge University Press, 1979.

Dutton, A. Richard. *Ben Jonson: To the First Folio*. Cambridge: Cambridge University Press, 1983.

Ferry, Anne. *All in War with Time: Love Poetry of Shakespeare, Donne, Jonson, Marvell*. Cambridge: Harvard University Press, 1975.

Fowler, Alastair. "The Locality of Jonson's *To Penhurst*." In *Conceitful Thought*. Edinburgh: University of Edinburgh Press, 1975.

Gibbons, Brian. *Jacobean City Comedy.* Cambridge: Harvard University Press, 1968.

Gilbert, A. H. "The Function of the Masques in *Cynthia's Revels.*" *Philological Quarterly* 22 (1943): 211–30.

———. *The Symbolic Personages in the Masques of Ben Jonson.* Durham, N.C.: Duke University Press, 1948.

Gilman, Ernest. *The Curious Perspective.* New Haven: Yale University Press, 1978.

Gordon, Donald J. *The Renaissance Imagination.* Berkeley and Los Angeles: University of California Press, 1975.

Guibbory, Achsah. "Ben Jonson: Stoic Constancy and Cyclical Vicissitude." In *The Map of Time: Seventeenth Century English Literature and Ideas of Pattern in History,* 102–36. Urbana: University of Illinois Press, 1986.

Harding, Robert. "Corruption and the Moral Boundaries of Patronage in the Renaissance." In *Patronage in the Renaissance,* edited by Guy Fitch Lytle and Stephen Orgel, 54–56. Princeton, N.J.: Princeton University Press, 1981.

Hawkins, H. "Folly, Incurable Disease, and *Volpone.*" *Studies in English Literature 1500–1900* 8 (1968): 335–48.

Heffner, Ray L. "Unifying Symbols in the Comedy of Ben Jonson." In *English Stage Comedy,* edited by W. K. Wimsatt, 74–97. New York: Columbia University Press, 1955.

Jackson, Gabriele B. *Vision and Judgment in Ben Jonson's Drama.* New Haven: Yale University Press, 1968.

Kernan, Alvin B. *The Cankered Muse.* New Haven: Yale University Press, 1959.

———, ed. *Two Renaissance Mythmakers: Christopher Marlowe and Ben Jonson.* Baltimore: Johns Hopkins University Press, 1977.

Knights, L. C. *Drama and Society in the Age of Jonson.* London: Chatto & Windus, 1937.

Lawry, Jon S. "A Prospect of Jonson's *The New Inn.*" *Studies in English Literature* 23 (1983): 310–27.

Leggatt, A. *Ben Jonson: His Vision and His Art.* New York: Methuen, 1981.

Levin, Harry. "Jonson's Metempsychosis." *Philological Quarterly* 22 (1943): 231–39.

Loewenstein, Joseph. *Responsive Readings: Versions of Echo in Pastoral, Epic, and the Jonsonian Masque.* New Haven: Yale University Press, 1984.

Meagher, John C. *Method and Meaning in Jonson's Masques.* Notre Dame, Ind.: University of Notre Dame Press, 1966.

Newton, Richard C. "'Goe, quit 'hem all': Ben Jonson and Formal Verse Satire." *Studies in English Literature* 16 (1976): 105–16.

Noyes, R. G. *Ben Jonson on the English Stage.* Cambridge: Harvard University Press, 1935.

Orgel, Stephen. *The Illusion of Power: Political Theatre in the English Renaissance.* Berkeley and Los Angeles: University of California Press, 1975.

———. *The Jonsonian Masque.* Cambridge: Harvard University Press, 1968.

Ornstein, Robert. *The Moral Vision of Jacobean Tragedy.* Madison: University of Wisconsin Press, 1965.

Parfitt, George. *Ben Jonson: Public Poet and Private Man.* London: Dent, 1976.

Partridge, Edward B. *The Broken Compass: A Study of the Major Comedies of Ben Jonson.* New York: Columbia University Press, 1958.

Perkinson, R. H. "*Volpone* and the Reputation of Venetian Justice." *The Modern Language Review* 35 (1940): 11–18.

Peterson, Richard S. *Imitation and Praise in the Poems of Ben Jonson*. New Haven: Yale University Press, 1981.

———. "The Iconography of Jonson's *Pleasure Reconciled to Virtue*." *Journal of Medieval and Renaissance Studies* 5 (1975): 123–53.

Redwine, J. D., Jr. "Beyond Psychology: The Moral Basis of Jonson's Theory of Humour Characterisation." *ELH* 26 (1961): 316–34.

Rhodes, Neil. *Elizabethan Grotesque*. London: Routledge & Kegan Paul, 1980.

Salinger, L. G. "Farce and Fashion in *The Silent Woman*." *Essays and Studies* 20 (1967): 29–46.

Slights, W. W. E. "*Epicoene* and the Prose Paradox." *Philological Quarterly* 49 (1970): 179–87.

Spanos, William V. "The Real Toad in the Jonsonian Garden: Resonance in the Non-Dramatic Poetry" 68 (1969): 1–23.

Summers, Claude J. and Ted-larry Pebworth, eds. *Classic Cavalier: Essays on Jonson and the Sons of Ben*. Pittsburgh: University of Pittsburgh Press, 1982.

Sweeney, John G. III. "*Sejanus* and the People's Beastly Rage." *ELH* 48 (1981): 61–82.

Talbert, Ernest W. "Classical Mythology and the Structure of *Cynthia's Revels*." *Philological Quarterly* 22 (1943): 192–210.

Thayer, C. G. *Ben Jonson: Studies in the Plays*. Norman: University of Oklahoma Press, 1963.

Trimpi, Wesley. *Ben Jonson's Poems: A Study of the Plain Style*. Stanford: Stanford University Press, 1962.

Wells, Susan. "Jacobean City Comedy and the Ideology of the City." *ELH* 48 (1981): 38–39.

Wilson, Edmund. *The Triple Thinkers*. New York: Farrar, Straus & Giroux, 1976.

Winner, Jack D. "Ben Jonson's *Epigrammes* and the Conventions of Formal Verse Satire." *Studies in English Literature* 23 (1983): 61–76.

Young, R. V. "Style and Structure in Jonson's Epigrams." *Criticism* 17 (1975): 201–22.

Zender, Karl F. "The Unveiling of the Goddess in *Cynthia's Revels*." *JEGP* 77 (1978): 37–52.

Zitner, S. P. "The Revenge of Charis." In *The Elizabethan Theatre*, edited by George Hibbard, 128–40. London: Edward Arnold, 1970.

Acknowledgments

"The Double Plot in *Volpone*" by Jonas A. Barish from *Modern Philology* 51, no. 1 (August 1953), © 1954 by the University of Chicago. Reprinted by permission of the University of Chicago Press.

"The Allusiveness of *Epicoene*" by Edward B. Partridge from *ELH* 22, no. 2 (June 1955), © 1955 by the Johns Hopkins University Press, Baltimore/London. Reprinted by permission of the Johns Hopkins University Press.

"The World's Proportion: Jonson's Dramatic Poetry in *Sejanus* and *Catiline*" by Geoffrey Hill from *Jacobean Theatre* (Stratford-upon-Avon Studies 1), © 1960 by Edward Arnold (Publishers) Ltd. Reprinted by permission of St. Martin's Press.

"The Jonsonian Masque and the Limits of Invention" (originally titled "The Limits of Invention") by Stephen Orgel from *The Jonsonian Masque* by Stephen Orgel, © 1965 by the President and Fellows of Harvard College, © 1986 by Stephen Orgel. Republished in 1981 by Columbia University Press. Reprinted by permission of Columbia University Press.

"The Venter Tripartite in *The Alchemist*" by William Blisset from *Studies in English Literature 1500–1900* 8, no. 2 (Spring 1968), © 1968 by William Blisset. Reprinted by permission.

"Ben Jonson and the Centered Self" by Thomas M. Greene from *Studies in English Literature 1500–1900* 10, no. 2 (Spring 1970), © 1970 by Thomas M. Greene. Reprinted by permission.

"Ben Jonson Full of Shame and Scorn" by William Kerrigan from *Ben Jonson: Quadricentennial Essays* (Special Issues of *Studies in the Literary Imagination*) 6, no. 1 (April 1973), © 1973 by the Department of English, Georgia State University. Reprinted by permission.

"The Significance of Jonson's Revision of *Every Man in His Humour*" by A. Richard Dutton from *Modern Language Review* 69, no. 2 (April 1974), © 1974 by the Modern Humanities Research Association. Reprinted by permission.

"Festivity and the Dramatic Economy of Jonson's *Bartholomew Fair*" by Jonathan Haynes from *ELH* 51, no. 4 (Winter 1984), © 1984 by the Johns Hopkins

University Press, Baltimore/London. Reprinted by permission of the Johns Hopkins University Press.

"*Sejanus:* History and *Realpolitik*" (originally entitled "*Sejanus* (1603): History and *Realpolitik*") by Jonathan Dollimore from *Radical Tragedy: Religion, Ideology, and Power in the Drama of Shakespeare and his Contemporaries* by Jonathan Dollimore, © 1984 by Jonathan Dollimore. Reprinted by permission of the University of Chicago Press and the Harvester Press Ltd./Wheatsheaf Books Ltd.

"Echoic Presence and the Theatrical Court: *Cynthia's Revels*" by Joseph Loewenstein from *Responsive Readings: Versions of Echo in Pastoral, Epic, and the Jonsonian Masque* by Joseph Loewenstein, © 1984 by Yale University. Reprinted by permission of Yale University Press.

"The Brave Infant of Saguntum: The Self in Jonson's Verse" (originally entitled "Authors-Readers: Jonson's Community of the Same") by Stanley Fish from *Representations* no. 7 (Summer 1984), © 1984 by the Regents of the University of California. Reprinted by permission of the Regents.

"Ben Jonson and the Modality of Verse" by John Hollander from *Vision and Resonance* by John Hollander, © 1985 by Yale University.

"Forms of Ceremony in Ben Jonson's Masques" by Marijke Rijsberman, © 1987 by Marijke Rijsberman. Published for the first time in this volume. Printed by permission.

Index

69–70; setting of main masque, 68–70; use of conventions in, 72
New Inn, The, 51–52, 95
Newcastle, earl of, 213
News from the New World, 237
Nicholson, Marjorie, 90
Nietzsche, Friedrich Wilhelm, 2

Oberon: antimasque world of, 56–60; difficulties in, 60–63, 69, 70, 77; dramatic elements of, 77; homiletic approach of, 233–34; king's role in, 61–63, 234–35; occasion for writing, 56, 57; palace as world of masque in, 60–63; parody of masque conventions in, 59; poetry in, 57–59; role of Silenus in, 57–58
"Of Innovations" (Bacon), 4
Old Wives' Tales (Peele), 29
"On My First Sonne," 127
"On The Townes Honest Man," 198–99, 200
"On the Union," 94
Orgel, Stephen, 217, 223, 225, 234, 235
Ovid, 169, 172, 174, 183, 184, 211

Palmer, John, 129
Paradise Lost (Milton), 83
Passionate Shepherd (Marlowe), 44
Paul, St., 118, 121–22
Peele, George, 29, 183
Pepys, Samuel, 158, 159
Peterson, Richard, 200
Petrarch, 212
Petronius, 211
Pilgrim's Progress, The (Bunyan), 201
Plato, 209
Plays. *See* titles of plays
Pleasure Reconciled to Virtue, 70, 216–17, 237–38
Pliny, 214
Poetaster, 98
Poetry: alternate world of patronage in, 202–3; Aristotle's view of, 3; awkward beginnings of, 191–92; Bacon on, 1, 3, 6; classical influences on, 208, 209–11, 214–15, 220; classical verse, 211; comparison between Jonson and Donne, 206–8; couplets, 218; court poet and, 190–91; criticism of, 205–6, 208; function of, 202, 212–13, 217; ideal of, 94, 202; images of circle and center in, 92–96, 123–25, 203–4; imitativeness of, 219–21; inability to describe objects of,

197–99, 202; interchangeability of persons in, 203; Jonson's contributions to, 221, 222; Jonson's relationship with God, 115–24; Jonson's views of, 6; later works, 110; lyrics, 218; modern, 222; role in masques, 74; self in, 203–4; Sidney on, 3, 6; sonnets, 218; sources of, 219–20; two types of, 199; use of iambic pentameter, 211–12. *See also* specific poems
Poggioli, Renato, 4
Poly-Olbion (Drayton), 211
Pope, Alexander, 40, 44, 212
Poulet, George, 90
Pound, Ezra, 211
Professionalism, 189–90

Raab, Felix, 167
Rabelais, Francois, 141, 142, 143, 156
Rabelais and His World (Bakhtin), 141, 143
Raleigh, Sir Walter, 164
Rawe, Thomas, 94
Renaissance: marketplace and, 142–43; patronage system, 190–91; view of human self, 106–7
Reynolds, Henry, 2
Rhetoric as a Dramatic Language in Ben Jonson (Sackton), 23
Rhodes, Neil, 156–57
Richard II (Shakespeare), 164
Rilke, Rainer Maria, 222
Rise of Professionalism, The (Larson), 189
Roe, William, 96, 110
Roman tragedies. *See Catiline; Sejanus*

Saccio, Peter, 171
Sackton, Alexander, 23
"Sacrifice, The" (Herbert), 123
Sad Shepherd, The, 99, 109–10
Satiromastix (Dekker), 171, 187
Sejanus: Coleridge on, 47–48; domestic invasion in, 98; dual role of Sejanus, 42; ethical and sexual abnormality in, 41; historical realism of, 164–67; language in, 36–37, 44; liberty in, 38; political power in, 164–67; role of Lepidus in, 97–98; self-abuse in, 42; viewed as seditious, 163–64
Selden, John, 93, 216
Seneca, 112–13, 114, 183, 186
Shakespeare, William: Bacon's view of, 1; comedies of, 81, 111; compared to Jonson, 134, 135, 136, 174, 206; demands